BASIC CHRISTIAN DOCTRINES

CONTEMPORARY EVANGELICAL THOUGHT

BASIC CHRISTIAN

DOCTRINES

✚

OSWALD T. ALLIS   WILLIAM M. ARNETT   G.C. BERKOUWER
GEOFFREY W. BROMILEY   F.F. BRUCE   J. OLIVER BUSWELL, JR.
EDWARD JOHN CARNELL   HERBERT M. CARSON   RALPH EARLE
FRANK E. GAEBELEIN   J. NORVAL GELDENHUYS   JOHN H. GERSTNER
J. KENNETH GRIDER   ANTHONY A. HOEKEMA   PHILIP E. HUGHES
W. BOYD HUNT   FRED H. KLOOSTER   HAROLD B. KUHN
GEORGE E. LADD   ADDISON H. LEITCH   CALVIN D. LINTON
H.D. MCDONALD   JULIUS R. MANTEY   OTTO MICHEL
SAMUEL J. MIKOLASKI   LEON MORRIS   J.A. MOTYER
J. THEODORE MUELLER   WILLIAM A. MUELLER   JOHN MURRAY
ROGER NICOLE   M. EUGENE OSTERHAVEN   JAMES I. PACKER
BERNARD RAMM   WILLIAM CHILDS ROBINSON
ROBERT PAUL ROTH   ANDREW K. RULE
HENRY STOB   MERRILL C. TENNEY
J.G.S.S. THOMSON   CORNELIUS VAN TIL
JOHN F. WALVOORD   WAYNE E. WARD
WALTER W. WESSEL

EDITED BY CARL F.H. HENRY

HOLT, RINEHART AND WINSTON

NEW YORK | CHICAGO |

SAN FRANCISCO

Designer: Ernst Reichl
83580–0112
Printed in the United States of America

CONTENTS

✦   1192667

INTRODUCTION

✚

Theologians and evangelists were looked upon not too long ago either as eccentrics or as quacks. If no novelist caricatured the theologian like Sinclair Lewis libeled the evangelist in *Elmer Gantry*, it was probably because the theologian could pursue his relationship with God privately.

But why, after all, should modern man have been overawed by theology, when scholars who claimed some private wire to the supernatural world woefully disagreed over its content and meaning? So penetrating was the impact of secular speculation and religious philosophy, moreover, that some theologians were playing back very little that the actual foes of theology would not endorse.

Then followed what is now familiarly known as the exciting rediscovery of biblical theology. This trend emphasized a new examination of the Scriptures and of their unique testimony to Jesus Christ. The Judeo-Christian tradition rose to new vigor with its singular message of the self-revealing Creator-Redeemer God, who promises salvation to his fallen and sullied image-bearer and fulfills that promise through the atoning work of the God-man.

Modern intellectuals steeped in the secular tenets of the day suddenly realized that in the crisis of the times the Great Tradition enjoyed fresh relevance. They were now pressed to a sustained reappraisal of the history of thought and to lively involvement in the questions of salvation history and of Scripture's special import. Suddenly, such long-ignored themes as the inspiration and authority of the Bible, the divinity and humanity of Jesus Christ, sin and atonement, Christ's death and resurrection, end-time and second coming and Kingdom once again were lively and current topics of discussion.

Now it became clear that the modern revolt against theology had not arisen primarily because of rationalized charges of metaphysical quackery and of disagreements among the religionists. The basic issue to emerge was the modern bias against the reality of the supernatural, a bias encouraged by the tenets of secularism, scientism, and naturalistic philosophy. Sharp dissension raged over what means our tormented generation could and should trust to transform society. For scientism, experimental techniques represented the only mediator between yesterday's and tomorrow's values. Communism looked to political violence and revolution to sweep life and society into the orbit of state absolutism; it became increasingly impatient with its own expectation of dialectical materialism to achieve proletarian objectives automatically and mechanically. Meantime, political democracy sought social change through gradual rather than swift transition, and replaced its former reliance on education with an ever-enlarging confidence in legislation to advance its ends. By its far deeper demand, the Christian message discredited all others; it called for *a new race of men*. "Ye must be born again!" Without denying God's providential purpose in the background of scientific control of nature and of political preservation of order, Christianity proclaimed the absolute indispensability of the new birth.

This claim involved many related concepts. It implied a special view of God and His universe, and of man's place in it. It gave special perspective to the purpose and goal of history, to redemptive revelation and the message of the Bible. It exposed the tragic destiny of mankind in sin, and spoke of God's ongoing witness to a lost world through the church, that body of regenerate believers whose head is the slain and risen Christ.

Among the most gratifying features of this awakening interest in Bible study and theological reflection is its widening inclusion of the layman and his participation. Historians have noted that in the Protestant Reformation the laity grappled with theological concerns more deeply than did many of the clergy. Our century has served theological skim milk to both churchmen and churchgoers; to the masses outside, non-milk, non-nutritious substitutes. Even in its elementary stages, therefore, a new interest in Bible doctrine is heartening indeed.

One sure sign of theological renewal will be revived interest in a systematic theology that rests on the fixed norm of biblical authority. At present, only the barest outlines of such a development are discernible on the religious horizon; much of the current theological discussion is still limited and selective.

First published as a series in *Christianity Today*, and now appearing in book form, the essays in *Basic Christian Doctrines* have at least the merit of a comprehensive overview. Competent evangelical scholars of interdenominational and international stature have shared the task of preparing these studies. A supplementary essay by Dr. Roger Nicole on the various disciplines of theology has been added to challenge the reader to explore also the larger areas of theological learning.

Publication of these essays in the "Contemporary Evangelical Thought" series makes them all immediately available in permanent form to both the ministry and the laity. Holt, Rinehart and Winston are to be commended for issuing the work in a format matching the companion symposium volumes *Contemporary Evangelical Thought* (1957) and *Revelation and the Bible* (1958). My colleague, Dr. Frank Farrell, is due special commendation for careful reading of the original manuscripts and for assistance in editing them for publication.

This present collection of theological table talks with many of the devout scholars of our day is a feast for mind and heart. Here and there, special denominational traditions may shine through. But what the various contributors share in common as committed evangelicals far outweighs their differences. This basic agreement is only proper in a united theological effort that would stimulate renewed and devoted study of those priorities which determine the destiny of our world.

CARL F.H. HENRY

Editor, *Christianity Today*

I

THE KNOWLEDGE OF GOD: GENERAL AND SPECIAL REVELATION

✚

ADDISON H. LEITCH

Addison H. Leitch, Professor of Philosophy and Religion at Tarkio College, Tarkio, Missouri, received his general and theological education at Muskingum College (B.A., 1931; D.D., 1947), Pittsburgh-Xenia Theological Seminary (B.D., 1936; Th.M., 1937), Cambridge University, England, and Grove City College (D.D., 1947; Litt. D., 1955). He is the author of *Beginnings in Theology*, *Meet Dr. Luke*, and *Interpreting Basic Theology*.

It is the psalmist who sings "The Heavens declare the glory of God; and the firmament showeth his handiwork. Day unto day uttereth speech, and night unto night showeth knowledge. There is no speech nor language, their voice is not heard." Men have known these things for generations. They have gloried in the glory of a God Who manifests Himself in His wondrous works. No speech nor language is spoken; it is not in the words of Greek or Hebrew or German or English; yet every day speaks and every night shows knowledge. The apostle adds in a later day, "the invisible things of him from the creation of the world are clearly seen, being understood by the things that are made, even his eternal power and godhead; so that they are without excuse." Psalmist and apostle declare what no man can deny: that there is a God Who can be known through His works, and when we refuse to see Him there we are without excuse.

Such knowledge of God forced on us by the world around us has been recognized and accepted by believers in every generation. In some fashion it is the approach of Plato as he moves level upon level to his supreme Idea, an idea which, according to Plato's thinking, necessarily has moral qualities which can be defined as an Ideal. In some fashion it is the approach of Aristotle as his system carries us from utter matter to perfect form or from the inanimate world to the high reaches of the Unmoved Mover. More specifically, in the Christian tradition men have discovered in the world around them "proofs" for God, reasons for faith, necessities for believing, and, at least in the direction of their thinking, they have been forced toward some knowledge of God. Arguments for the existence of God and in support of the nature of God are very old ones. They have been subjected to much criticism and therefore to considerable refinement in the history of thought. In spite of such criticism, however, they keep cropping up in one form or another, one argument, or one way of stating the argument, appealing to one generation more than to another; but none of the arguments ever quite disappears. That these arguments keep reviving is probably a reason for their fundamental strength; men feel under some duress to define what they know must be true about God from the evidence of the external world.

FROM EFFECTS TO THEIR CAUSE

Keeping in mind that these arguments say something about God's attributes as well as giving reasons for His existence, we are justified in using them as supports in natural theology for our knowledge of God. In general, the arguments move under at least four titles: the cosmological, the teleological, the anthropological, and the ontological. These arguments all allow somewhat the same scheme, namely that an effect must have a cause equal to or greater than the effect itself. In the general scheme of things you cannot get something from nothing and, surely, one can observe a great deal of something in the world of nature; the question is, therefore: what is "the source, the support, and the end" of all these things about us? What is the explanation of their existence?

The easiest argument is the *cosmological*. It argues from the existence of the Cosmos, the universe, what C.S. Lewis calls "the whole show." Man does not need to be either clever or subtle merely to wonder about the world around him. How can one account for all these things he sees and experiences—the birds, the rocks, the trees, and the stars in their courses? This first argument in "natural" theology finds us unable to escape the belief that back of all this Cosmos there is some thing or some one equal to bringing into existence (by what method we need not argue here) the universe within us, around us, and above us.

The *teleological* argument is more reflective regarding the universe. Here, our interest is focused on design and purpose, as we discover the amazing intricacy with which all things are interlocked as if united in some grand mutual interdependency, some basic design. These interlocked designs and purposes point to a designer, some intelligence with creative purpose. There are no isolated data, there is no item so small that it is not somehow interrelated with every possible other thing. Nothing ever "just happens." You can never really say of anything that "it doesn't really matter." Butler in his *Analogy*, Paley in his *Evidences*, and in these latter days F.R. Tennant in *Philosophical Theology* found this argument from design almost conclusive for the existence and the nature of God.

In his master work, *Nature, Man and God*, William Temple sets himself to examine the world of nature only to discover that nature includes man and that nature and man together point us to God. In some such fashion the *anthropological* argument grows out of the teleological argument, for nothing points more clearly to intelligence and design than the fact of man himself, man who is able to understand the design and to appreciate the designer. But beyond this is man as person. Man as a person has what we call personality. Will anyone seriously argue that personality can arise from some impersonal source? Will anyone seriously support accidents or material or both as sufficient to account for all the wonders in man? Since man is so creative himself, was the ground of his existence uncreative? Thus the argument runs. We cannot get something from nothing; we have something personal in man; we cannot believe that this personal end product comes from impersonal sources.

The *ontological* argument points to perfection or more exactly to the idea of perfection which we find inescapable in our ways of thought. To use our thinking about God as an example, how is it possible for us to talk about the perfections of God without some idea of perfection as a point of reference? Yet we are imperfect ourselves; we think imperfectly; we are surrounded by a world of imperfections. Since, once again, we cannot get something from nothing and since assuredly we have ideas of perfection which cannot be accounted for in the immediacies of our surroundings, the conclusion suggests itself that this *idea* of perfection must come directly from the perfect source, namely, from God Himself.

It would appear from this brief treatment that we have at least four reasons for believing in God. (Some add the moral argument, that is, the inescapable sense of "oughtness" common to all men, Kant's *categorical imperative*. We believe that the moral argument which we have not here expanded can find a natural place in the anthropological argument.) These tell us some very definite things about God's nature: He is mighty enough to account for the universe itself; He is intelligent enough to satisfy its design; He is personal enough to account for man as person; and He is the ground of all our understanding and perfection. If we add creativity and morality as necessary to man as person, we may presume to have found as necessary a God Who is almighty, intelligent, personal, creative, moral, and perfect. We are not far from the kingdom!

FROM NECESSARY PRESUPPOSITIONS

What has been said thus far usually comes under the heading of *a posteriori* reasoning, that is, reaching our conclusions inductively. There are others who prefer the *a priori* approach; this is, as a matter of fact, the approach of much of the theology of our day. Knowledge of God with this approach is not so much the result of our thinking as it is the starting place of our thinking. The starting place is always there, described sometimes as a first truth, and it is only in personal intellectual maturity or perhaps in the maturity of the race that man gets around to analyzing the nature of his starting place. Living as we do in an age dominated by scientific method, it is difficult for us to accept the fact that we operate, even in science, even in our "proofs," from the foundation of various presuppositions. For many, the fact of God is one of the necessary presuppositions.

All of us must accept some first truths about ourselves from the outset. We are alive and awake and sane; such truths about ourselves we cannot prove objectively, but merely accept as starting places. On a deeper level we base our thinking on the assumption that there are certain foundations of truth and reason from which we operate and to which we constantly return. We believe that truth has an interrelatedness in a *universe* (which is a single organizational principle of truth).

All serious thinking, especially the most objective scientific research, upholds the necessity of absolute honesty in methods and in findings, appealing, therefore, to a moral ground built into the structure of reality. In other directions our words betray us: "It stands to reason" or "That doesn't make sense." Thus, we are insisting that our thinking, as well as our experimenting, demands a frame of reference that is sensible. Moreover, we appeal to one another on the grounds of a common acceptance of these necessary fundamentals. Notice the presupposition of this paragraph recently published in the "Science" section of *Time* magazine where the discussion has to do with the possibility of interplanetary conversations: "But what message would aliens send that could be understood by earthlings? Dr. Drake suggests a familiar series of numbers, such as 1, 2, 3, 4. Professor Purcell believes that a simple on-off signal would be more logical as a starter. After that the messages could progress to *Mathematical relationships, which are surely the same in all planetary systems....*"* [Italics supplied.] Note how normal it is for scientists to assume an underlying rational system.

FROM SPECIAL REVELATION

From this *a priori* approach it is interesting to note that we are talking again about a reality at the source of things, showing attributes of truth, reason, and morality. We are being pressed to the conclusion again, namely, that in what is called natural theology there are strong reasons for knowing that there is a God and knowing something of His attributes. But, "can a man by searching find out God?" Only is this possible when God is pleased to reveal Himself and to answer finally and authoritatively man's deepest questions. This is not natural revelation but special revelation. This is the Bible record of God's mighty

* *Time* magazine, "Science—Project OZMA," April 18, 1960, p. 53.

acts and His authoritative Word about the revelatory acts and about Himself. This is the climax and fulfillment of God's Word to us in the Living Word, even Jesus Christ. Natural revelation gives us direction and confidence in our search for God; God's special revelation gives us final authority and assurance regarding His own nature and His will for man. As Calvin suggests, in the Bible we have the "divine spectacles" which bring the truths of natural theology into focus.

BIBLIOGRAPHY

In addition to classic systematic theologies by C. Hodge, A.H. Strong, L. Berkhof, and others, we suggest the following:

R. Flint: *Evangelical Theism* [an old standard work]
J. Gerstner: *Reasons for Faith* [popular and sound]
S.M. Thompson: *A Modern Philosophy of Religion*
H. Heppe: *Reformed Dogmatics*
K. Barth: *Die kirchliche Dogmatik* [dialectical]
F.R. Tennant: *Philosophical Theology* [liberal but surprisingly firm in its objective approach]

2

THE KNOWLEDGE OF GOD:

THE SAVING ACTS OF GOD

✚

GEORGE E. LADD

George E. Ladd, Professor of Biblical Theology at Fuller Theological Seminary, Pasadena, California, received his general and
theological education at Gordon College (Th. B., 1933), Gordon
Divinity School (B.D., 1941), and Harvard University (Ph.D.,
1949). He is the author of *Crucial Questions about the Kingdom
of God and The Blessed Hope,* and is a contributor to *The
Biblical Expositor.*

The uniqueness and the scandal of the Christian religion rest in the
mediation of revelation through historical events. The Hebrew-
Christian faith stands apart from the religions of its environment because it is an historical faith, whereas they were religions rooted in
mythology or the cycle of nature. The God of Israel was the God of
history, or the *Geschichtsgott,* as German theologians so vividly put it.
The Hebrew-Christian faith did not grow out of lofty philosophical
speculation or profound mystical experiences. It arose out of the historical experiences of Israel, old and new, in which God made Himself
known. This fact imparts to the Christian faith a specific content and
objectivity which set it apart from others.

At the same time, this very historical character of revelation raises an acute problem for many thinking men. Plato viewed the realm of time and space as one of flux and change. History by definition involves relativity, particularity, caprice, arbitrariness, whereas revelation must convey the universal, the absolute, the ultimate. History has been called "an abyss in which Christianity has been swallowed up quite against its will."

REVELATORY HISTORY

How can the Infinite be known in the finite, the Eternal in the temporal, the Absolute in the relativities of history? From a purely human perspective this is impossible, but at precisely this point is found perhaps the greatest miracle in the biblical faith. God is the living God, and He, the eternal, the unchangeable, has communicated knowledge of Himself through the ebb and flow of historical experience.

The problem is well nigh insoluble for the man who takes his world view from modern philosophies rather than from the Bible. Yet there can be no doubt about the Bible's claim for the historical character of revelation. This can be seen in the historical character of the Bible itself. From one point of view, the Bible is not so much a book of religion as a book of history. The Bible is not primarily a collection of the religious ideas of a series of great thinkers. It is not first of all a system of theological concepts, much less of philosophical speculations. Nowhere, for instance, does the Bible try to prove the existence of God; God simply *is*. His existence is everywhere assumed. Nowhere does the New Testament reflect on the deity of Christ. Christ is God, and yet God is more than Christ. The Father is God; Christ is God; the Holy Spirit is God; and yet God is one, not three. The New Testament does not try to synthesize these diverse elements into a theological whole. This is the legitimate and necessary task of systematic theology.

Neither is the Bible primarily the description of deep mystical experiences of religious geniuses, although it includes profound religious experience. Much of the New Testament is indeed the product of the religious experience of one man: Paul. Yet the focus of Paul's epistles is not Paul and his experience, but the meaning of Jesus of Nazareth, resurrected and exalted at God's right hand.

The Bible is first of all the record of the history of Abraham, of Isaac, of Jacob, of the twelve tribes of Israel and their settlement in Palestine, of the kingdom of David and his successors, of the fall of the divided kingdom, and of the return of the Jews from Babylon. It resumes its history with the life, death, and resurrection of Jesus of Nazareth, and the establishment and extension of the early Church in the Graeco-Roman world.

Yet history is not recorded for its own sake. History is recorded because it embodies the acts of God. The evangelistic preaching of the early church did not attempt to demonstrate the superiority of Christian truth over the teachings of pagan philosophers and religious teachers. It did not rest its claim to recognition in a higher ethic or a deeper religious experience. It consisted of a recital of the acts of God.

The bond which holds the Old and New Testaments inseparably together is the bond of revelatory history. Orthodox theology has traditionally underevaluated or at least underemphasized the role of the redemptive acts of God in revelation. The classic essay by B.B. Warfield acknowledges the fact of revelation through the instrumentality of historical deeds, but rather completely subordinates revelation in acts to revelation in words.

However, as Carl F.H. Henry has written, "Revelation cannot... be equated simply with the Hebrew-Christian Scriptures; the Bible is a special segment within a larger divine activity of revelation.... Special revelation involves unique historical events of divine deliverance climaxed by the incarnation, atonement, and resurrection of Jesus Christ."[1]

The greatest revelatory act of God in the Old Testament was the deliverance of Israel from bondage in Egypt. This was no ordinary event of history, like the events which befell other nations. It was not an achievement of the Israelites. It was not attributed to the genius and skillful leadership of Moses. It was an act of God. "You have seen what I did to the Egyptians, and how I bore you on eagles' wings."[2]

This deliverance was not merely an act of God; it was an act through which God made Himself known and through which Israel was to know and serve God. "I am the Lord, and I will bring you out from under the burdens of the Egyptians, and I will deliver you from their bondage . . . , and *you shall know that I am the Lord your God*."[3]

In the later history of Israel, the Exodus is recited again and again as the redemptive act by which God made Himself known to his people. Hosea appeals to Israel's historical redemption and subsequent experi-

[1] J.F. Walvoord, ed.: *Inspiration and Interpretation*, pp. 254 f.
[2] Exod. 19:4.   [3] Exod. 6:6–7.

ences as evidence for the love of God. "When Israel was a child, I loved him, and out of Egypt I called my son.... I led them with the cords of compassion, with the bands of love."[4]

History also reveals God in wrath and judgment. Hosea goes on immediately to say that Israel is about to return to captivity because of her sins. Amos interprets Israel's impending historical destruction with the words: "Therefore thus I will do to you, O Israel; because I will do this to you, prepare to meet your God, O Israel!"[5] The revelation of God as the judge of His people in historical events is sharply reflected in the designation of Israel's historical defeat by the Assyrians as the Day of the Lord.[6]

Israel's history is different from all other history. While God is the Lord of all history, in one series of events God has revealed Himself as He has nowhere else done. German theologians have coined the useful term *Heilsgeschichte* to designate this stream of revelatory history. In English, we speak of "redemptive history" or "holy history." To be sure, God was superintending the course of Egypt and Assyria and Babylon and Persia; but only in the history of Israel had God communicated to men personal knowledge of Himself.

The New Testament does not depart from this sense of holy history. On the contrary, the recital of God's historical acts is the substance of Christian proclamation. The earliest semblance of a creedal confession is found in I Corinthians 15:3 ff., and it is a recital of events: Christ died; He was buried; He was raised; He appeared. The New Testament evidence for God's love does not rest on reflection on the nature of God, but upon recital. God so loved that He gave.[7] God shows His love for us in that Christ died for us.[8] The revelation of God in the redemptive history of Israel finds its full meaning in the historical event of the life, death, and resurrection of Christ.

One aspect of this holy history must be emphasized. Sometimes the revelatory event assumes a character which the modern secular historian calls unhistorical. The God who reveals Himself in redemptive history is both Lord of history and Lord of creation, and He is, therefore, able not only to shape the course of ordinary historical events but to act directly in ways which transcend usual historical experience.

The most vivid illustration of this is the resurrection of Christ. From the point of view of scientific historical criticism, the resurrec-

---

[4] Hos. 11:1, 4.   [5] Amos 4:12.
[6] Amos 5:18.   [7] John 3:16.
[8] Rom. 5:8.

tion cannot be "historical," for it is an event uncaused by any other historical event and it is without analogy. With this judgment the Bible record agrees. God, and God alone, is the cause of the resurrection. It is, therefore, causally unrelated to all other events. Furthermore, nothing like it has occurred elsewhere. The resurrection of Christ is not the restoration of a dead man to life, but the emergence of a new order of life—resurrection life. If the biblical record is correct, there can be neither "historical" explanation nor analogy of Christ's resurrection. Therefore, its very offense to scientific historical criticism is a kind of negative support for its supernatural character.

The underlying question is a theological one. Is such an alleged supernatural event consistent with the character and objectives of the God Who has revealed Himself in holy history? Is history, as such, the measure of all things, or is the living God indeed the Lord of history? The biblical answer to this question is not in doubt. The Lord of history is transcendent over history, yet not aloof from history. He is, therefore, able to bring to pass in time and space events which are genuine events, yet which are "suprahistorical" in their character. This merely means that the revelation of God is not produced by history, but that the Lord of history, Who stands above history, acts within history for the redemption of historical creatures. The redemption of history must come from outside of history: from God himself.

While revelation has occurred in history, revelatory history is not *bare* history. God did not act in history in such a way that historical events were eloquent in and of themselves. The most vivid illustration of this is the death of Christ. Christ died. This is a simple historical fact which can be satisfactorily established by secular historical disciplines. But Christ died for our sins. Christ died showing forth the love of God. These are not *bare* historical facts. The cross by itself did not speak of love and forgiveness. Proof of this may be found in the experience of those who watched Jesus die. Was any of the witnesses overwhelmed with a sense of the love of God, conscious that he was beholding the awesome spectacle of atonement being made for the sins of men? Did John or Mary or the centurion or the high priest throw himself in choking joy upon the earth before the cross with the cry, "I never knew how much God loved me!"

DEED-WORD REVELATION

The historical events are revelatory *only when they are accompanied by the revelatory word*. Theologians often speak of deed-revelation and word-revelation. This, however, is not an accurate formulation if it suggests two separate modes of revelation. The fact is that God's word is His deed, and His deed is His word. We would therefore be more accurate if we spoke of the deed-word revelation.

God's deed is His word. Ezekiel describes the captivity of Judah with the words, "And all the pick of his troops shall fall by the sword, and the survivors shall be scattered to every wind; and you shall know that I, the Lord, have spoken."[9] Captivity was itself God's word of judgment to Israel. The event is a word of God.

Yet the event is always accompanied by spoken words, in this case, the spoken words of the prophet Ezekiel. The event is never left to speak for itself, nor are men left to infer whatever conclusions they can draw from the event. The spoken word always accompanies and explains the revelatory character of the event. Therefore, not the deed by itself, but the deed-word is revelation.

This is equally true in the New Testament. *Christ died* is the deed; Christ died *for our sins* is the word of interpretation that makes the act revelatory. It was only after the interpretative word was given to the disciples that they came to understand that the death of Christ was revelatory of the love of God.

We must go yet a step further. God's word not only follows the historical act and gives it a normative interpretation; it often precedes and creates the historical act. The test of whether a prophet speaks the word of the Lord is whether his word comes to pass.[10] For when God speaks, something happens. Events occur. "I, the Lord, have spoken; surely this will I do to all this wicked congregation . . . they shall die."[11] "I the Lord have spoken; it shall come to pass, I will do it."[12] "You shall die in peace. . . . For I have spoken the word, says the Lord."[13]

The revelatory word may be both spoken and written. Jeremiah both spoke and wrote down the word of the Lord. Both his spoken and written utterance were "the words of the Lord."[14] It is against this background that the New Testament refers to the Old Testament Scriptures as "the word of God."[15] It is for this reason that the orthodox theologian is justified, nay, required to recognize the Bible as the Word of God.

[9] Ezek. 17:21.
[11] Num. 14:35.
[13] Jer. 34:5.
[15] John 10:35.

[10] Deut. 18:22.
[12] Ezek. 24:14.
[14] Jer. 36:4, 6.

Revelation has occurred in the unique events of redemptive history. These events were accompanied by the divinely given word of interpretation. The word, both spoken and written, is itself a part of the total event. The Bible is both the record of this redemptive history and the end product of the interpretative word. It is the necessary and normative explanation of the revelatory character of God's revealing acts, for it is itself included in God's revelation through the act-word complex which constitutes revelation.

BIBLIOGRAPHY

J.G.S.S. Thomson: *The Old Testament View of Revelation*
P.K. Jewett: *Emil Brunner's Concept of Revelation*
C.F.H. Henry, ed.: *Revelation and the Bible*, "Special Revelation as Historical and Personal," by P.K. Jewett
B. Ramm: *Special Revelation and the Word of God*

3

THE KNOWLEDGE OF GOD:

THE INSPIRATION OF

THE BIBLE

✠

PHILIP E. HUGHES

Philip E. Hughes, editor of *The Churchman* (London), received his general and theological education at the University of Cape Town (B.A., 1937; M.A., 1939; D. Litt., 1955)
and the University of London (B.D., 1947). He is the author of
Receive Us Again, The Divine Plan for Jew and Gentile, and
Scripture and Myth, among other volumes, and is a contributor
to such volumes as *Dictionary of Theology* and *The Biblical Expositor.*

It is only in modern times that leaders within the Christian church
have assailed the doctrine of the inspiration of the Bible. Over the
centuries, of course, enemies have not been lacking who have assailed
it from without; but today it has become fashionable in many church
circles to deny the inspiration of the Bible in the classical sense. The
Bible is, indeed, now widely regarded as a book of human, not divine,
origin—inspired only in the humanistic sense that the Hebrews, who

wrote it, had a genius for religion, just as the Greeks had a genius for philosophy and the Romans a genius for government. The evolutionary interpretation of reality, which has so powerfully influenced the thinking of the Western world, assigned the Bible, in its different parts, a place within the supposed gradual development of religion from the crude apprehensions of primitive man in his cave-dwelling to the refined concept of ethical monotheism of our day. This viewpoint inevitably accords the Bible a position of purely relative significance, in radical conflict with the high conception of it as the inspired Word of God addressing a unique revelation of truth to fallen (not rising) man, and therefore *absolute* in its significance.

Again, it is characteristic of the so-called neo-orthodox theology of our day, with its emphasis on "encounter," to define the Bible as a word of man which may, at certain times and under certain circumstances, *become* the Word of God to me; that is, God may speak or reveal some truth to me through it, so that at that point in my experience it, or some portion of it, functions as a Word of God to me. Correlative with this outlook are the conceptions of the Bible as not in itself the Word of God, but as *containing* the Word of God, as conveying truth through the "kernel" of myth, independently of whether or not the "outer shell" in which the myth is enclosed is historically true, and even as—by a strange quirk of divine providence—conveying truth through error. Conceptions of this kind are marked by a subjectivism which contrasts noticeably with the classical view of the Bible as an *objective* revelation given by God.

What, then, are we to believe about the inspiration of the Bible? Three main witnesses have a claim upon our attention: the witness of the Bible to itself, the witness of history, and the witness of God.

THE WITNESS OF THE BIBLE TO ITSELF

Some people take exception to the procedure whereby the Bible is allowed to witness to itself. Certainly, the argument "the Bible claims to be the inspired Word of God; therefore it is the inspired Word of God" is not by itself admissible. But it is a commonplace of legal justice that any person standing trial has the right to engage in self-testimony. By itself—that is, in the absence of the independent witness of other persons or of circumstances—that self-testimony may or may not be true. The point is that *it may be true,* and so it must not be stifled. In the case of the Bible, it bears witness to itself in terms which, if true, are of the most vital consequence for the whole of mankind. Its witness must, therefore, be heard.

All who read the Old Testament cannot help being struck by the theme which so often and so extensively recurs that it may properly be described as the leading theme, namely, the assertion that it is *God*, not man, who is speaking. This impression is conveyed by the use of characteristic expressions, such as "Thus saith the Lord . . ." and "The word of the Lord came unto me, saying. . . ."

The implication of such expressions is fully corroborated by the witness of the New Testament to the Old. Thus, the Apostle Paul affirms that all Scripture is given by inspiration of God (or, literally, is "God-breathed");[1] the author of the Epistle to the Hebrews declares that it was God Who spoke in time past in the prophets;[2] and Peter asserts that the ancient prophets "spake from God, being moved by the Holy Spirit."[3] And what could be more significant for the Christian than the attitude of Christ Himself (with which, of course, the attitude of His apostles is fully consonant)? He emphasized not only that He had not come to destroy the law and the prophets but to fulfill them, but also that not one jot or tittle would pass away until all things were accomplished.[4] The Scripture was for Him something that could not be broken.[5] In the temptation in the wilderness, the devil is on each occasion repulsed, without further argument, by a quotation from the Old Testament, "It stands written . . .," the plain inference being that it is the absolutely authoritative Word of God.[6] It was the Old Testament Scriptures, viewed in their entirety—"the law of Moses, and the prophets, and the psalms"—which the risen Saviour expounded to His disciples, emphasizing the necessity that all things written in them concerning Him should be fulfilled.[7] Throughout the New Testament, indeed, the whole of Christ's life, death, and resurrection is seen in the light of the fulfillment of Holy Scripture, and therefore as a vindication of the Bible as the inspired Word of God.

But, it may be asked, what of the New Testament? It, too, is not without its own self-testimony. If the Old Testament bears witness pre-eminently to the One Who is to come, the New Testament bears witness to the One Who *has* come. It testifies to Him Who, in his person

[1] II Tim. 3:16.
[2] Heb. 1:1.
[3] II Pet. 1:21.
[4] Matt. 5:17 f.
[5] John 10:35.
[6] Matt. 4:4, 7, 10.
[7] Luke 24:44 ff.

and action as well as in His teaching, is the Word of God incarnate. The New Testament is the record of the imperishable truth which Christ brought and taught. Christ Himself proclaimed that heaven and earth would pass away, but that His words would not pass away.[8] Moreover, He promised to His apostles that the Holy Spirit would teach them all things and bring to their remembrance all that He had spoken to them, and would lead them into all truth and reveal to them things that were to come.[9] This is the very keystone of the New Testament and of the claims which it makes for itself. Accordingly, it is a mark of consistency to find John affirming that the witness of his Gospel is true[10] or Peter classifying Paul's epistles along with "the other scriptures."[11]

THE WITNESS OF HISTORY

The witness of history to the Bible is the witness of the history of the Christian church. Until modern times, as has already been said, the Bible was always acknowledged by the church to be the inspired Word of God. The significance of this fact can hardly be overemphasized. The definition of the canon of Holy Scripture—and especially of the New Testament, since that of the Old was already established—in the period that succeeded the age of the apostles, so far from being the result of the assertion of an authority superior to the Bible (as though the books of the Bible became canonical because the church pronounced them to be so), was in fact a recognition of this very principle of the divine inspiration of the Bible. It was a recognition of an authority vested in the biblical books, which is unique and normative precisely because together they constitute the Word of God written. If there was one external factor which played a decisive role in the fixing of the New Testament canon, it was the equating of canonicity with apostolicity. Books which were not of apostolic origin were not admissible as canonical. In other words, the authority vested in the apostles is now vested in their writings, through which they continue to govern the church.

But there was no question of this authority of the apostles being *human authority;* for, inasmuch as it was derived from Christ, their divine Master, theirs was a divine authority, and their teaching (handed down in their writings) again was not their own, but Christ's, in accord-

8 Matt. 24:35. 9 John 14:26; 16:13.
10 John 21:24. 11 II Pet. 3:15 f.

ance with His promise that the Holy Spirit would bring to their remembrance all that He had taught them and would lead them into all truth. In defining the canon of Scripture, therefore, the church, with the instinct of faith, was acknowledging and submitting herself to this authority, which, even more than apostolic, was dominical; for, ultimately, the authority involved is none other than that of the Lord Himself.

Although the unanimous consent of the Fathers is in the main an ecclesiastical fiction, yet there was at least one doctrine in which they were united, namely, that the Bible is the inspired Word of God. It was far from them to claim for their own writings the inspiration which they attributed to Scripture. And the same is to a particular degree true of the Age of the Reformation, when, in the light of the biblical revelation, which then shone forth again after centuries of spiritual darkness, all pretended authorities were exposed as spurious except insofar as they were subject to the supreme authority of the Word of God. Also worthy of notice is the inconsistency of modern liberal authors who, while denying the objectivity of the Bible as the Word of God, nonetheless commonly seek to authenticate the theology they propound by adducing statements and quotations from the Bible, as though it were in fact objectively authoritative.

Mention may also be made of the history of persecution. Men and women from generation to generation have given proof of the inspiration of the Bible by the radical transformation which the reception of its message has produced in their lives, so much so that they have held the Bible to be more precious than any other possession and have been willing to suffer torture and death rather than deny its truth, by which they have been set free. Attempts also to destroy the Bible, to burn it, to ban it, or in any other way to obliterate it from society, have ever proved futile. Not only does it continue unchallenged year after year as the world's best seller, but it is beyond doubt the greatest force for good and blessing in every sphere of human society.

The witness of history to the inspiration of the Bible is indeed massive, and it powerfully confirms the witness of the Bible to itself. When, as at the present time, the church is tempted to leave the old paths and to disparage this witness of her history, she should ask herself whether she is not in fact thereby in danger of ceasing to be the church, and bartering her heritage for something that is not of God but of the devil.

THE WITNESS OF GOD

Here we come face to face with that testimony which is absolutely conclusive and inexpungeable. The witness of God is greater than the witness of man. It needs no support, but stands firm by itself. Briefly stated, the position is this: if the Bible is in reality the inspired Word of God, it must as such be self-authenticating; it is in no need of human sanction. God Himself witnesses to the truth of the Bible. As its Author, He also authenticates it to the heart and mind of every believer. It is by the operation of the Holy Spirit that we are brought to faith in Christ, and that saving faith is founded upon the good news proclaimed in the pages of the Bible, *and nowhere else*. It is by the internal witness of the Holy Spirit that we acknowledge and appropriate the biblical message, and are assured daily and constantly that "all scripture is inspired of God."

As the witness of the Holy Spirit, this testimony is objective; as an internal witness within the believer, it is subjective. As at the same time both objective and subjective, this witness is completely impregnable. He who experiences it cannot gainsay it. He who gainsays it has not experienced it, and should search his heart as to why this is so.

In all charity and humility we would invite those to whom this internal witness of God, the Holy Spirit, is something strange to consider whether they are not lacking one of the essentials of genuine Christianity and whether, consequently, they are in any proper position to assail the doctrine of the inspiration of the Bible. We would urge them to pray that God will grant them the witness of the Holy Spirit, to convince and enlighten both heart and intellect.

Finally, let us ever remember that the primary purpose and function of Scripture is to lead us to Christ, that its proper place is within the framework of God's plan for our redemption. Hence, Paul advised Timothy that the Holy Scriptures were able to make him "wise unto salvation through faith which is in Christ Jesus";[12] Peter reminds his readers that "the word of the Lord abideth for ever," adding that "this is the word of the gospel which was preached unto you";[13] and John, in describing the purpose of what was possibly the last in time of the biblical writings, asserts: "These things are written that you may believe that Jesus is the Christ, the Son of God, and that believing you may have life in his name."[14]

[12] II Tim. 3:15.   [13] I Pet. 1:25.
[14] John 20:31.

"The Scripture," wrote the reformer and martyr William Tyndale, to whom, more than anyone else, we owe the priceless treasure of our English Bible, "is that wherewith God draweth us unto him, and not wherewith we should be led from him. The Scriptures spring out of God, and flow unto Christ, and were given to lead us to Christ. Thou must therefore go along by the Scripture as by a line, until thou come at Christ, which is the way's end and resting-place." May God grant us to use this holy book for this holy purpose.

BIBLIOGRAPHY

L. Boettner: *The Inspiration of the Scriptures*
J. Calvin: *Institutes of the Christian Religion*, I, vii
J. Jewel: *A Treatise of the Holy Scriptures*
C.F.H. Henry, ed.: *Revelation and the Bible*
J. Orr: *Revelation and Inspiration*
B.B. Warfield: *The Inspiration and Authority of the Bible;* and, in particular, the introductory essay by C. Van Til
W. Whitaker: *A Treatise of the Holy Scriptures*

4

THE ATTRIBUTES OF GOD:

THE INCOMMUNICABLE

ATTRIBUTES

✛

FRED H. KLOOSTER

Fred H. Klooster, Associate Professor of Systematic Theology at Calvin Theological Seminary, Grand Rapids, Michigan, received his general and theological education at Calvin College (B.A., 1944), Calvin Theological Seminary (B.D., 1947), Westminster Theological Seminary (Th.M., 1948), and the Free University of Amsterdam (Th.D., 1951). He is the author of *The Incomprehensibility of God in the Orthodox Presbyterian Conflict*, *Calvin's Doctrine of Predestination*, and *The Significance of Barth's Theology*.

The *Westminster Shorter Cathechism* beautifully describes God as "Spirit, infinite, eternal, and unchangeable, in his being, power, holiness, justice, goodness, and truth" (Question 4). The Belgic Confession of Faith begins similarly: "We all believe with the heart and confess with the mouth that there is one only simple and spiritual Being, which we call God; and that He is eternal, incomprehensible, invisible, immutable, infinite, almighty, perfectly wise, just, good, and the overflowing fountain of all good" (Article I). Most of these terms are called the attributes or the perfections of God.

The attributes may be defined as those perfections of God which are revealed in Scripture and which are exercised and demonstrated by God in His various works. Reformed and Evangelical theologians have frequently distinguished communicable and incommunicable attributes. The *communicable* attributes of God are those which find some reflection or analogy in man who was created in God's image, while the *incommunicable* attributes of God find little or no analogy in man. The latter—unity, independence, eternity, immensity, and immutability —emphasize the transcendence and exalted character of God.

PRELIMINARY CONSIDERATIONS

(1) It is important to recognize that all of the attributes, both communicable and incommunicable, are the attributes of the one only true and living God—Father, Son, and Holy Spirit. The attributes of God may not be discussed as if they were attributes of deity in general, in order then to move on to consider the triune God as one God among many. Christianity is rightly monotheistic, and therefore all the attributes are attributes of the only true God of Scripture. The recognition of this uniqueness of the living God has sometimes been discussed under the incommunicable attribute of the unity of God (*unitas singularitas*).[1]

(2) Since the only true God is the triune God of Scripture, the communicable, as well as the incommunicable, attributes belong equally to the Father, the Son, and the Holy Spirit. There is therefore no absolute necessity for discussing the attributes prior to the doctrine of the Trinity. There is a good reason for doing so, however, since the attributes characterize the divine nature of the triune God. However, the incommunicable attributes of God must not be confused with the "incommunicable property" of each divine Person, that is, with generation, filiation, and spiration.

(3) Discussion of the attributes must also acknowledge the incomprehensibility of God. Finite man can never comprehend the infinite God. The believer will not even be able fully to understand all that God has revealed concerning His attributes.

(4) The attributes must be regarded as essential characteristics of

[1] Cf. Deut. 6:4; I Kings 8:60; Isa. 44:6; Mark 12:28 ff.; Eph. 4:6; I Tim. 2:5.

the Divine Being. It is not man who attributes these perfections to God, God Himself reveals His attributes to us in Scripture. The attributes are objective and real. They describe God as He is in Himself. Hence they are also exercised or demonstrated in the works which God performs in creation, providence, and redemption.

Again, these various attributes must not be regarded as so many parts or compartments of God's being. Each of the attributes describes God as He is, not just as part of His being or simply what He does. Furthermore, there is no scriptural warrant for elevating one attribute, such as love or independence, to pre-eminence and making others mere subdivisions of it. While there is a mutual relationship and inter-relationship between the various attributes, there is a divinely revealed difference between the eternity of God and the immutability of God, between the love of God and the holiness of God, for example. These themes are often considered under the attribute of simplicity (*unitas simplicitas*).

DISCUSSION OF SPECIFIC ATTRIBUTES

Attention will now be directed to a brief consideration of specific incommunicable attributes. The unity and simplicity of God have been discussed. We shall now consider the independence, eternity, immensity, and immutability of God. (The source and norm of our assertions here, as everywhere in theology, must be exclusively the inspired and inerrant Word of God.)

(1) *Independence* (*Aseity*). Scripture indicates the independence of God in various ways. When Moses was sent to Israel and Pharaoh, it was "I am that I am"[2] who sent him, the living God Who has "life in himself."[3] God is not "served by men's hands, as though he needed anything, seeing he himself giveth to all life, and breath and all things."[4] He works "all things according to the counsel of his will"[5] and His counsel "standeth fast forever."[6] In this light, the independence of God may be defined as that perfection which indicates that God is not dependent upon anything outside of Himself, but that He is self-sufficient in His whole being, in His decrees and in all His works.

Although God has the ground of His existence in Himself, He is not self-caused or self-originated, for the eternal God has neither beginning

2 Exod. 3:14.   3 John 5:26.
4 Acts 17:25.   5 Eph. 1:11.
6 Ps. 33:11.

nor end. The independence of God includes more than the idea of God's *aseity* or self-existence. His independence characterizes not only His existence, but His whole being and His attributes, His decrees and His works of creation, providence, and redemption.

The biblical view of God's independence does not permit one to identify the God of Scripture with the abstract philosophical concept of the Absolute of Spinoza or Hegel. The self-existent, independent God of Scripture is the living God Who is not only exalted above the whole creation, but is at the same time its creator and sustainer. And in governing the world, God entered into fellowship with man before the fall, and after the fall He established a new fellowship in the covenant of grace. Although God works all things according to the counsel of His will, He sometimes performs His will through immediate and secondary causes. He uses men, for example, in the all-important task of publishing the Gospel.

(2) *Eternity*. The infinity of God is sometimes considered as an absolute perfection which characterizes all God's attributes as limitless and perfect. In this sense, all the communicable attributes would be characterized by the incommunicable attribute of infinity. It is primarily with reference to time and space, however, that the infinity of God is considered as the eternity and the immensity of God.

Scripture speaks of "the eternal God" Who is our dwelling place.[7] He is "the King eternal,"[8] existing before the foundation of the world "from everlasting to everlasting,"[9] "the Alpha and the Omega."[10] He "inhabiteth eternity,"[11] His "years shall have no end";[12] and "one day is with the Lord as a thousand years, and a thousand years as one day."[13]

Eternity may be defined as that perfection of God which expresses His transcendence with respect to time. God has neither beginning nor end. He does not undergo growth, development, maturation. He existed before the world, He dwells even now in eternity, and He will continue as the eternal God even when history has ended.

Although we must acknowledge that God is not subject to the limitations of time, we must also recognize that time is God's creation and that He is the Lord of history. History is the unfolding of His

[7] Deut. 33:27.
[8] I Tim. 1:17.
[9] Ps. 90:2.
[10] Rev. 1:8.
[11] Isa. 57:15.
[12] Ps. 102:27.
[13] II Pet. 3:8.

sovereign counsel. It was in the "fulness of time" that "God sent forth his son."[14] Time is meaningful for the eternal God, for it was on a Friday that Christ died on the cross and on Sunday morning that He rose from the grave. The risen Christ told His disciples, "Lo, I am with you always, even unto the end of the world."[15] The Christian, therefore, confidently confesses: "My times are in thy hand."[16]

(3) *Immensity and Omnipresence.* God is a God both at hand and afar off so that no one can hide himself in a secret place: "Do not I fill heaven and earth? saith Jehovah."[17] Heaven is His throne and the earth is His footstool.[18] Therefore no one can escape the omnipresent and omniscient God.[19] "He is not far from each one of us; for in him we live, and move, and have our being."[20]

In the light of such passages, the immensity of God may be defined as that perfection of God which expresses His transcendence with respect to space. And omnipresence expresses the fact that this transcendent God is yet present everywhere in heaven and earth.

Here again one must seek to grasp the positive implications of this incommunicable attribute. God is spirit; He has no body and hence is not limited by space. Therefore, we are not bound to Jerusalem or any other place in our worship of the true God.[21] On the other hand, it was into this world that God sent His only begotten Son. And Christ, Who now governs the whole cosmos, will come again physically at the end of history to judge the living and dead.

(4) *Immutability.* God is described in Scripture as "the Father of lights, with whom can be no variation, neither shadow that is cast by turning."[22] "For I, Jehovah, change not"[23] is His own affirmation. And by an oath He has "immutably" witnessed to the immutability of His counsel."[24]

Immutability is that perfection which designates God's constancy and unchangeableness in His being, decrees, and works. He remains forever the same true God, faithful to Himself, His decrees, His revelation, and His works. He undergoes no change from within, nor does He undergo change due to anything outside of Himself.

It is necessary to ask whether the immutability of God can be

---

14 Gal. 4:4.   15 Matt. 28:20.
16 Ps. 31:15.   17 Jer. 23:23 f.
18 Isa. 66:1.   19 Ps. 139.
20 Acts 17:27 f.   21 John 4:21 ff.
22 James 1:17.   23 Mal. 3:6.
24 Heb. 6:17 f.

maintained in the face of several scriptural assertions concerning a certain "repentance" of God. For example, with respect to the unfaithfulness of Saul, God told Samuel: "It repented me that I have set up Saul to be king."[25] However, there is a specific statement in the same chapter which indicates that God cannot repent. After telling Saul that God was taking the kingdom from him and giving it to another (David), Samuel adds: "And also the Strength of Israel will not lie nor repent."[26] It appears then that God's "repentance" must be understood in an anthropomorphic sense to describe the depth of His displeasure and grief in relation to the horrible sins of men. At the same time, the faithfulness, constancy, and immutability of God stand out in His taking the kingdom from Saul and giving it to David, for the sake of keeping His faithful covenant.

There are also instances in which the "repentance" of God is related to a condition, either expressed or implied. The general rule in such instances is expressed in Jeremiah 18: "If that nation, concerning which I have spoken, turn from their evil, I will repent of the evil that I thought to do unto them . . . if they do what which is evil in my sight, that they obey not my voice, then I will repent of the good, wherewith I said I would benefit them."[27] Thus, with respect to Nineveh, Jehovah "saw their works, that they turned from their evil way; and God repented of the evil which he said he would do unto them; and he did it not."[28] Similar references to God's "repentance" occur in Amos and Joel.[29] In these instances also the word "repentance" is used in an anthropomorphic way to express God's faithful response to the meeting of a condition, either expressed or implied in His promise or threat. Rather than contradict the immutability of God, this "repentance" in the total context of Scripture emphasizes that God is faithful and true to His word and promise forever. There is no "holy mutability of God," as Karl Barth claims. "The Lord hath sworn and will not repent,"[30] and His "counsel shall stand."[31]

The immutability of God does not mean, however, that God is immobile or inactive. The Christian God is always active, never unemployed or incapacitated. He not only sustains or preserves all that He has created, but He actively governs it in accord with His sovereign

[25] I Sam. 15:11.
[27] Jer. 18:8 ff.
[29] Amos 7:3, 6; Joel 2:13 f.
[31] Isa. 46:10.

[26] I Sam. 15:28 f.; cf. Num. 23:19.
[28] Jonah 3:10; cf. 3:9; 4:2.
[30] Ps. 110:4.

and immutable counsel. In all His works, the eternal and sovereign God executes His decree and shows Himself "the same yesterday, and to-day, yea and forever."[32]

CONCLUSION

The incommunicable attributes describe the transcendent greatness of the triune God. He is self-sufficient and all-sufficient, transcendent above time and space and yet present everywhere in heaven and and earth; He remains forever the same true God, unchangeable in His being, wisdom, power, holiness, justice, goodness, and truth. Since all theology concerns God and His relations with men, one's entire theological position is reflected in the doctrine of the attributes of God. Therefore, a biblical doctrine of the attributes of God should reflect itself in the whole of one's theology.

BIBLIOGRAPHY

Reformed

H. Bavinck: *The Doctrine of God*
L. Berkhof: *Systematic Theology*
S. Charnock: *The Attributes of God*
A.A. Hodge: *Outlines of Theology*
C. Hodge: *Systematic Theology*, I
W.G.T. Shedd: *Dogmatic Theology*, I

Neo-orthodox

G. Aulén: *The Faith of the Christian Church*
K. Barth: *Die kirchliche Dogmatik*, II, 1
E. Brunner: *The Christian Doctrine of God*

[32] Heb. 13:8.

5

THE ATTRIBUTES OF GOD:

THE COMMUNICABLE

ATTRIBUTES

✝

ANTHONY A. HOEKEMA

Anthony A. Hoekema, Professor of Systematic Theology at Calvin Theological Seminary, Grand Rapids, Michigan, received his general and theological education at Calvin College (B.A., 1936), University of Michigan (M.A., 1937), Calvin Theological Seminary (B.D., 1942), and Princeton Theological Seminary (Th.D., 1953).

God's attributes cannot be separated from His Being. God and His perfections are one. We may not think of love and righteousness as incidental aspects of God's character; on the contrary, God is with His whole Being love and righteousness, grace and holiness. Because this is so, one attribute cannot be limited by another. We may not say, for example, that God is not infinitely righteous because He is love. Though the attributes are many, God is one. While we distinguish the attributes for purposes of study, we can never separate them.

This essay will concern itself with the so-called communicable attributes of God. We may define these as attributes to which some analogy is found in man (the incommunicable being those to which no analogy is found in man). It should be remembered, however, that the difference between these two groups of attributes is relative. God possesses all His communicable attributes in an incommunicable way. Whatever we find in man by way of analogy is but a faint reflection of these perfections as found in God.

The following division of the communicable attributes has been adapted from Berkhof's *Systematic Theology*: 1. intellectual attributes: knowledge and wisdom; 2. moral attributes: goodness, love, grace, mercy, longsuffering, veracity (including faithfulness), holiness, righteousness; 3. volitional attributes: the sovereign will of God and the sovereign power of God.

INTELLECTUAL ATTRIBUTES

Under the intellectual attributes, we note first the *knowledge* of God. Scripture tells us that "God is light and in him is no darkness at all."[1] This designation tells us that God knows all things.[2] God knows Himself thoroughly and completely. Further, God knows all that exists outside Himself. To this attribute, we give the name of God's *omniscience*. It includes the minutest details, even the numbering of the hairs of our heads.

God's *wisdom*, though related to His knowledge, is to be distinguished from it. Wisdom means the application of knowledge to the reaching of a goal. God's wisdom implies that God uses the best possible means to reach the goals He has set for Himself. The Old Testament Psalmist was impressed with the evidence of God's wisdom in creation: "O Jehovah, how manifold are thy works! In wisdom hast thou made them all."[3] Joseph in Egypt saw the wisdom of God revealed in the providential ordering of his life,[4] whereas Paul particularly saw that wisdom displayed in the plan of salvation.[5]

MORAL ATTRIBUTES

Under the moral attributes, we list first of all the *goodness* of God. By this we understand "that perfection of God which prompts Him to

[1] John 1:5. [All quotations from ASV.]
[2] I John 3:20.   [3] Ps. 104:24.
[4] Gen. 50:20.   [5] I Cor. 1:18, 24.

deal bountifully and kindly with all his creatures."[6] This goodness is spoken of in such passages as Psalm 145:9[7] and Acts 14:17. By some theologians, this goodness of God is called His "common grace," in distinction from His special grace shown only to His elect people.

The *love* of God is very prominent in Scripture, especially in the New Testament. The three persons of the Trinity exist in an eternal fellowship of love,[8] but in and through Christ, God reveals His love to man. In this connection, John 3:16 comes to mind, as well as many other memorable New Testament passages. All the blessings of salvation are the fruits of God's love: "Behold what manner of love the Father hath bestowed upon us, that we should be called children of God."[9]

One of the major questions in the area of the attributes today is: How can we properly relate the love and the righteousness of God? The liberal theology of the nineteenth century virtually cancelled out the righteousness of God. Ritschl, it will be recalled, said that there was no such thing as the wrath of God, and that anyone who thinks so is laboring under a delusion. In contemporary neo-orthodox theology, this old liberalism has supposedly been repudiated. As we examine the doctrine of the attributes, however, noting what neo-orthodox theologians teach particularly about the love and righteousness of God, we shall have occasion to ask ourselves whether the liberal rejection of the wrath of God has *really* been abandoned by these men, or whether it has simply been restated in a different form.

Contemporary theologians describe love as the center and core of God's revelation. Karl Barth, in fact, divides God's attributes into "The Perfections of the Divine Loving" and "The Perfections of the Divine Freedom," insisting that we must not begin with attributes which concern the being or essence of God and then go on to speak of His love, but that we must begin by discussing the love of God.[10] When Barth goes on to define God's love, he includes in its scope all men and all of creation: "God is He who in His Son, Jesus Christ, loves all His children, in His children all men, and in men His whole creation."[11]

Emil Brunner, like Barth, stresses that love is the very nature of God[12] and quotes with approval Luther's statement that God is "an

[6] Berkhof, *op. cit.,* p. 70.
[7] "Jehovah is good to all."
[8] John 3:35; 17:24.
[9] I John 3:1.
[10] K. Barth: *Die kirchliche Dogmatik,* II, 1, pp. 348 ff.
[11] *Ibid.,* p. 351.
[12] E. Brunner: *The Christian Doctrine of God,* p. 185.

abyss of eternal love."[13] Brunner describes this love as *agape* (love poured out on those who are worthless; love which does not desire to get but to give) in distinction from *eros* (love of someone because he is worthy of being loved). At this point, Brunner acknowledges his indebtedness to Anders Nygren.[14]

These men have much to teach us. However, when we note Brunner's insistence that, for Paul, the righteousness and mercy of God are identical,[15] and when we look again at Barth's definition of love, we begin to wonder whether both of them do not assume that *agape* requires God to treat all men alike. Our Lord Jesus Christ, however, clearly taught that there is a wrath of God which is to be revealed against those who reject God and refuse to believe in His Son. Christ speaks of the outer darkness, of the place where the fire is not quenched, of a hell into which one may be cast, and of the disastrous consequences of losing one's soul.

Associated with God's love are His *grace*—God's love shown to those who have not deserved it, but have rather deserved its opposite— His *mercy*—God's love shown to those who are in misery or distress— and His *longsuffering*—that aspect of God's love whereby He endures evil men in spite of their disobedience, and seeks to lead them to repentance.

By the *veracity* of God, we mean His truthfulness. God is the source of truth, true in His revelation and true in His promises. In this connection, it is particularly the *faithfulness* of God which is to be stressed: He keeps his promises, and is ever faithful to His covenant people.[16]

We come next to the *holiness* of God. The origin of the Hebrew root QADASH (the Hebrew word for holy) is obscure; its basic meaning, however, seems to be that of apartness. Thus, God's holiness means first of all that He is other than the creature, infinitely exalted above His creation. In this sense, the holiness of God is not so much a separate attribute as a qualification of all that God is and does. As an attribute, however, God's holiness means, negatively, that He is "of purer eyes than to behold evil"[17]; that He is free from all that is impure and hates all sin. Positively, God's holiness denotes His moral excellence, the fact that He perfectly embodies all that is pure and good.

13 *Ibid.*, p. 168.
15 *Ibid.*, p. 301.
17 Hab. 1:13.

14 *Ibid.*, p. 185 ff.
16 *See* II Tim. 2:13.

When we take up the *righteousness* of God, we touch upon an attribute which is the object of much contemporary discussion. The basic idea of righteousness is that of becoming conformed to a rule or law. God may therefore be called righteous because He acts in accordance with law, not a law above Him but a law which is within Him, of which He Himself is the author. By God's rectoral justice, we mean God's rectitude as the Ruler of the Universe, particularly of His moral creatures. By His distributive justice, we mean His rectitude in the execution of His law. In this connection, we think first of God's remunerative justice, which distributes rewards not on the basis of merit but solely by grace. Paul speaks of this in Romans 2:6 and 7: "Who will render to every man according to his work: to them that by patience in well-doing seek for glory and honor and incorruption, eternal life." By retributive justice, we mean God's infliction of penalties upon those who disobey Him; this justice is an expression of His wrath. Paul speaks of this in verses 8 and 9 of Romans 2: "But unto them that are factious, and obey not the truth, but obey unrighteousness, shall be wrath and indignation, tribulation and anguish, upon every soul of man that worketh evil."[18] Although it is true that in Scripture the righteousness of God is generally applied to the salvation of sinners (think of what Paul says about justification in Rom. 3:21-28), the Bible teaches unequivocally that there is such a thing as retributive righteousness or the wrath of God.[19]

Since this is a matter of crucial importance, let us see what contemporary neo-orthodox theologians teach about the righteousness of God. Barth treats God's mercy and righteousness together, as "Perfections of the Divine Loving." Citing both Luther and Anselm, he stresses the identity of God's righteousness and mercy.[20] For Barth, the great message of the Bible is: "There is no righteousness of God which is not also mercy and no mercy of God which is not also righteousness."[21] In distinction from Ritschl, Barth maintains that there is such a thing as a punitive righteousness in God.[22] In a discussion of the significance of Good Friday, Barth goes on to show that God's retributive or punitive righteousness is wholly satisfied by the crucifixion of His Son.[23] While appreciating the profound insights offered here,

18 Cf. also Rom. 1:32 and II Thess. 1:8.
19 *See* W.G.T. Shedd: *Dogmatic Theology*, I, pp. 380 ff.
20 Barth, *op. cit.*, pp. 377 ff.   21 *Ibid.*, p. 380.
22 *Ibid.*, pp. 382, 391.   23 *Ibid.*, pp. 395-406.

we look in vain for any suggestion that God's retributive righteousness is also to be expressed at the last day in the punishment of the lost. In fact, Barth asserts that it is characteristic of heathen but not of scriptural eschatology to put "these two ways" before our eyes: the way of eternal glory and the way of everlasting fire.[24] The conclusion seems inescapable that, for Barth, there will be no final punishment of those who are lost. Barth's teachings on election, in fact, have led Brunner to designate Barth's views as "the most thoroughgoing doctrine of universalism that has ever been formulated."[25]

So far as Brunner's own teachings are concerned, he quotes approvingly Luther's affirmation that the revelation of God's wrath is his "strange work," whereas the revelation of God's love is His "proper work."[26] Like Luther, Brunner holds that the wrath of God reached its climax on the cross, but that here faith sees God's love behind His "strange work."[27] When, however, we ask about Brunner's view of retributive justice, culminating in eternal punishment for the lost, we get an equivocal answer. Brunner, while sharply critical of Barth's view of election,[28] joins Barth in rejecting double predestination.[29] Brunner firmly rejects universal salvation[30] and says that we cannot eliminate a final judgment of wrath from the New Testament.[31] Yet he expresses his doubts about eternal punishment[32] and elsewhere suggests that to die without Christ is equivalent to being annihilated.[33]

We see that, in this respect, Brunner is not as radical as Barth. Yet Brunner hesitates about eternal punishment, a doctrine which Nels Ferré decisively rejects.[34] As we reflect upon the views of these contemporary theologians, we cannot suppress the following questions: Does God's retributive righteousness and particularly God's wrath really come into its own in the views of these men? Or do we have here a repetition of the liberal subordination of the wrath of God to His love? Does not this contemporary treatment of God's wrath rob the Gospel message of its deepest earnestness? Does it do justice to the teaching of our Lord, Who spoke some of the sternest words about the wrath of God?

[24] *Ibid.*, p. 293.
[25] Brunner, *op. cit.*, p. 314.
[26] *Ibid.*, p. 169.
[27] *Ibid.*, p. 173.
[28] *Ibid.*, pp. 348 ff.
[29] *Ibid.*, pp. 345 ff.
[30] *Ibid.*, p. 352.
[31] *Ibid..* p. 349.
[32] *Ibid.*, p. 353.
[33] E. Brunner: *Faith, Hope, and Love*, p. 56.
[34] N. Ferré: *The Christian Understanding of God*, pp. 217 ff.

VOLITIONAL ATTRIBUTES

Coming finally to the volitional attributes, we distinguish between God's *sovereign will* and His *sovereign power*. By God's *sovereign will*, we mean His directing of the events of the universe and of the actions of His creatures in accordance with His plan. Needless to say, this sovereign will is the final cause of all that happens.[35] To suggest that things may happen which are not under the ultimate direction of God's will is to detract from His sovereignty and thereby from His majesty.

What do we mean by God's *sovereign power*, also called His *omnipotence?* To say that God can do all things is to open the door to all kinds of foolish questions, such as: Can God sin? Can God make a stone too heavy for Himself to lift? It is better to define omnipotence as that power by virtue of which God can do whatever He wills to accomplish.[36]

God's omnipotence must not be so conceived as to leave no room for human decision or to reduce man to the dimensions of a radio-guided missile. Divine omnipotence establishes human freedom and responsibility. It is precisely this fact which makes the sovereignty of God so deeply mysterious that man cannot fathom it.

BIBLIOGRAPHY

Standard systematic theologies by H. Bavinck, L. Berkhof, C. Hodge, and W.G.T. Shedd
References to neo-orthodox works found cited above
S. Charnock: *The Attributes of God*

[35] Eph. 1:11: ". . . who worketh all things after the counsel of his will . . ."
[36] *See* Matt. 19:26.

6

THE HOLY TRINITY

✛ 1192667

J. KENNETH GRIDER

J. Kenneth Grider, Associate Professor of Theology at Nazarene Theological Seminary, Kansas City, Missouri, received his general and theological education at Olivet Nazarene College (B.A., 1944, Th.B., 1945), Drew Theological Seminary (B.D., 1948, M.A., 1950), Glasgow University (Ph.D., 1952). He is the author of *Psalms* in the Aldersgate Biblical Series and a contributor to *The Biblical Expositor* and *Dictionary of Theology*.

Off with our shoes, please, for the Holy Trinity is holy ground. Away with finely figured syllogisms and ordinary arithmetic: here, logic and mathematics do not suffice. The need is rather for a listening ear, an obedient heart,[1] rapt adoration, a careful engagement with the Holy Scriptures.

That the one God is three-personed is an audacious conception. Yet it is the confidence which has possessed us Christians ever since it dawned upon us in the days of His sojourn that Jesus Christ too was divine. We have understood that God is three persons existing in a single, uncompounded nature, in structural togetherness; the mid-numbered one in this eternal society being an actual *alter ego*, as is the

---

[1] John 7:17.

Holy Spirit as well; there being three "Hims," three centers of con-sciousness, but one nature, essence, substance, Godhead.

Call it an intellectual elixir if it must be called that. Discount it as an "incomprehensible jargon," as Thomas Jefferson did. Throw it off as "the fairytale of the three Lord Shaftesburys," as did Matthew Arnold. Nonetheless, this is our confidence.

We cannot comprehend with our natural faculties this threeness in oneness, oneness in threeness. In part, this is because we have no anal-ogies of it where our native faculties are accustomed to function. No three human persons are structurally one, without any hindrance to a full interpenetration of personal life; always there is a core of privacy about human persons. Nor is a human person, even with his intellect, feeling, and will, of such distinct threeness as we understand to obtain in God. We cannot therefore conceive the One Divine Three in man's image.

BIBLICAL BASIS

The doctrine that God is three persons in one substance or essence is first of all an attempt to explain what is revealed in the Holy Scrip-tures. The unity of God is certainly the indispensable starting point. In the Hebraic-Christian faith there is but one God. Not three, as Roscellin[2] was inclined to say, but only one. Irenaeus, Tertullian, Athanasius, Augustine, the Fathers in general, and the Schoolmen (ex-cepting Roscellin) and the Reformers—all saw it plainly taught in the Scriptures that there is but one God. Those three New Testament "unity" passages used in the Socinian Racovian Catechism to oppose the threeness,[3] are simply enfolded into the Trinitarian conception, which admits that there is but one God.

And yet the Scriptures differentiate the Deity in a three-personal way. The most common designations are, of course, the Father, the Son, and the Holy Spirit. The three are referred to at Jesus' baptism.[4] Our baptism, too, is to be in the name of the three, according to Matthew 28:19. Paul's benediction enumerates them in II Corinthians 13:14. The three are spoken of in John 14-16; Ephesians 2:18; I Peter 1:21, 22, and so on. The Son is called God in John 1:1 and 20:28, I Timothy 3:16, Hebrews 1:8. That the Holy Spirit is God is implied in Hebrews 9:14, I Peter 3:18, II Peter 1:21.

[2] Roscellin was condemned for tritheism at Soissons in 1092.
[3] John 17:13; I Cor. 8:6; Eph. 4:6.   [4] John 1:27-33.

After the nature of God was floodlighted by the New Testament revelation, Christians began to see that in the Old Testament there are numerous lesser lights thrown upon God which point to His tri-personality. One of them is the "holy, holy, holy" of Isaiah's vision in 6:3, when coupled with the "who will go for us?" of 6:8. Another is the plurality of persons possibly implied in the plural *Elohim*, used so often, even in the Deuteronomy 6:4 "unity" passage; and certainly suggested in such passages as "let us make man in our image"[5] and "let us go down, and there confound their language."[6]

CREEDAL STATEMENT

Secondarily, the doctrine of the tri-unity has been devised in order to explain our common experience of God. This common experience, shared in great part because of the scriptural disclosure, has been made express in the Apostles', the Nicene, and the Athanasian creeds. The Apostles' Creed is not clearly Trinitarian. From that compact formula, taken by itself, you might think that only the Father is God, as in Arianism and adoptionism. You might read into it Sabellianism, with the Creed's simple, successive mentions of the Father, Jesus Christ, and the Holy Spirit. But the formulation does not state that the three are one, nor that Jesus Christ and the Holy Spirit are divine. It might be taken as implying that they are not, since the Father and only the Father is referred to as God.

But when you get to the second of the three ecumenical creeds which Western Christianity espouses, the Nicene of 325 A.D., and when you read it with what was added to it on the Holy Spirit in 381, you have a Trinitarianism in which the three are divine and are of one substance. The Athanasian Creed centuries later, named for the fourth century figure most vigorous with a "Nay" to Arius, spells out both the oneness and the threeness much as an anthem conveys and re-conveys its message. At one point that Creed affirms, "So the Father is God; the Son is God; and the Holy Ghost is God. And yet there are not three Gods but one God." It contains the important formula, "neither confounding the persons, nor dividing the substance."

In Eastern Christianity, such as Greek Orthodoxy, it is taught, from the earlier version of the Nicene-Constantinople Creed, that the Holy Spirit "proceedeth from the Father," and not from the Son. In the Athanasian Creed and in Western Christianity in general, it has been

5 Gen. 1:26.   6 Gen. 11:7.

taught that the "Holy Ghost is of the Father and of the Son; neither made, nor created, nor begotten; but proceeding." This surely helps to explain why both "the Spirit of God" and "the Spirit of Christ" appear in Romans 8:9—although some say that the Spirit of Christ is Christ's spirit, meaning Christ himself, which might tend to a binitarianism (as in the Shepherd of Hermas and in the fourth century Macedonian Heresy), but is actually used to a unitarian purpose. The Western view is also suggested in I Peter 1:10, 11, where "the Spirit of Christ," that is, Who proceeds from Christ, is evidently the Holy Spirit and not Christ, because through the prophets He "testified beforehand the sufferings of Christ." A passage in John can be taken as teaching either the single or the double procession of the Spirit, for Jesus says, "But when the Comforter is come, whom I will send unto you from the Father, even the Spirit of truth, which proceedeth from the Father."[7]

MYRIAD IMPUGNERS

There have been opposers aplenty as the centuries have passed. Some have been like Sabellius of the early third century, teaching that the Father, the Son, and the Holy Spirit are three successive ways in which the uni-personal God has manifested Himself. Many have been either adoptian or Arian, the latter being in a sense closer to the Trinitarian view, in teaching not simply that a man was adopted as God's son in a special way, but that Christ was the first and highest created being, of like substance with the Father, and the Holy Spirit a less exalted creature. But in neither of these is there participation in human life on the part of the Deity; in neither of them does a God-man die for our sins. God remains alone and aloof, unhurt by our humanity.

Faustus Socinus[8] was conspicuous for his anti-Trinitarianism and fathered the Unitarians, who have now joined organically with the Universalists. The English Deists, such as Lord Herbert and John Locke, impugned the doctrine, and soon Leibniz and Wolff in Germany were also "enlightened." That country's Kant, Schleiermacher, and Hegel opposed the doctrine also, generally in the direction of adoptionism or an impersonal pantheism—although Schleiermacher considered himself to be Sabellian.

The late William Adams Brown of Union Theological Seminary in New York figured that the threeness is simply the way we think about

[7] John 15:26.   [8] Faustus Socinus, 1539–1604.

God, not the way in which he exists.[9] One of the most articulate recent oppositions to the doctrine has come from another Union professor, Cyril C. Richardson.[10] Richardson likes to speak of the three as "symbols," not persons. Frequently, he calls them "terms."[12] He supposes that the doctrine "often beclouds[13] the vital concerns of the Christian faith." To him it is "an artificial threefoldness."[14] If you are a "thoughtful Christian," you are not supposed to believe in it.[15]

Richardson properly credits Leonard Hodgson with giving us one of our superb studies of Trinitarian doctrine.[16] But while Hodgson says that there are three centers of consciousness in God, and that this makes for a more "intensive" unity, such as obtains in organisms but not in arithmetic,[17] Richardson admits the possibility of the three making for a more intensified unity, but asks why Hodgson stops with three centers of consciousness. Richardson suggests, "The logic of this should perhaps have driven Hodgson to posit an *infinite* number of persons in the Trinity."[18] Hodgson posits only three because both Scripture and the creeds stop there—although Hodgson is, like many others, so vocal in our time in holding that revelation is in events conceived as divine disclosures rather than also in the biblical records of those events. Like Barth, Hodgson is more orthodox on this doctrine than on the Bible itself.

Not as many are impugning the doctrine of the Trinity now as, say, a generation or two ago, although the eternality of the three persons is often lost in merely modal views. During the late summer of 1960, the ninety-member central committee of the World Council of Churches voted to recommend to the 1961 New Delhi World Council meeting that all member denominations confess faith not only in "Jesus Christ as God and Saviour," as at present, but, along with a few other changes, in "the one God, Father, Son, and Holy Spirit."

A PRIZE TO PROMULGATE

The doctrine of the Trinity, scripturally supportable and spelled out particularly in the historic creeds, is no doubt the one basic Chris-

[9] W.A. Brown: *Dogmatics in Outline*, p. 156.
[10] C.C. Richardson: *The Doctrine of the Trinity*, 1958.
[11] *Ibid.*, p. 111.   [12] *Ibid.*, p. 98.
[13] *Ibid.*, p. 14.   [14] *Ibid.*, p. 15.
[15] *Ibid.*, p. 14.
[16] L. Hodgson: *The Doctrine of the Trinity*, 1944.
[17] *Ibid.*, p. 96.   [18] *Ibid., p.* 113.

tian belief, when it is thought of comprehensively so as to include re-demption. In one of the few choice books on the subject, Charles W. Lowry calls the conception "....at once the ultimate and the supreme glory of the Christian faith."[19]

There is a richness in the dogma. It means that God is no bare monad, but an eternal fellowship. It is exciting to realize that God did not exist in solitary aloneness from all eternity, prior to the creation of the world and man, but in a blessed communion.

Although Jesus Christ is the proper magnetic center of our faith, and although faith in Him distinguishes ours from other religions, such as Judaism and Unitarianism, we evangelical Protestants are sometimes prone to relegate the Father and the Holy Spirit to lesser importance. It is to be expected that we would feel close to the one Who "pitched his tent" among us, Who bit dust for us, wept for us, died for us, is coming to translate us. Stressing the deity of Christ as we need to do, we might tend to make the Begotten One the first instead of the second person of the Trinity. The three are of equal dignity, majesty, glory, power, eternity. Each has all the divine attributes. But the Father has a priority in eternally generating the Son, and the Holy Spirit proceeds from the Father and the Son. The fact that the incarnated Son obeys the Father, along with the biblical portrayal of the Holy Spirit as pe-culiarly characterized by personal self-effacement, also points to a priority of the Father. Whereas Jesus said that He and the Father are one,[20] He also said, "My Father is greater than I."[21] He declared, "For I have not spoken of myself; but the Father which sent me, he gave me a commandment, what I should say, and what I should speak."[22]

One way in which we have tended to give Christ the first-numbered position is by so often directing our prayers to Him. Actually, prayer may be made to any one of the persons. But, ordinarily, according to our biblical precedent, we should address the Father in Christ's name and as the Spirit urges us, both in private and in public prayer. Very frequently, however, our private prayers, and often our public ones, are directed to Christ. Often, when directed to "God" or to the "Father," they are concluded "in Thy name"—which probably means that we have thought of the prayer as directed to Christ.

A similar tendency to error in evangelical Protestantism lies in the

[19] C.W. Lowry: *The Trinity and Christian Devotion*, 1946, p. xi.
[20] John 10:30.   [21] John 14:28.
[22] John 12:49.

common practice of asking Christ to forgive. He can forgive sins, according to the New Testament.[23] But according to the same New Covenant Scriptures, we are ordinarily to think of the Father as forgiving the sinner, because Christ by his death assuaged the Father's holy wrath.[24]

Our tendency to give priority to the middle person may be reflected also in our making next to nothing of Trinity Sunday. It is doubtful if a high percentage of evangelical Protestant ministers even know that this festival falls the first Sunday after Pentecost. Because it was inaugurated in the West in 1305 and universally observed after 1334, and since we of the Reformation faith share the belief that God is triune, we might well mark the festival as do the Romanists and the Anglicans.

BIBLIOGRAPHY

P. Schaff, ed.: *Nicene and Post-Nicene Fathers*, "On the Holy Trinity" by Augustine
R.S. Franks: *The Doctrine of the Trinity*
L. Hodgson: *The Doctrine of the Trinity*
C.W. Lowry: *The Trinity and Christian Devotion*
B.B. Warfield: *Studies in Tertullian and Augustine*

[23] Mark 2:10.   [24] Rom. 3:24–26.

7

THE DECREES OF GOD

✚

GEOFFREY W. BROMILEY

Geoffrey W. Bromiley, Professor of Church History at Fuller
Theological Seminary, Pasadena, California, received his general
and theological education at Emmanuel College, Cambridge
(B.A., 1936; M.A., 1940), and the University of Edinburgh
(Ph.D., 1943; D. Litt., 1948; D.D., 1961. He is the author of
Reasonable Service: Baptism and the Anglican Reformers,
Thomas Cranmer, Theologian, and *Doctrine of the Sacraments*,
among other works. He was also the editor and translator of
Karl Barth's *Church Dogmatics*.

In definition of the decree or decrees of God, the *Westminster Confession*[1] maintains that "God from all eternity did, by the most wise and
holy counsel of his own will, freely and unchangeably ordain whatsoever comes to pass; yet so as thereby neither is God the author of
sin, nor is violence offered to the will of the creatures, nor is the liberty
or contingency of secondary causes taken away, but rather established."[2]

The decree of God is thus equivalent to the effective resolve or purpose, grounded in His free wisdom, by which God eternally controls
His creation. It refers not merely to predestination, to salvation or per-

[1] 1647.

[2] *Westminster Confession*, Chapter III.

dition, but to all God's action in the creation and direction of the world. As the *Shorter Catechism* puts it, "The decrees of God are his eternal purpose according to the counsel of his will, whereby, for his own glory, he hath foreordained whatsoever comes to pass."[3]

IMPORTANT DETAILS ARE TO BE NOTED

First, the decrees are eternal, and are not therefore subject to temporal conditions nor variable in the light of changing situations. Second, they accord with God's wisdom, and cannot therefore be dismissed as the capricious decisions of naked sovereignty. Third, they allow for secondary wills and causes, so that they are not a mere fate, nor deterministic nexus, nor Islamic will. Fourth, they serve God's pleasure, and therefore are neither meaningless nor discordant with the righteous love which characterizes God and redounds to His glory.

The reference of the decrees is specifically to creation, providence, and election. "God executeth his decrees in the works of creation and providence."[4] "By the decree of God some angels and men are predestinated unto eternal life, and others foreordained to everlasting death."[5] In this respect, Westminster follows Calvin's *Institutes*, which speak both of the general decrees of God[6] and then of his special decree of election.[7] Within the same understanding, the order of the decrees formed the subject of the great infralapsarian-supralapsarian debate of the seventeenth century, the one party ranging the decree of election after the decrees of creation and the fall (within God's providential ordering), the other ascribing priority to the decree of predestination. From the order of treatment, both Calvin and Westminster tend to the infralapsarian view, which implies a logical succession of decrees rather than a primary decree subserved by others. This emerges more clearly in the *Catechism*.

At the same time, there is an obvious hesitation to use the plural, even at Westminster. Strictly, indeed, the *Confession* speaks only of the decree of God, and the real theme of chapter VI is quickly seen to be predestination. This is more consonant with the earlier Reformation tradition, as may be seen from statements such as the *Belgic Confession*,[8] the *Thirty-Nine Articles*,[9] and even Dort,[10] with its reference

[3] *Shorter Catechism*, Question 7.   [4] *Shorter Catechism*, Question 8.
[5] *Westminster Confession*, Chapter III, 3.
[6] J. Calvin: *Institutes*, I, XVII, XVIII.
[7] *Ibid.*, III, XXII–XXIV.   [8] 1561, *Article XVI*.
[9] 1563, *Article XVII*.   [10] 1619.

to the one decree of election and reprobation grounded in the divine good pleasure. Obviously this does not mean a negating of the sovereignty of God in creation and providence. It does not imply that the decree of God cannot be multiple and varied in operation. It suggests, however, that there is a higher right in supralapsarianism, so long as it is not artificially entangled in temporal conceptions. The purpose or decree of God is ultimately one, namely, the establishment of gracious covenant and fellowship with a chosen people as fulfilled in the saving work of Christ. Necessarily, the basic decree carries with it other general or detailed decrees, just as the unity of God includes a wealth of perfections. In itself, however, it is one and supreme. Hence, it is perhaps better to keep to the singular of Westminster and the earlier confessions, not ranging creation, providence, and so forth under a wider genus "decree," but interpreting them in relation to the "eternal and immutable decree from which all our salvation springs and depends."[11]

But is it right even to use the term "decree" in this context? As in the opening definition, it obviously has to be carefully safeguarded to prevent misunderstanding. In the Bible it is used for the most part of the arbitrary, inflexible, and often vexatious orders of despotic rulers rather than the resolve of God. Perhaps this underlies the sparing use, often in verb form, in the earlier confessions. It is hardly conceivable that, for example, the *Helvetic* or *Gallican Confessions*, or the *Heidelberg Catechism*, should devote a special section to the divine decree or decrees. On the other hand, the term seems in practice to be unavoidable. It turns up in almost every document. Even the Remonstrants refer to God's "eternal and immutable decree" in their first *Article*,[12] and more blatantly Arminian statements only limit the range of the divine decree; for example, that "God does not decree all events which he knows will occur."[13] Similarly, the Lutheran *Formula of Concord*[14] distinguishes between foreknowledge and foreordination,[15] but in relation to predestination or election it states that God "in his eternal counsel has decreed."[16] There thus seems to be good reason for the judgment of Karl Barth, no enthusiast for the word, that it "describes something which cannot be denied," and is not therefore to be erased or abandoned.[17]

[11] 1560, *Scots Confession*, Article VII.   [12] 1610.
[13] 1834, *Free Will Baptist Confession*.   [14] 1576.
[15] Lutheran *Formula of Concord, Article* XI, 1.
[16] Lutheran *Formula of Concord, Article* XI, 12.
[17] K. Barth: *Die kirchliche Dogmatik*, II, 2, p. 182.

The dangers of the term are easy to see. Even in Scripture it has associations with the arbitrarily, rather than the righteously and meaningfully, sovereign. In itself it emphasizes sheer power instead of holy, wise, and loving power. It suggests harsh enforcement rather than beneficent overruling. It implies that which is fixed and static, so that man is an automaton and God himself, having made his decree, is unemployed and uninterested; that is, the God of deism Who simply leaves things to take their decreed course. Perhaps it is not insignificant that the heaviest casualties to Unitarian deism seemed to be suffered in churches which emphasized the decrees. Perhaps it is not for nothing that Lutherans detected a Turkish or Islamic impulse in Reformed teaching. Perhaps it is with reason that some Reformer apologists are still ill-advised enough to find support in scientific or Mohammedan determinism. There are, in fact, real dangers in the term and its use.

Nevertheless, no single word is so well adapted to express the true sovereignty, constancy, and infallibility of the divine counsel, purpose, and resolve; and therefore biblical and evangelical expositors have little option but to use it. Safeguards are no doubt required. It does not, perhaps, form a genuinely suitable heading, as at Westminster. It is best handled in the text where there can be proper qualification. Yet that which God wills and purposes is, in a true sense, decreed by Him. His wise and omnipotent resolve constitutes His free, sovereign, and incontestable decree.

Most of the difficulties derive, perhaps, from a failure to remember that the decree is genuinely eternal, and cannot, therefore, be a lifeless, deistic fiat. No doubt much of the wonder of eternity is that it is pre-temporal. To this extent, an eternal decree is rightly seen to be, prior to its fulfillment, belonging to the past before the beginning of all things. But eternal does not mean only pre-temporal. It also means co-temporal and post-temporal. The decree of God is thus present and future as well as past. It is with and after the fulfillment, as well as before it. Deistic conceptions can arise only out of an ill-balanced and unhealthy over-concentration on the one aspect of eternity, which is also what gives such unreality to the famous infralapsarian-supralapsarian discussion. The truly eternal decree is just as alive and relevant today and tomorrow as it was yesterday. Made in eternity, it has been made, but is still being made and still to be made. The decree accompanies and follows, as well as precedes its fulfillment. It cannot, then, be regarded merely as a lifeless foreordination. It is really the decree of God, and therefore an eternal decree in the full and proper sense.

Even if the deistic threat is averted, however, the difficulty of apparent arbitrariness remains. It is, in fact, heightened by some of the confessions, with their references to the inscrutability of the decree. Thus the *Westminster Confession* speaks of the "secret counsel" of God in election, and his "unsearchable counsel" in reprobation.[18] Dort warns against inquisitive prying into "the secret and deep things of God."[19] The *Gallican Confession*[20] and the *Thirty-Nine Articles*[21] both refer to secrets or secret counsels; and the *Belgic* uses the term "incomprehensible."[22] Now, it is true that according to Scripture the ways of God in nature and history take an astonishing course, so that the detailed decrees of God might well be called unsearchable or inscrutable. It is also true that sinners cannot perceive the things of God, so that even the primary decree, which the others serve and express, may aptly be termed a mystery. Yet the question arises whether this mystery is not revealed in Jesus Christ. Are not believing eyes opened, in part at least, to the ways of God by the Holy Spirit? Can we really say that the basic decree of God, for all the strangeness of its outworkings, is inscrutable, secret, or incomprehensible in the primary and ultimate sense?

The question is pertinent, for it forces us to ask what we really mean by this decree. In the earlier confessions, this seems to be clear. It is God's "eternal and unchangeable counsel, of mere goodness" to elect certain men to salvation in Jesus Christ.[23] It is his "everlasting purpose ... to deliver ... those whom he hath chosen in Christ."[24] This aspect naturally remains in later statements, as we may see from the *Canons of Dort*, I, 7 and the *Westminster Shorter Catechism*, question 20. But a new element tends to emerge. The decree of God comes to be identified specifically with the pre-temporal discrimination between the elect and the reprobate, which we cannot foresee, which is not based on any good works or foreknown response, and which is therefore necessarily inscrutable and apparently arbitrary. This profound, merciful but just acceptance or rejection of men equally involved in ruin is the real decree of God at the beginning or end of his ways, which we can only

---

[18] *Westminster Confession*, III, 5, 7.   [19] Dort, I, 12.
[20] *Gallican Confession*, VIII.   [21] *Thirty-Nine Articles*, XVII.
[22] *Belgic Confession*, XIII.   [23] *Ibid.*, XVI.
[24] *Thirty-Nine Articles*, XVII.

accept since we have neither the means to understand nor the right to challenge it.

The question arises whether this is a justifiable equation. Will not a "special prudence and care"[25] lead us, not to this sorting of individuals, but to Jesus Christ, in whom God's grace and wrath are manifested? If Jesus Christ is really the mirror of election, as also, we might add, of reprobation, are we not to seek the basic decree in Him, whom to see is to see the Father? When we ask concerning the ultimate decree, surely we are still to concentrate on Him in whom the fullness of Godhead dwells, rather than looking abroad to other mysteries.

In other words, the decree of God must be strictly related to Jesus Christ. The *Formula of Concord* puts this well: "This predestination of God is not to be searched out in the hidden counsel of God, but is to be sought in the Word of God ... but the Word of God leads us to Christ.... In Christ, therefore, is the eternal election of God to be sought."[26] The *Remonstrant Articles* also display a fine judgment in their initial definition that "God, by an eternal, unchangeable purpose in Jesus Christ his Son ... hath determined ... to save in Christ for Christ's sake, and through Christ, those who, through the grace of the Holy Ghost, shall believe on this his Son Jesus."

These statements are vitiated, however, by their tendency to make salvation dependent, in the last resort, on the human decision of faith, and their virtual ignoring of the element of reprobation inseparable from the divine decree. We may thus refer again to the fine passage in the *Institutes*, in which Calvin teaches us to seek our election in Christ as the Eternal Wisdom, the Immutable Truth, the Determinate Counsel of the Father.[27] And we may close the whole discussion with some noble sentences from the widely adopted *Second Helvetic Confession*, penned in 1576 by the aging Bullinger of Zürich: "We therefore condemn those who seek otherwhere than in Christ whether they be chosen from all eternity, and what God has decreed of them before all beginning.... Let Christ, therefore, be our looking-glass, in whom we may behold our predestination. We shall have a most evident and sure testimony that we are written in the Book of life if we communicate with Christ, and he be ours, and we be his, by a true faith. Let this comfort us in the temptation touching predestination, than which there is

[25] *Westminster Confession*, III, 8.
[26] Lutheran *Formula of Concord*, Article XI, 5–12.
[27] J. Calvin: *Institutes*, III, XXIV, 5.

none more dangerous: that the promises of God are general to the faithful."[28] "For the ultimate reality of the decree of God, our Lord Jesus Christ, was from all eternity predestinated and foreordained of the Father to be the Saviour of the world."[29] In sum, Jesus Christ Himself is the purpose and decree of God. In Him we see God's righteousnesses both to condemn and to save. Incorporated into Him by faith, we have the assurance that the basic decree to which all others are subject, while it carries with it the condemnation and judgment of sin, is, as such, a decree of grace and life, of fellowship and glory.

BIBLIOGRAPHY

K. Barth: *Die kirchliche Dogmatik*, II, 2; III, 3
J. Calvin: *Institutes*, I, xvi, xxvii; III, xxi–xxiv
H. Heppe: *Reformed Dogmatics*, pp. 137 ff.
C. Hodge: *Systematic Theology*, I, 9
P. Schaff: *The Creeds of Christendom*, Volume III
W.G.T. Shedd: *Dogmatic Theology*

[28] Bullinger: *Second Helvetic Confession,* X.
[29] *Ibid.,* XI.

8

PREDESTINATION

✤

WILLIAM CHILDS ROBINSON

William Childs Robinson, Professor of Historical Theology at Columbia Theological Seminary, Decatur, Georgia, received his general and theological education at Roanoke College (B.A., 1917), the University of South Carolina (M.A., 1919; D.D., 1928), Columbia Theological Seminary (B.D., 1920), Princeton Theological Seminary (Th.M., 1921), and Harvard University (Th.D., 1928). He is the author of *The Certainties of the Gospel*, *What Is Christian Faith*, and *The World of the Cross*, among numerous works.

For Christian faith, predestination is a vision of the King in the glory of His grace, and a warning against transposing the revelation of the majesty of His mercy into any concatenated scheme of human logic. It proclaims the freeness of God's saving grace in Christ, without making of His will an arbitrary fatalism. The ways of Him who predestines are past our tracing out, and the mystery thereof bids us worship where we cannot fathom.

Historically, Augustine of Hippo formulated triple predestination, that is: general predestination or providence, which magnifies God's wisdom in governing all things; special predestination or election in which His free grace is seen in the choice of His people; and preterition

or reprobation by which He passes by and leaves other sinners to the
due desert of their guilt for the manifestation of His power and justice.

In the English Bible, the verb predestinate occurs in the eighth chapter of Romans and in the first chapter of Ephesians. The Apostle intro-
duces us to this high theme from the viewpoint of a pastor and in the
context of a congregation, rather than as a logician of a philosophical
school. In this setting, we confront not abstract decrees set and established in the distant past, but the living God and Father of our Lord
Jesus Christ predestining and gathering to Himself His family, adopting
them in the Son of His love, and leading them to the praise of the glory
of His unspeakable grace. Thus considered, predestination is *personal,
Christocentric*, and *gracious*. This revelation of the living God, Who
personally predestines, delivers us from an impersonal petrification of
predestination. Its center in Christ gives us the assurance of faith and
saves the believer from that deadly labyrinth which swallows up the
speculative thinker. And its sheer grace protects from Pelagianism and
Pharisaism and fills the heart with gratitude. The rhythm of grace and
gratitude, of *God for us* and consequently of *us for God* is the Christian life.

PREDESTINATION IS
THE PERSONAL DECISION OF THE GOD WHO ELECTS

The most important thing in the Apostle's statements on predestination in Romans and in Ephesians is that it is God who chooses. The
doctrine is not primarily predestination, but God who predestines; the
decrees are only after God's decreeing. In Ephesians 1:3, it is God
who is showering His blessings upon us. In verse 4, the Greek verb
is a middle which indicates God selecting for Himself, as an old patriarch might look over his heirs—including his in-laws, adopted children,
and grandchildren—and say to them all: You are just the ones Mother
and I chose for ourselves to make up this, our whole family. Since
God's choosing was before the foundation of the world, when He
alone existed, this can be nothing but God's own act. The fifth verse
continues the stress on the decision and action of the divine personality, by declaring it to be according to the good pleasure of His own
will.

In Romans 8, God is working all things for good to those who are
called according to His own purposes. The golden chain which ties together the acts of God, from their foundation in His eternal purpose to

their consummation in His making us who are sinners like unto the image of His Son, is nothing else than just *God Himself*. He loved us; He foreknew us; He predestined us; He called us; He justified us; He glorified us. It is God Who is for us. It is God Who justifies. In the hands of Paul, as of Augustine, Luther, Calvin, and Edwards, this teaching brings God into the center of the picture—God, the Person who wills, who decides, who acts for us, even for our salvation.

A speculative consideration of the eternal decrees may well issue in a mode of thinking that treats them as abstractions apart from God and thereby depersonalizes them. And when either decree or grace is construed without God Himself, then the quest for a personal element lights upon man, and what started as God's free grace ends as man's decisive will. Eternal predestination according to decrees established before the foundation of the world may be turned into a form of "orthodox" deism. On the other hand, the sovereignty of God meant for Luther and Calvin God in action here and now, His hand at the helm even in the most violent storm. God has not gone fishing or golfing or to an Ethiopian banquet. He is not asleep. He is not otiose. He is *activissimus*. We are not following the Reformers when we treat God as an absentee deity. Their God was the God of Elijah.

Indeed, the thought of God who personally wills, decides, and acts is close to the heart of the Gospel. It rings in the finite verbs in the Creed. It shines in the great passives by which John Wesley describes the strange warming of his own heart. It is a genuine part of the re-study of the *kerygma*, which is blessing the Church today.

Again, this God, who personally predestines, acts in His love. In mercy, He chose for adoption into His family of children even us rebellious sinners. The man who wrote Romans and Ephesians describes himself as the chief of sinners. In Ephesians 1:5, the choice to be God's children is according to the purpose of His own will, with which the phrase *in love* may well be linked. Or, if that phrase belongs to verse 4, nevertheless in Ephesians 2:4, the riches of God's saving mercy rest upon "his great love wherewith he loved us." In Romans, the verb predestinate occurs in the context of God working all things for good, of both the ascended Christ and the Holy Spirit interceding for the saints, and of the purpose of God bringing them into the fellowship and likeness of Jesus Christ. In Ephesians, the God who blesses His people with every spiritual blessing, according to His choosing of them before He made the worlds, is none other than *the Father of our Lord*

Jesus Christ. The God Who predestines is the God before Whom Jesus lived, in Whom He trusted, to Whom He prayed "Abba," and to whose right hand as Lord and Christ He has been exalted that He may actively accomplish the loving program of eternal election in the history of world affairs and carry the host of His redeemed into the gates of the New Jerusalem.

PREDESTINATION IS IN JESUS CHRIST

According to Romans 8, we are predestined to be conformed to the image of His Son that He may be the firstborn among many brethren, and we know that God is for us by His not withholding His own Son. According to Ephesians 1:3, Christ is the ground and reason of the divine blessing; in 1:4, He is the meritorious cause of our election; in verse 5, through His mediation, our adoption is realized; and in verse 6, the grace of God is revealed and bestowed. Salvation is the act of the Holy God doing justice to His own righteousness at any cost to Himself. In Christ we have redemption through His blood—the forgiveness of sins through His giving of Himself for us.

Augustine turned away from that neo-Platonic scheme, in which the "lower parts" of God and the "higher parts" of man somehow make contact, to Jesus Christ, Who as man is the way and as God is the goal of man's pilgrimage. Staupitz told Luther to find himself in the wounds of Christ, and then predestination would be to him inexpressibly sweet. To the request of a troubled woman, Luther replied, "Hear the Incarnate Son. He offers thee Himself as Predestination."

Likewise, Calvin exhorts men "to flee straight to Christ in whom the salvation is set forth for us which otherwise would have lain hidden in God." That we may call boldly on God as our Father, "our beginning is not at all to be made from God's determination concerning us before the creation of the world, but from the revelation to his fatherly love to us in Christ and Christ's daily preaching to us by the Gospel."[1] Calvin prays that we may be "led to Christ only as the fountain of election," even as truly God, He is "the author of election" and as truly man, He is "the brightest example of election." And, "it is beyond all controversy, that no man is loved by God but in Christ; He is the Beloved Son in Whom the love of the Father perpetually rests, and then diffuses itself to us so that we are accepted in the Beloved."[2]

[1] *Concensus Genevensis.*
[2] J. Calvin: *Institutes*, III, xxii, 7; III, xxii, 1; III, ii. 32.

One may compare this with the declarations of neo-orthodoxy in the *Scottish Journal of Theology*,[3] to the effect that election is *in Christo* in the sense that Christ is the Chooser; that it is *per Christum* in that He is the Chosen One who imparts salvation to those committed to Him, the Head who communicates to His members; and that it is *propter Christum* because He takes upon His shoulders our condemnation and bears for us the damnation we deserve.

The neo-orthodox, however, extend this last point further than do the classical Augustinians. Indeed, their view of Christ, as taking reprobation for the whole human race, would seem to leave no place for any discriminatory choice by God. When all is said and done, there remains the biblical picture of God Who chooses, God Who elects, God Who predestines in Christ and for His sake saves a great host that no man can number, including the last, the least, and the lowest of those who take refuge under his wings; but He does not save those who continue to love darkness rather than light, because their deeds are evil; nor those for whom the preaching of the Gospel is a savor of death unto death; nor those who despise the riches of his goodness, long-suffering, and forebearance, and fail to consider that the goodness of God leads to repentance. When the cities of His day rejected Jesus, He rejoiced in the Father's sovereign discrimination, and continued to sound forth His gracious invitation: "Come unto *me*, and find rest for your souls."

PREDESTINATION IS THE ELECTION OF FREE GRACE

The Lord of the hosts whom He predestines to be His children in Jesus Christ is the God of grace. In Ephesians, predestination is rooted in and magnifies the sheer grace of God.

Ephesians begins as it ends, with grace. God has blessed us with all spiritual blessings in Christ. All these flow from His gracious choosing. He predestines according to His loving purpose, to the praise of *the glory of His grace* which He has *graciously* bestowed upon us in the Beloved, in Whom we have redemption through His blood, even the forgiveness of our sins according to *the riches of His grace* which He has lavished upon us.

There is no place here for human conceits. God did not bestow His electing love upon us before the foundation of the world because of any fancied "infinite value of the human soul." We had no value;

---

[3] *Scottish Journal of Theology*, I, pp. 179–181.

indeed, we had no existence. God, Who alone was before creation, is the God of love, of pure grace. The riches of His mercy were bestowed upon us *on account of His great love wherewith He loved us*. There was no goodness nor worthiness in us to cause Him to choose us. Rather were we hateful and hating one another, when the kindness and love of God toward men appeared in Christ. God so loved the world, which slew the babies of Bethlehem and crucified Jesus, that He gave for it His only begotten Son. In Ephesians, it is quite definite that God foresaw us and must needs have seen us only in Christ in order to choose such rebellious sinners to be holy and without blame before Him in love.

Grace means that God is for us, yes, for us even when we were against Him. In sheer grace He chose to create men who were capable of denying the love which He bears them. The unfathomable depths of that grace are revealed in God's giving for this rebellious race the Son of His bosom. It is Christ coming into the world to save sinners, to identify Himself with us, to pick up the ticket for our responsibilities, to give Himself on the cross as the ransom price for our deliverance—the propitiation which diverted from us the divine wrath.

Those who come to Christ were already God's sons in His heart while they were yet in themselves enemies. Again and again that grace is made conspicuous. The risen Christ intervenes to confront His chief opponent and turn him into His trusted friend. Grace is Christ's love for Saul of Tarsus, even when Saul was persecuting Him in the treatment he was meting out to Jesus' brethren. Thus, grace is prevenient; it comes first, before any response by the sinner. We were dead in trespasses and sins, but God made us alive and raised us up together with Christ. Thus were we born "not of the will of man but of God," born of the Spirit who works faith in us and thereby unites us to Christ in our effectual calling.

Grace is the heart and center of the Gospel. It is the expression of the electing love of God and the parent of faith. It issues in the inward work of the Holy Spirit, illuminating our hearts to appropriate the love of God revealed in Christ dying for the ungodly. It is this love reaching out to forgive the guilty. It is not that we loved Him, but that He loved us and sent His Son to be the propitiation for our sins. It is the forgiveness which justifies the ungodly, through the redemption that is in Christ Jesus. It is the Father's welcome to the prodigal, which gives him a place in the family of God by adoption and by regeneration.

Because it is *sola gratia*, therefore, it can only be *sola fide*. Grace leads to faith, to unwavering trust of the heart in Him Who has given Himself to us as our Father and our Saviour in Jesus Christ. Faith wrought by the grace of the Spirit lays aside trust in self; denies all self-confidence, renounces any thought of merit even in our faith; and entrusts the believer as a helpless, undeserving, ill-deserving, hell-deserving sinner wholly to the goodness, mercy, love, kindness, and grace of God revealed in Jesus Christ.

BIBLIOGRAPHY

Augustine: *Predestination*
J. Calvin: *Institutes*
K. Barth: *Die kirchliche Dogmatik*, II, 2

9

CREATION

✛

HAROLD B. KUHN

Harold B. Kuhn, Professor of Philosophy of Religion at Asbury
Theological Seminary, Wilmore, Kentucky, received his general
and theological education at John Fletcher College (B.A., 1939),
Harvard University (Ph.D., 1944), and the University of Mu-
nich. Each summer Dr. Kuhn has been active in refugee work in
West Germany and Austria.

Among the basic affirmations of the Christian faith is that "God the
Father Almighty" is "Maker of heaven and earth." This affirmation answers to a deep requirement and a deep questioning upon the part of
the human mind. The doctrine has a profound significance for the entire structure of Christian thought, and specifically for our understanding concerning His freedom, His self-sufficiency, and His uniqueness as an eternal Existent. As F.R. Tennant points out, the existence of
a "general order of Nature" forces upon the human mind the conviction that the universe is the outcome of intelligent design. It will not
do to dismiss this as a lingering echo of eighteenth-century rationalism.
This generalization is as well established and as widely recognized as
any generalization of science.[1]

[1] F.R. Tennant: *Philosophical Theology*, Volume II, pp. 79 f.

NON-CHRISTIAN SYSTEMS

These have tended to view "creation" in one of the following ways: they have regarded the universe as being the result of self-origination; they have imagined it to be some sort of unfolding or emanation of a divine being; they have posited some form of eternally existing chaos, which an intermediate "creator" fashioned into a cosmos; or they have regarded the visible universe as an illusion. These find a common denominator of sorts in the belief in the eternity of matter or of "pre-matter." Ancient paganism could rise no higher than this. Its systems proved to be unstable, particularly in their attempt to defend the belief that the universe contained two eternals, two absolutes, two infinites. Slowly, the human mind came to perceive the metaphysical impossibility of such a position.

Historically, the Christian assertion of an absolute creation by a transcendent God was not only a scandal to the pagan mind (for example, the Graeco-Roman mind), but it represented as well a threat to the entire thought world of ancient civilization. As Galen, of the second century after Christ, says: "Moses' opinion greatly differs from our own and from that of Plato and all the others who among the Greeks have rightly handled the investigation into nature. To Moses, it seems enough that God willed to create a cosmos, and presently it was created; for he believes that for God everything is possible. . . . We however do not hold such an opinion; for we maintain, on the contrary, that certain things are impossible by nature, and these God would not even attempt to do. . . ."[2]

This we quote to point out that opposition to the biblical account of an absolute origination of the universe by God is by no means contemporary. True, some contemporary alternatives are based upon slightly other grounds. At the same time, opposition has been in the name of a form or type of world view which seemed to be threatened by the Christian teaching at this point.

THE CHRISTIAN AFFIRMATION

With reference to the origination of the universe, the basic Christian affirmation is that God is the Author of the whole cosmos. This is found in the Old Testament and in the Judaism which emerged from Old Testament times. It is continued in the Christian system. The basic elements of the Christian teaching concerning creation are the

[2] Galen: *De Usu Partium Corporis Humani*, XII, p. 14.

following: that the universe has its beginning and end in God's spontaneous will; that the universe is in no sense independent of Him, but that its maintenance represents a continuing exertion of His creative power and ability; and that God made the universe not out of some type of pre-existent "stuff" but out of nothing. This assumes that prior to the "moment" of creation, God existed in self-sufficient and majestic aloneness. It is just here that the Christian understanding of God differs profoundly from that of classical paganism, which assumed, at best, the co-existence of God and the material universe (or its proto-elements); or from radical forms of moral dualism, which assumed that evil (or the factors which make for it) were co-eternal with God.

The Christian understanding of God involves the conviction that while God is One, He is not for that reason *one thing*. Within the fundamental unity of His Godhead there exists a Trinity of Persons; He contains within Himself three centers of personal activity, each capable of being denoted by personal pronouns. This means that there is an incomprehensible richness in the inner life of God, and that creation is one of the expressions of this inner richness of self-determination. Karl Barth summarily suggests that the doctrine of creation assumes the tri-unity of God's being.[3] In any case, God's eternal self-existence and self-sufficiency do not imply a precreation life of motionlessness upon His part. They do assert that God is in no sense dependent upon His world and in no sense under compulsion to create, except as a spontaneous manifestation of His love.

The Christian understanding of creation implies, we repeat, that prior to the "moment" of creation, God existed in sovereign self-sufficiency. It suggests also that there came a "point" in the divine life in which He determined to project into being that which was not Himself and yet which was dependent upon Him for its continuing being and existence. This *projection* represents an absolute origination, that is, it implies a beginning and bringing out of nothing (*ex nihilo*) and not any mere fashioning of some pre-existent matter or pre-matter. The accent falls here upon His freedom, upon His sovereign intelligence. The consequent universe is real; it is no illusion. Its reality is a *conferred* reality, which is always relative to His upholding Word. The universe is distinct from God; it is not, properly speaking, continuous with Him. That is, in creation, God set over against Himself in the realm of being that which was *not Himself*.

[3] K. Barth: *Church Dogmatics*, III, 1, pp. 46 ff.

At this point it must be noted that the biblical account of creation has two aspects: there is the aspect of absolute origination in the initial creation, indicated by the words, "In the beginning God created the heavens and the earth." This denotes the calling into being, in the dateless past, of the basic "finite" which is our universe. Then, there is the second and detailed aspect, sketched in the first two chapters of Genesis in terms of six successive creative days,[4] and specialized in the account of human origins.[5]

OBJECTIONS

It should be noted here that the Christian affirmation has been challenged upon several grounds. Some have felt that it represents a too-narrow monotheism. We have given brief attention to this objection earlier in this study. Others suggest that the "Let it be" or fiat of creation is too simple, that it describes in a few words what was in reality most complex. It must be recalled in this connection that the account of Genesis is designedly simple. The New Testament does, however, show an increased awareness of the issues for human thought which the teaching concerning creation implies and involves. Others object to what they consider to be the "childishness" of the Old Testament account, which divides creation, rather creative activity, into six successive days. This objection loses much of its force in the light of two things. First, the creative sequence indicates progress in the formation of the world, progress which upon closer study may not be, after all, illogical. Second, it is recognized in nearly all evangelical circles that in Hebrew the term "day" is used to denote more than one quantity of time. In some contexts, the term "day" denotes an era or an epoch. This may be illuminated by the words, "These are the generations of the heavens and of the earth" in Genesis 2:4. Reverent scholars allow for the possibility that the "days" of Genesis 1 may be generic periods.

There have been objections to the Christian doctrine of creation upon more directly philosophical grounds. Some have asserted in more "modern" form the view of Greek paganism, to the effect that prior to and behind the cosmos existed some primordial "world-stuff," variously understood as Prime Matter or as "the receptacle"—a formless precondition of all reality. Jakob Boehme,[6] regarded as the first writing

---

[4] Gen. 1.   [5] Gen. 2.
[6] Jakob Boehme, 1575–1624.

philosopher in the German language, has offered on this point a Germanic version of the general view of ancient Greek thought (that is, Platonic thought). He suggests: "We understand that without [outside of] nature there is an eternal stillness and rest, viz., the Nothing, and then we understand that an eternal will arises in the nothing, to introduce the nothing into something, that the will might find, feel, and behold itself."[7]

This quotation is significant in that it is a prototype of more modern views raised in objection to the historic Christian view of creation. These more modern opinions are, in general, directed at the objective of absolving God from responsibility for the existence of evil in the world. Now, no one will pretend that the existence of evil in the universe is something to be shrugged off. No division of the question (as, for example, into terms of "natural" and "moral" evil) will eliminate the problem. But the Christian can scarcely content himself with such an explanation as is advanced by Nicholas Berdyaev, who, in the general tone of Boehme, suggests that prior to and outside of God there existed a primal *Ungrund*, which accounts for the irrational "freedom" which in turn accounts for evil and which exists in God as a "tragic conflict" within His nature.[8] Nor can the Christian content himself with the view, advanced in our country by Edgar S. Brightman, that within the being of God, there exists a "Given" which is irrational and disorderly and which is an ever-present internal obstacle to the realization of His purposes.

The Christian understanding of God cannot divorce freedom from God, nor can it locate evil with God's being. The doctrine of creation presupposes God's sovereign self-determination. Any proper solution to the "problem of evil" must be found elsewhere than in a limitation of God's sovereignty. In the last analysis, any light cast upon this tragic problem must be found in the self-giving of the divine Son upon the cross.

GOD'S FREE WILL

In reality, the heart of the Christian world view is revealed in this aspect of the Christian understanding of creation. The biblical record is clear at the point of ascribing to God the ultimate and sole *will* in the

---

[7] J. Boehme: *Signatura Rerum*, p. 14.
[8] N. Berdyaev: *The Destiny of Man*, p. 177.

matter of creation. Creation reflects and represents His own freedom in action.

It needs to be noted that modern objections to the Christian understanding of creation have been raised at the point of the relation of creation to time. If we reject the classic pagan view of the eternity of matter, we must yet consider the question of whether creation was, after all, eternal. If we reply that the biblical doctrine implies an *origination*, a beginning of the universe, we answer this question in the negative. The question then arises: did creation occur in time? Christian thought has, in general, suggested that we know too little of the matter of sequence in the career of God to offer a final answer at this point. Some early thinkers (Origen, for example) felt that God's self-determination to create must have been eternal. Others held that creation was an act which did not fall within the categories of time and space as we understand them. Augustine held that the universe was not created in time, but that time was created along with the universe. This means that time (as we know it) was something which became manifest at the point at which the universe was projected. Perhaps this is the best available answer.

CONCLUSION

We have noted seriatim some of the alternatives which have been proposed to the Christian affirmation of creation, the basic content of the Christian teaching, some of the objections raised to it, and something of the larger bearings of the doctrine. We need to note, finally, that the doctrine creates no new mysteries. The mysteries are already present and confront the thoughtful with a perennial challenge. Nor does the Christian doctrine suggest that the concept of absolute creation is an easy one. It is ultimately an article of faith, based upon the acceptance of divine revelation. However, as the reverent mind ponders the alternatives, it finds nothing comparably satisfying to the answer given by the Christian faith.

The Christian Scriptures do not attempt to describe the "how" of creation. They do assure us that the entire Trinity was active in the production of the universe. While it is God the Father Who is, in the broad sense, Creator of heaven and earth, it was through the agency of the Word, the eternal Son, that all things were made. During the creative process, it was the Holy Spirit who moved upon "the face of the waters," bringing order out of the formless and empty chaos.

At the core of the doctrine of creation stands the mighty assertion that the universe is the product of the release of creative energies of an infinitely free and completely holy God, utterly self-sufficient in His being and infinite in His ability to perform that which His heart of love dictates. And in the person of the eternal Son, the activities of creation and redemption meet and conjoin.

BIBLIOGRAPHY

J. Orr, ed.: *International Standard Bible Encyclopedia*, Volume II, articles "Creation" and "Creator" by J. Lindsay

S.M. Jackson, ed.: *The New Schaff-Herzog Encyclopedia of Religious Knowledge*, Volume III, article "Creation and Preservation of the World" by O. Zöckler

R.S. Foster: *Creation*

K. Heim: *Christian Theology and Natural Science*

C. Hodge: *Systematic Theology*, II

L.H. Keyser: *The Problem of Origins*

A.H. Strong: *Outlines of Systematic Theology*

F.R. Tennant: *Philosophical Theology*, Volume II

IO

ANGELS

✠

BERNARD RAMM

Bernard Ramm, Professor of Systematic Theology at California Baptist Theological Seminary, Covina, California, received his general and theological education at the University of Washington (B.A., 1938), Eastern Baptist Theological Seminary (B.D., 1941), and the University of Southern California (M.A., 1947; Ph.D., 1950). He is the author of *Problems in Christian Apologetics, Protestant Biblical Interpretation, Protestant Christian Evidence, Types of Apologetic Systems, The Christian View of Science and Scripture*, and *Special Revelation and the Word of God*, among other works.

The omission of a discussion of angels in almost every book on the philosophy of religion reveals the gulf between modern mentality and the biblical revelation. Philosophers of religion discuss God, the soul, and nature, but stop short of any serious discussion of angels. Skeptics will spend much time in refuting the proofs of the existence of God and the immortality of the soul, but will not even wet the pen to refute the existence of an angelic host. In contrast to this treatment of angels on behalf of philosophers (religious or skeptical) are the profuse references to angels in sacred Scripture.

It must be admitted, however, that there are certain problems or ambiguities attending the discussion of angels, and Calvin himself expressed a great reserve and caution on the subject.[1] It is this discrepancy between modern mentality and the biblical disclosure about angels that causes Barth to begin his discussion of angels with so much hesitation.[2]

NO RATIONAL OBJECTION

Mankind has no handbook titled *A Guide to All Possible Creations*. It has no information about creation, apart from the data afforded by this creation. The *how* and the *why* and the *what* of creation can be gained only from the concrete character and concrete givenness of creation. Humanity has no *a priori* principles for judging the character or composition of a creation. And in that angels are creatures of God, what applies to creation in general applies to angels in particular.

Whether there shall be angels or not cannot be determined by any concept of necessity or fitness of things. There is nothing in the constitution of the human mind which enables it to judge this issue. If there is any necessity or any fitness to the existence of angels, it is known and determined by the divine Majesty.

In a word, modern man can have no *a priori* objection to the existence of angels based upon some sort of principle of necessity or fitness. The existence or nonexistence of angels can be based only upon an *a posteriori* judgment arising out of the concrete character of creation itself.

The root of Christian theology is the knowledge of God conveyed to man through special revelation. This is the nerve of Christian theology, and if it is cut, theology atrophies into mere religious chatter (even though it be learned chatter). This knowledge of God takes the concrete form of a canon, a Scripture, or, in the technical language of the New Testament, a *graphe*. The New Testament uses this term *graphe* to indicate the ink and parchment embodiment of the revelation of God. It is this *graphe* which informs the church of the structures of creation, insofar as these structures pertain to our proper understanding of God, ourselves, and the character of our creaturely and

It is from the *graphe* that the church comes to know the reality of angels. The real conflict with modern man and Christianity conspiritual lives.

---

[1] J. Calvin: *Institutes*, I, xiv, 3, for example: "It is also our duty cheerfully to remain in ignorance of what is not for our advantage to know."
[2] K. Barth: *Die kirchliche Dogmatik*, III, 3, Sec. 51.

cerning angels is not really whether the concept of angels is rational or not, but whether the *graphe* bears an authentic knowledge of God which expresses itself with regard to angels. Modern man has no criterion within himself to judge this issue, apart from Scripture.

NO DIVINELY GIVEN SENTIMENT

Furthermore, mankind has no divinely given *sentiment* whereby it can judge whether angels are proper or not. Why this refusal to discuss angels by the philosophers of religion, if there is not rooted deeper than reason a sentiment which is antipathetic toward angels? Is there not here an unwritten or unspoken appeal to a sense of propriety, a sense of fittingness, which boggles at the doctrine of angels?

In the universe of electrons and positrons, atomic energy and rocket power, Einsteinian astronomy and nuclear physics, angels *seem* out of place. They *seem* to intrude upon the scene like the unexpected visit of the country relatives to their rich city kinfolk. Atoms *seem* at home in our contemporary thinking, but not angels! The prospect of some interplanetary *Beagle* cruising among the planets gathering scientific data surprises no educated man of today. But if such a man were called upon to comment upon angels, he would either act very nervous or else he would pompously deny that angels existed. He knows the principles whereby he can reasonably imagine a scientific cruise of the planets by a space-age Darwin, but he has no principles whereby he may discuss angels. So he prefers to dismiss the concept of angels as mythological.

The serious question which confronts the Christian theologian in view of modern man's squeamish attitude toward angels is whether or not there is a logical or theological justification for this attitude. Christian theology would be faced with a serious logical problem if angels and atoms competed with each other in natural law. It is true that God does make angels as winds and as fires,[3] but the angels are never part of the scriptural explanation of the *order* or *ordering* of natural things. Angels and atoms do not compete! There can be then no formal logical objection to the existence of angels.

Christian theology would be confronted with a serious theological problem if it could be shown that the concept of angels is inappropriate to the notion of God. But this could only be the case if mankind had

[3] Heb. 1:7.

an innate criterion by which to judge what is appropriate with reference to God. But as already indicated, man is not gifted with this sentiment, and therefore the only possible mode of judging this question is
by the revelation of the knowledge of God in sacred Scripture.

The root of modern man's objection to the reality of angels is not
logical nor theological but psychological. It is a psychological squeam-
ishness which stems from the antisupernaturalism of modern mentality. The medieval theologian-philosopher Occam affirmed that no more
principles should be employed in explanations than those which are
absolutely necessary. This principle has been called "Occam's Razor."
Modern man *feels* (for he cannot make his case from logic) that Occam's Razor enables him to trim off all supernatural principles and all
superhuman beings in accounting for the sum total of phenomena in
the universe.

To frame this another way, modern mentality may be likened to a
decorator's motif. Only certain colors and styles harmonize in the
house, and furniture which does not harmonize is hauled out! Angels
do not match the modern *décor*, so they are discarded.

Karl Barth has noted that there is one basis for modern man's hesi-
tations about angels. Angels are servants and have no reality or purpose
in themselves. We can imagine people without servants, but we cannot conceive of servants without people. The rationale of servants is
the rationale of people. There is no rationale for servants *in themselves*.
We can imagine God as existing without angels, but it is meaningless
to imagine a universe with angels but no God. The rationale for angels
is that they are servants of God and man in the interest of the redemption provided by God.

THE STRUCTURE OF DIVINE MEDIATION

Creation is that order, that space-time reality, which is created by
God and is thereby different from God. His omnipotent word spoke it
into existence.[4] There is, therefore, an ineradicable difference between
God and the creature. In the language of categories, it is the eternal
contrasted with the temporal, the infinite with the finite, the uncreated with the created, and so on. The communication between this
great God and finite, limited man must thus always be a *mediated*
communication.

This is not a judgment about the "impurity" of the world, which

[4] Heb. 11:3.

would force God to communicate indirectly lest he contaminate himself with the world. It is based upon the *transcendence* of Creator over the creature. Therefore, when God comes to humanity in revelation, He comes through *mediators*. The prophetic word is a *mediated* word. The theophany is a *mediated* manifestation of God. The Incarnation is the glory of God, *mediated* through the human nature of Christ.[5] *Angels are part of the complex structure of the divine mediation.*

With reference to this divine mediation man has no *a priori* understanding of it. Man does not know if there shall be one or a million mediators. He has no esthetic power whereby he can evaluate one scheme of mediation over another. If man wishes, he may reject the notion of angels. Barth cites Goethe as saying, "Let me name for you an appendage: What you call angels."[6] But the necessity of mediation remains, and if the divine Majesty shall say something to His creatures, it must be a mediated word!

In this matter, there is only one point of judgment. In the concrete data of revelation, either the mediatorial role of angels is set forth or it is not. At this point the witness of scriptural record[7] is accepted or rejected. To speculate about angels apart from the concrete, historical, and specific character of revelation is like attempting to fly in a vacuum. We have no *a priori* principle to judge this matter; we have no innate esthetic sense to assess its fittingness. We either rest upon the contents of revelation or we pass the question by.

THE HEAVENLY SERVANTS OF GOD

If angels function in the schema of divine mediation, their role is essentially that of *servant*.[8] The service of angels in special revelation and divine redemption is the second scriptural rationale for angels. Man is the earthly servant of God; Jesus Christ is the theanthropic servant of God;[9] and the angels are the heavenly servants of God, for they are always represented as coming from heaven and returning to heaven.

Angels serve God in the administration of his kingdom and his redemption.[10] The range of their service is phenomenal. From the Old Testament incidents in which they appear like ordinary men,[11] we move through the biblical record of their actions to the great

[5] John 1:14.
[6] *Ibid.,* p. 436.
[7] Cf. Acts 7:53; Gal. 3:19; Heb. 2:7.
[8] Heb. 1:14.
[9] Phil. 2:5 f.
[10] Dan. 8:16; Luke 1:19, 26; and so forth.
[11] Judges 13.

dramatic pictures of the book of Revelation, where angels assume cosmic powers. The association of Jesus Christ with angels is remarkable—compare His birth narratives, His temptation, His experience in Gethsemane, His resurrection, His return with great hosts of angels.

In this connection is the remarkable Old Testament revelation of the angel of the Lord. Because the angel of the Lord is both a representation and a type there is some obscurity attached to the subject matter which an honest exegesis will not overlook. But the angel-form of the Mighty One who comes in the service of God is a happy anticipation of Philippians 2:5 ff.; where the exalted Son of God empties himself to take the form of a servant.

One other remark is pertinent to the servant role of angels: everywhere in Scripture their worship or veneration is sternly rebuked.[12]

THE GLORY OF GOD

The third rationale for angels is to be seen in the manner in which they surround the throne of God.[13] One of the names of God is *the Lord of Hosts*. He is pictured in Scripture as surrounded by an innumerable company of angels.[14] One of the primary means by which Scripture represents to us the glorious nature of God is always to surround Him with an endless host of powerful and majestic angels, particularly the seraphim who cry "holy, holy, holy" day and night.[15] If the angelic hosts are deleted from our representation of God, then one of the strongest possible modes of representing the glory, the might, the majesty, and the holiness of God is lost. Just as the royal palace, the fabulous furnishings, and the royal court are all part of the means of expressing the dignity and royalty of an *earthly* king, so the visions of heaven and the majestic court of glorious angels are part of the biblical method of impressing the human mind with the glory of God. The abstract listing of divine attributes may be theologically precise, but such a list can never do for the human imagination what is done by the biblical presentation of God surrounded with an innumerable host of great, glorious, and powerful angels.

If men have entertained angels unawares,[16] theologians should be the first to attempt to make their visit welcome, and their stay desirable.

---

[12] Cf. Col. 2:18; Rev. 19:10.   [13] Heb. 12:22.
[14] Rev. 5:11, ". . . numbering myriads of myriads and thousands of thousands."
[15] Isa. 6:3.   [16] Heb. 13:2.

BIBLIOGRAPHY

K. Barth: *Die kirchliche Dogmatik*, III, 3, Sec. 51 [Historical and theological materials found in remarkable fullness]

G. Kittel, ed.: *Theologisches Wörterbuch zum Neuen Testament*, Volume I, article *"aggelos, archaggelos, isaggelos"* by W. Grundmann, G. von Rad, G. Kettel.

A Greek-English Lexicon of the New Testament, article "Angels" by W.F. Arndt and F.W. Gingrich

E. Harrison, ed.: *Dictionary of Theology*, article "Angel" by G.W. Bromiley

F.L. Cross, ed.: *The Oxford Dictionary of the Christian Church*, article "Angel"

Dionysius: *The Celestial Hierarchy* [Historically has played a fantastically large role]

T. Aquinas: *Summa Theologica*, Volume I, 50–64, 106–114

————: *Summa Contra Gentiles*, Volume II, 91–101

J. Calvin: *Institutes*, I, xiv [Where he remarks that Dionysius' treatment is "mere babblings"]

F. Schleiermacher: *The Christian Faith* [Comments upon the abstract possibility of angels, but of their religious dispensability]

H.W. Bartsch, ed., R.H. Fuller, tr.: *Kerygma and Myth*, article "New Testament and Mythology" by R. Bultmann [Rejection of spirits, good or evil]

II

SATAN AND THE DEMONS

✛

G. C. BERKOUWER

G.C. Berkouwer, Professor of Dogmatics and History of Dogma at the Free University of Amsterdam, received his general and theological education at the Free University of Amsterdam (Th.D., 1932). He is the author of the important volume *The Triumph of Grace in the Theology of Karl Barth* and has completed twelve volumes in the series *Studies in Dogmatics*.

One could wonder about the propriety of setting *demonology* within a series on basic Christian doctrines. Satan, the dark power of evil, who appears sometimes as an angel of light,[1] and whose designs are not unknown to us[2]—where does he fit into the system of Christian doctrine? Doctrine is an attempt to set forth the interrelatedness of the Word of God. But do we not have in demons the power that breaks the unity seen in the Word? In dogmatic theology we speak of our task as that of systematic reflection on the message of the Word. What can we systematize in the work of demons? Is not the *diabolos* the very personification of destruction and confusion, the direct opposite of system and order, especially the good order of God's creation?

When we try to be systematic and orderly in regard to a study of Satan and his works, we are tempted to fit Satan into a legitimate and

---

[1] II Cor. 11:14.   [2] II Cor. 2:11.

proper place within creation. We may also be tempted to use him as an explanatory principle of evil, principle which leads, if we are not careful, to an excusing of ourselves. For instance, the dualistic schemes of Persian religions set two eternal powers of good and evil in opposition, the good one causing the good and the bad one causing the evil of the world. This was a simple scheme. But the net result in practice was the same as that of any rational explanation of evil. The personal guilt of men was hidden in the shadow of the explanation of evil. And where personal guilt is obscured, the grace that frees men from guilt is obscured also.

Evil has often been systematized so rationally that the chaotic world of evil actually looked orderly. When evil is brought into a rational system that explains its existence, its evilness is always toned down. At times, thinkers have dared to seek the origin of evil in God, in spite of the Church's most emphatic conviction that God may never be called the cause of evil. (*Deus non causa peccati.*) This conviction comes from the Bible, which states the point with perfect clarity: "This then is the message which we have heard of him ... that God is light, and in him is no darkness at all."[3] When one is inclined to excuse himself on the ground that he is tempted of God, he is warned by the Word: "Let no man say when he is tempted, I am tempted of God."[4] The point is made in many ways by the Scriptures: sin does not find its origin in God.

We see this in God's wrath against sin, in His judgment upon sin, and especially in His redemptive action by which He brings grace to light in the punishment of sin upon the cross. The cross reveals the soundness of the church's conviction that God is not the origin of evil. We also see in the cross that the dualism which hypnotized Augustine for nine years is wholly unacceptable. For the cross reveals that God does not eternally face an independent power of evil, but rather that God conquers evil and sets it within His service. The terrible evil accomplished by Judas, Israel, and the Gentiles around the cross is taken up into the triumphant fulfillment of God's redemptive plan.

THE POWERS OF DARKNESS

In regard to all this, it is still possible to speak about the powers of darkness with real meaning, as long as we speak the language of the

---

[3] I John 1:5.   [4] Jas. 1:13.

Bible. It is not our concern to pursue an academic curiosity about evil. This kind of interest in evil has often been too keen. Consider the large Roman Catholic book on Satan, which fills 666 pages with a huge attempt to shed light on the demonic powers afoot in all phases of life. One gets an impression in such a book that evil is a triumphant, dynamic force, crusading unhindered through history. The Bible, to be sure, calls us to be aware of Satan's craft. But the biblical summons in regard to Satan is not at all like an answer to our curiosity. The Bible sounds a warning. It never suggests that evil is an invincible power to which we are hopelessly and fatally captive. We hear indeed of the reality of temptation and rebellion, of resistance and disobedience, of confusion and destruction, but these are a reality over which God is surely triumphant.

God's triumph is particularly manifest in the New Testament where the Apostles tell us that Christ has conquered and dethroned Satan.[5] Resistance again arises threateningly at the appearance of the antichrist. But his very name suggests that Satan is not a primary figure; he gets his significance only as an opponent of Him Who has already conquered. When Satan falls out of heaven as lightning, he rebels against the defeat that the cross and resurrection of Christ inflict on him.[6]

This is why we meet Satan and his demons in the environment of Jesus Christ. Satan manifests himself especially during the earthly ministry of our Lord. He is active among the people of Israel and in the world of the Gentiles whom he blinds.[7] In the Book of Revelation, the dark appearance of the dragon on the scene is set back of the foreground of the Lamb Who conquers. And it is the Lamb to Whom it is given to open the locked book of history, Who is the central figure of the spiritual course of human history.

But we still have to reckon with the power of Satan. "Your adversary the devil goes about as a roaring lion, seeking whom he may devour."[8] But this is not dualism, as though we were pawns in a battle between God and Satan, with the outcome still uncertain. For there is, in Christ, the power of resistance to Satan. "Resist the devil and he will flee from you."[9] We must not fall prey to a superficial judgment that underestimates the power of Satan. Resistance to him is possible only in the immediate fellowship of the Lord of lords and King of

[5] Col. 2:15.   [6] Luke 10:18.
[7] II Cor. 4.   [8] I Pet. 5:8.
[9] Jas. 4:7.

kings. Without Him, we should discover to our woe that Satan is a foul spirit who possesses the power to overcome us: "how God anointed Jesus of Nazereth with the Holy Ghost and with power: who went about doing good, and healing all that were oppressed of the devil, for God was with him."[10]

SATAN'S FRUSTRATION

But at the same time, given the fellowship of Jesus Christ, there is no reason to overestimate the power of Satan either. He is not free to pursue his own destiny. He cannot and has not frustrated God. God has frustrated him once and for all at Calvary. Our only danger is that we try to frustrate Satan within the limitations of our own power.

In our day, largely because of the many catastrophic outbreaks of evil in the world, theology has turned its attention anew to demonology. This concern with demons has not always been biblically oriented. But the old optimism about the conquest of evil is surely gone. (Long before Bultmann, Schleiermacher insisted that modern insights made serious acceptance of the reality of demons untenable, even though Satan still kept a place in the church's hymns.) Attention is also once again directed to the antichrist figure of the New Testament. The question is asked how we are to relate the victory of Jesus Christ over Satan to the present power that Satan seems to exercise in the world. Does it not seem that evil is a constantly resurgent power? Are not we and all the world subject to this power? In considering such questions, we can easily be overcome with pessimism and lose sight of the triumphant theme of the Gospel. We must not, however, forget that when our Lord saw Satan fall from heaven, the triumph over Satan was already at hand. The preaching of the Gospel in our time must be clear on this point. Against human optimism, it must point up human inability to resist the power of evil, while at the same time proclaiming the full power of the Gospel to accomplish this.

THE CHRISTIAN'S STRATEGY

The Bible, in reference to the demons, calls us to responsibility and prayer. Think, for instance, of the Lord's Prayer. The last petition asks for deliverance from evil. But the prayer does not begin with evil; it speaks of evil only after guilt has been confessed. Satan is not an explanatory principle that does away with our guilt. The reality of

[10] Acts 10:38.

Satan's power does not undo the reality of our personal responsibility in evil. But when we have prayed for forgiveness of our own sin, we also pray for resistance against the evil power, against him who has only a little time left,[11] who seeks to lead men astray, who accuses the brethren before the throne of God, and who strives mightily to blind men to the great salvation that has really come into the world.

For this reason, we shall not be able to do battle with the evil of the world in our own time by means of the armament of human morality and plans for world improvement. For Satan's ways are not unknown to us—so says Paul[12] in warning the congregation. His designs can be summed up in one word: *anti*. He is anti-creation and anti-redemption. The antichrist shall appear to be *for* many things. He shall be for culture, for human religions, for the earth, for development of life. But he shall be *anti*-Jesus Christ. In this sense, the power of Satan is a negative power. It is a power that shall be revealed as nothing when the *parousia* of Jesus Christ confronts the *parousia* of the antichrist.[13] The basic weakness of Satan since the cross will then be made manifest.

We fail to see this now. The power of Satan appears undiminished and Satan appears unconquerable at times. But our failure lies in part with the fact that Satan appears now as an angel of light. The false prophets, against whom Paul warns, bring this to the Apostle's mind. Satan stands before the entrance to a dry desert and proclaims it as the gateway to Paradise. He witnesses to the light with signs and wonders, but is really bidding men to follow him into darkness. Only in the light of Him who is the Light of the World does it become wholly clear that Jesus Christ is indeed the powerful conqueror of Satan.

Scripture and the faithful preaching of the church warn us against doing away with evil by finding an explanation of it. We are warned against explaining evil away by saying that God is its origin. We are warned against any dualism which makes a minor god the cause of evil. We are warned against making Satan an overpowering force who takes away our responsibility for our own sin. The Bible does not give us a rational explanation of everything about evil. But it is gloriously clear in showing the way that a man can travel in life. It is the way of faith and prayer and, in the power of the Gospel, the way of resistance to evil. In the perfect prayer, the right perspective is beautifully manifest. We pray for forgiveness of personal guilt and then go on to a

[11] Rev. 12:12.   [12] II Cor. 2:11.
[13] II Thess. 2:9.

doxology. "For thine is the kingdom and the power and the glory forever. Amen." Whoever prays this prayer with his whole heart has grasped the inner meaning of the doctrine of evil.

BIBLIOGRAPHY

Besides the many handbooks of theology, *see:*

B. Noack: *Satanas und Soteria: Untersuchungen, zur N.T. Dämonogie*

R. Leiverstad: *Christ the Conqueror, Ideas of Conflict and Victory in the New Testament*

K. Barth: *Die kirchliche Dogmatik*, III, 3

G.C. Berkouwer: *De Zonde*, I

I 2

PROVIDENCE

AND PRESERVATION

✛

ANDREW K. RULE

Andrew K. Rule, Professor of Apologetics and Ethics at Louisville Presbyterian Seminary, Louisville, Kentucky, received his general and theological education at the University of New Zealand (M.A., 1916), Princeton Theological Seminary (B.D., 1919), and the University of Edinburgh (Ph.D., 1923).

The doctrine called providence pervades the Scriptures of both Testaments. It is not incidental or accidental, but it is rationally integral to the scriptural system of truth and joyfully integral to its way of life. The term comes from the Latin *pro* and *videre*, meaning to look ahead, to foresee, and thus to plan in advance. But as here used, it also means to carry out the plan. And, since the agent of providence is the all-knowing, all-powerful God, literally everything is included. Although for purposes of analysis (following the order of the historical unfolding of God's purpose) we properly distinguish between creation, providence, redemption, and fulfillment, they all are simply stages in one eternal and unchanging purpose, the several historical stages of which are completely harmonious with, and fully support, each other.

In a brief article such as this, such a claim obviously cannot be fully documented. However, anyone who may doubt it should read the Scriptures with this claim in mind, and allow them to make their own impression on his mind. He will find that certain passages, as Psalm 139, express this doctrine sharply and powerfully, but the calm assurance with which the Scriptures as a whole either refer to it or simply assume it should perhaps have an even more convincing effect. A briefer way of achieving the same result might be to read Dr. G.C. Berkouwer's delightful treatise on *The Providence of God*. It is open to anyone to doubt the truth of the doctrine, if the intellectual difficulties which it undoubtedly entails seem overwhelming; but it is not open to any candid mind to doubt that the Scriptures uniformly teach it and take it for granted, or that millions of intelligent believers live joyfully and triumphantly in the conviction of its truth.

INTEGRAL TO CREATION

This doctrine, as we have said, is integral to, harmonious with, and fulfills the doctrine of creation. Without it, the latter would be, as Calvin says, "jejune." For, as he also says, "unless we proceed to his providence, we have no correct conception of the meaning of the article 'that God is the Creator' " and "no one seriously believes that the world was made by God, who is not persuaded that he takes care of his own works." The Creator may not be thought to have made the world without any definite idea of what He intended to do with it, to discover that, when later his plans were matured, it was not well adapted to his purpose. What we can see, by revelation or by discovery, of His grand design shows clearly that central to it, so far as this world is concerned, is personal association. And so, from the beginning, He made the world so that it could be a responsive stage for, and a contributing instrument of, personal fellowship, having indeed a share in that fellowship according to its various levels of potentiality. It is, as Keats expressed it, "a vale of soul-making"; and this is true even if the absolute idealists, who made great use of this conception, failed to understand its true significance.

But this involved the precise balancing of two apparently opposite conditions. On the one hand, as deism and naturalism one-sidedly maintain, God gave the world an abiding existence with inherent organization and with stable operations according to law; the world and its several constituent parts exist in some sense in their own right, possess their own character, and operate with their own dynamism. Thus the created world can be understood by acquaintance with its individual parts and discovery of its (and their) laws; and it can normally be assumed, without fear, that it will not change its character and action irresponsibly and unpredictably. But if, as deism and naturalism further maintain, the natural world were a closed system with no possibility of influence by its higher levels on the lower, or by the Creator, then the possibility of personal fellowship within it would have been precariously provided for only within narrow circles, and the Creator would have been shut out. And so, as pantheism maintains, God made the world everywhere, always and in all its parts open to and dependent upon His presence; and, as the French occasionalists also insisted, though equally one-sidedly, He made it completely responsive in all its operations to His will. If the continuous divine energy were even momentarily withdrawn, creation would lapse into nothingness. This is not, as Barth teaches, because it would be overwhelmed by a mysteriously positive and aggressive "chaos," although a power and purpose and a personal kingdom of destruction do exist. But, were the divine providence withheld, the created world would lapse into nothingness even if no such kingdom of evil existed at all. It would be so because it was originally made to be continuously dependent upon the sustaining power of God, and it was so made in the service of His purpose of personal fellowship. The same conception may be stated in positive terms. Although God and the created world are not to be identified, yet the relationship is so intimate that God is everywhere present and active, so that any action of created being, or of a created being, is at the same time God's act.

BASIC TO REDEMPTION AND FULFILLMENT

Involved in what has already been said is the further fact that the doctrine of providence is basic to and completely harmonious with the doctrines of redemption and fulfillment. They simply represent, in view of the fact of evil, the further outworking of God's original and unchanging purpose of personal fellowship. God had them in mind when He created the world, and does now as He providentially sustains and governs it. The Lamb was slain from before the foundation of the world, and the world was so created and constituted and providentially governed that, in the fullness of the times, He would enter into it by way of incarnation, live and die in it, and rise again. This was no afterthought worked out in a world not already prepared for it. All history, including cosmic history, was from the beginning designed to be summed up in Christ by the power, wisdom, and grace of God, who is continuously immanent in the world as He is ever also transcendent to it.

God's providence embraces not only the whole, but its parts as well —"all his creatures and all their actions." This includes "free" creatures, their "free" actions (even their evil ones), and their sinful state. It is here that many who would disagree with what has already been said begin to hesitate or deny. Among the various reasons given for negative reaction at this point, two seem to be of basic importance, and another, not so generally recognized or admitted, is probably even more influential. The latter is simply the refusal of the sinful human heart to surrender to God and to rest joyfully in His sovereignty. Those who acknowledge it do not need that it be further discussed here, and to those who refuse to admit it, nothing that we can say would do much good. So we will turn to the other sources of difficulty. One of them is a certain dualism which assumes or asserts that if God rules in any action, then it is God's act *and not a free man's,* and if man acts freely, then it is man's act *and not God's.* A careful exposure of this unbiblical dualism is sorely needed, for by it much theological discussion (notably at this time discussion of revelation and inspiration) is vitiated. But such an exposure clearly lies beyond the limits of this discussion. Suffice it here to point out that the Scriptures nowhere present or endorse such a dualism. They freely attribute human actions to God, actions which, insofar as they are attributed to man, are judged to be good or evil. One and the same act is an act of self-hardening on Pharaoh's part and an act of hardening by God of Pharaoh's heart. One and the same act is a result of the evil purposes of Joseph's brethren and of the good purpose of God. Also, be it carefully noted, the relations between man and God, in these free human actions, is not simply a voluntary cooperation of two independent actors. It is much more intimate than that. Paul is in Christ and Christ is in Paul. We are to work out our own salvation, for it is God that worketh in us both the willing and the doing. A scriptural study of the work of the Holy Spirit *as possession* would be specially illuminating at this point. It would make it abundantly clear why the Scriptures are aware of no problem here, because they take for granted and affirm not this subtle dualism but God's providential and gracious rule.

THE PROBLEM OF EVIL

The other source of difficulty for many is the far profounder problem of evil. There are really two problems of evil. One, which may be called the *practical* problem of evil, asks: since evil there is, what can be done about it? The Gospel is the sufficient answer. The other may be called the *theoretical* problem of evil. In a world created and providentially sustained and governed by a God of infinite wisdom, goodness, and power, how could evil possibly be real? How could such a God be said to sustain and govern evil creatures in their continued being and in all their actions? The writer of the Book of Job, the Psalmist, and other Scripture writers are aware of some aspects of this theoretical problem, but, though some light is here and there thrown upon it, the Scriptures never attempt a theoretical answer to it. When some aspect of it is presented, it is always as a challenge to faith; and from the resulting struggle, faith emerges strengthened and deepened and expressing itself as doxology. Modern believers find themselves in the same situation. They freely acknowledge that no man knows the answer to this theoretical problem—an acknowledgment that is only confirmed by a study of Barth's ambitious attempt to solve the problem. Their faith is challenged, but it emerges singing, "This is my Father's world." They confess with Lewis F. Stearns, "If we only had the faith to apprehend, in the things seen and temporal, the things unseen and eternal, we should discover in every running brook and every breaking dawn, in every event of history and every experience of life, the presence of Our Saviour, working for human redemption." Or, as B.B. Warfield used to express it, "The devil thinks he is free; but he has the bit in his mouth, and God holds the reins."

Naturally, if some other god is substituted for the God and Father of our Lord Jesus Christ, this can become an unspeakably terrible doctrine. By any who know God in Christ but have rejected Him, this doctrine will also be fiercely rejected. If, forgetting the humility that is due in our situation of finiteness and sinfulness, we insist on having all the answers, this doctrine may well seem incredible. But if, knowing whom we have believed, we are ready to follow the light which He has revealed, we will find that this doctrine (which is light indeed in the midst of our darkness) will inevitably issue, together with all the other Christian doctrines with which it is harmoniously associated, in a life of gratitude and joy.

BIBLIOGRAPHY

For statements of this doctrine in the church creeds, *see:*

P. Schaff: *The Creeds of Christendom,* 3 volumes

For more detailed discussion, *see:*

J. Calvin: *Institutes,* I, xvi–xviii [Condensed into four pages in H.T. Kerr, Jr.: *Compend of the Institutes*]

C. Hodge: *Systematic Theology,* I, 11

For more modern monographs, *see:*

G.C. Berkouwer: *The Providence of God*

H.H. Farmer: *The World and God*

G. Harkness: *The Providence of God*

W.G. Pollard: *Chance and Providence*

I3

MIRACLES

✚

HENRY STOB

Henry Stob, Professor of Apologetics and Ethics at Calvin
Theological Seminary, Grand Rapids, Michigan, received his
general and theological education from Calvin College (B.A.,
1932), Calvin Theological Seminary (B.D., 1935), Hartford
Theological Seminary (Th.M., 1936), and the University of
Göttingen (Ph.D., 1938). He has been Associate Editor of *The
Reformed Journal* since 1951, and is the author of *The Christian
Concept of Freedom.*

The God Christians believe in is the Lord of all. He is the Creator of
the world and also its Sustainer. What He once made, He now controls
and continuously renews.

People who believe in this God are not much troubled about
miracles, for they see the effects of supernatural power in everything
around them. They see each thing not as a mere part or product of
some greater thing called nature, which God once fashioned and then
left to run "on its own" according to its immanent constitution; they
see each thing as God's *present* work, reflecting His uninterrupted
agency.[1] Everything is for them a "sign" of God, one of His "mighty

[1] Job 26:7-14.

deeds." Each is marvelous in their eyes, a "wonder," fit to evoke astonishment and praise.

What we call miracles are in the New Testament called "signs" (*semeia*), "mighty works" (*dunameis*), and "wonders" (*terata*). But what we call non-miraculous or natural events are in the Bible also viewed as signs and mighty works and wonders. In the biblical view, God is behind *everything*, the usual and the unusual, the common and the strange; and He is behind them equally. According to the Psalmists and the Prophets, the rain is God's doing and also the drought. So, too, are the movements of the planets and the tides. God "performs" all these, and more. Nothing is outside His jurisdiction; nothing moves except at His command. In everything that has being, He witnesses to Himself and to His power. Each is a "sign" He leaves of His presence and concern. All indicate that He "doeth great things and unsearchable."[2]

THE SOVEREIGNTY OF GOD

It would be premature to conclude from this that in the Christian view "all is miracle," but it would be right to say that in this view nature is no stranger to God's hand. Nature feels God's impulses constantly. It is always suffering His "invasions." Its processes but trace the contours of His will. Nature is pliable in His hands.

The reason is, of course, that God is Sovereign. He is Lord, and He is free—also in relation to nature. He traces His own paths through all that He has made; indeed, these tracings *constitute* what we call nature's "rule." The "laws of nature" which we formulate are nothing but our transcripts of God's "customary ways." They are not prior to but after God; they record His habits. They "hold" because God is wont to travel the same way; but they do not bind Him. God is free to plant His steps precisely where He will, and sometimes He plants them on unaccustomed ways. He does this, we may be sure, to serve some holy purpose. Perhaps He does it on occasion just to testify that He is free, and so "reveal his glory."

However this may be, He traces His own path always. Sometimes these paths seem very strange to us, as when He causes iron to float or a virgin to give birth or bread to multiply. With all our science, we could never have predicted He would take these courses; and after He took them, we can find no sufficient reason in the preceding causal

[2] Job 5:9.

nexus for His doing so. Strange events of this sort are beyond our science; they are miracles. Yet, in another sense, they are not so strange. In them, God merely celebrates the freedom which is always His but which in "ordinary" events is obscured by their scientific comprehensibility, that is, by their amenableness to the explanatory techniques we have developed precisely *in response* to events of like ordinariness.

Science builds itself up on observed constancies. In terms of our discussion this is but to say that it grows by observing and recording the general pattern of divine behavior, by noting God's "custom." This custom gives science its stability and worth and its predictive usefulness. It is quite unwarranted to suppose, however, that science can now turn about and *demand* that things behave in certain ways, that God keep to the accustomed paths and act according to the scientist's prescription. Science has no authority to prescribe. It does its work well only when it remains descriptive, when it follows after God as a reporter. Empiricism in science is therefore eminently Christian, if for no other reason than that it leaves God free, free to do great things which transcend our little systems and transgress the limits of our proud "a priories."

REJECTION OF MONISM

Because Christianity both allows and professes miracles, it repudiates all rationalistic naturalisms which, denying God, think that nature is "the all" and that miracle is impossible. But it also repudiates the more religious forms of monism: primitivism and pantheism—in both of which the miraculous seems to be given prominence.

In primitive religion or *animism* there are many gods or spirits, and they have power (*mana*) which they exercise in unpredictable ways. The animistic world is therefore full of mystery and apparent miracle; almost anything can happen at any moment. There is, of course, no real affinity between this view of things and that of Christianity. Animism is basically a monistic naturalism; the gods are nature spirits. Nature suffers no control here from outside itself; it is "on its own." There is no supernatural; hence there is no miracle, but only chaos. There is no nonnatural principle of order; hence there is no science, but only magic. This interconnection is worth observing. Miracles are possible only in a determinate universe, the kind of universe that makes science possible. Conversely, science is possible only in a universe that is under the control of an intelligent Creator, the kind of universe in which miracle is possible.

Extremes always meet, and that is why when "everything is God," as in *pantheism*, we have a universe quite like that in which "everything is nature." There is no real supernatural in either case. It is not surprising, therefore, that sophisticated pantheism exhibits the same ambiguity in respect of miracles that primitive animism does. On the one hand, there can be no miracles, for, since everything is God, there is no nature in which the miracle can occur; without nature, miracle simply cannot be domiciled. On the other hand, there can be nothing but miracle, for, since everything is God, all agency is, not merely ultimately but immediately and pervasively, divine; all is miracle. Here, miracle is either non-existent or only "the religious name for event," and thus all-encompassing. But if miracles are everywhere, they have lost all meaning. The two assertions of pantheism reduce therefore to the same thing: there are no miracles. In the gray twilight of this, and of every other monism, all real distinctions have evaporated, including the one at the very heart of Christianity: the distinction between the Creator and the creation. In consequence of this, all talk of miracles becomes meaningless.

REJECTION OF EXTREME DUALISM

The emphasis in all of the foregoing has been on God, on the true God of biblical revelation and on the spurious gods of primitivism and pantheism. But the universe contains more than God. There is beside Him another thing called nature, and no account of miracle can be acceptable which does not give this second thing its due.

On the existence of *nature* the scientist quite understandably insists. A wise scientist will acknowledge God, and if he is also Christian, he will acknowledge miracle, but he will not, therefore, part with nature; it is for him a datum, the very precondition of his vocation. He will, moreover, want to keep a certain kind of nature, the kind that is consonant with the scientific methods his success has vindicated. He will demand an impersonal, objectively existing nature with stable characteristics, open to observation, amenable to analysis, and operating in ways susceptible of mathematical formulation.

Because *deism*, without denying a transcendent God, supplies just such a nature, some Christians have been tempted to embrace this metaphysic. In its highest forms it seems to satisfy both the religious and the scientific needs of man. On the one hand, there is God, eternal and all-wise, who is the Maker and Sustainer of a world which by its order and design points unceasingly to its intelligent Creator. On the other hand, there is nature, possessing a fixed constitution and operating according to immanent and unalterable laws open to discovery and utilization. It would appear that within this scheme the worshiper and the investigator can both find room. It is not so, however. Here, as in monism, what is lacking is precisely miracle. It is excluded by an excess of dualism. Except at the point of origin, nature is isolated from God. Even when divine sustenance is acknowledged, it is conceived as merely general and external; providence never penetrates the world. Nature is constitutionally invulnerable; it can suffer no invasion. All that happens in it is exhaustively interpretable in terms of its own fixed properties.

Because of its intolerance of miracles, deism has not been able to win the allegiance of biblically informed Christians. Yet some Christians, when they posited miracles, thought of them as modifications of a nature deistically conceived. They conceived of nature as a vast interlocked system of things and events ruled by increated laws. Into this nature God sometimes entered to do miracles, but He did so only by "breaking" the laws He had once posited and by "disrupting" the order He had once established. This *semi-deistic* view of things is hardly Christian.

Of this, even its advocates seem to be vaguely aware, for when Heisenberg enunciated the principle of indeterminacy, many of them hailed the discovery with relief. It appears that before this time they were ill at ease with their implied suggestion that God sometimes repented of the cosmic arrangements He had made; they did not like to think that God by miracles disrupted the natural order He had once deliberately fixed. Now, however, there seemed to open up an avenue of escape from their distress. With Heisenberg a new "looseness," a kind of "lawlessness," was discovered in micro-nature, and this seemed to provide God with unobstructed access to macro-nature. A "god of the gaps" was accordingly conceived, a God whose miraculous power could be ushered into the world through the interstices of the atom. Passing through the lawless regions between sub-atomic particles, God's power became available for the performance of "mighty deeds," and yet it left every law unbroken and His original arrangements quite intact.

Apart from the question whether Heisenberg's principle really posits "objective lawlessness" within the atom, it is highly precarious to base a Christian apologetic upon an isolated, even if important, "scientific" discovery. What is required is a view of God and nature framed in positive dependence on the Bible and elaborated in organic relation to the total scientific enterprise, as this appears in the perspective of Christian theism.

NATURE AS DYNAMIC PROCESS

Nature is often likened to a book, even in Christian creeds. The figure is not meaningless, but it is misleading. Nature is hardly a completed manuscript in which each word is statically interlocked with every other, a manuscript to which the scientist goes simply in order to parse unalterable sentences. Nature is rather a dynamic process resembling a discourse now being spoken, and revealing at every turn the meanings and intentions of a living Speaker. What the Speaker says is not dictated by some necessity from outside; He speaks freely. No doubt His discourse is self-consistent, on which account nature may be contemplated as a harmonious whole. But the concept of the whole is not some lever man can manipulate to exclude supposedly inconsistent things like miracles. Miracles, in the Christian view, are *in* the whole called nature, and they help to constitute it. They are parts of the total discourse. They do not rupture nature; they complete and perfect it.

This becomes very evident when it is observed that nature is but a part of a still larger whole, the grand divine plan for all the cosmos. It pleased God to effect in nature some deeds which are crucial in this plan: the miracles of the Incarnation and the Resurrection, which all other miracles only anticipate or reflect. To suppose that these "destroy" nature is utterly to misconceive them. They "save" nature, because they redeem the whole of which nature is a part. They are not illusory events, nor are they real by accident only; they are the very clues to nature as to all else; they state the theme of the grand discourse of which nature is a chapter otherwise unintelligible.

So far as natural *things* go, there is no disposition in Christianity to deny that they are there, that they have recognizable qualities, and that a record of their behavior can be set down and utilized for prediction. Christianity insists only that these things were made by God, that they are still available to Him, and that all they are and do reflect His sovereign purposes. As Calvin says: "... respecting things inanimate ...

though they are naturally endued with their peculiar properties, yet they exert not their power any further than as they are directed by the present hand of God. They are, therefore, no other than instruments into which God infuses as much efficacy as he pleases, bending and turning them to any action, according to his will."[3]

CONCLUSION

To acknowledge miracle, and to appreciate science, nothing is required but to profess the God of Scripture and to accept the nature He has made and ceaselessly controls.

BIBLIOGRAPHY

J. Calvin: *Institutes*, I, xvi
R. Hooykaas: *Natural Law and Divine Miracle*
J. Kallas: *The Significance of the Synoptic Miracles*
C.S. Lewis: *Miracles*
A. Richardson: *The Miracle Stories of the Gospels*

[3] J. Calvin: *Institutes*, I, xvi, 2.

14

THE ORIGIN

AND NATURE OF MAN:

IMAGO DEI

✠

JOHN H. GERSTNER

John H. Gerstner, Professor of Church History at Pittsburgh Theological Seminary, received his general and theological education at Westminster College (B.A., 1936), Westminister Theological Seminary (B.D., B.Th., 1940), Harvard University (Ph.D., 1945), and Tarkio College (D.D., 1955). He is the author of *Ephesians, Steps to Salvation: The Evangelistic Message of Jonathan Edwards,* and *The Theology of the Major Sects,* among other works.

What is man? Man is a creature superior to all other creatures in this world—and therefore having rule over them—by virtue of his ability to know and love his Creator. This ability to know (mind) and love (will) is the *imago Dei* because in so knowing and loving God, man knows and does in finite measure what God knows and does in infinite measure. Implicit in this knowledge of God is the knowledge and love of all other creatures (man supremely, because man is the supreme creature) who are so many manifestations of God, directly or indirectly, consciously or unconsciously, rationally or nonrationally. Man as he now exists, apart from re-creation or regeneration, no longer possesses the *imago Dei* in this sense, but his present condition does not concern us here.

EXPOSITION

(1) *Creation.* In Genesis 1:27 it is recorded, "So God created man in his own image, in the image of God created he him." Thus, according to the Bible, God created man or made him out of nothing by the mere word of His power. We need not labor the point, it being almost universally granted, that the Bible does teach *ex nihilo* creation (though Barth denies it as a *"spekulative Konstruktion"* and in characteristic fashion gives it a new and novel meaning).[1]

(2) *Ideal Man.* If God created man and was pleased with His work, as the Bible says, then man was originally a far nobler creature as he came into being "trailing clouds of glory" than he is now after centuries of wallowing in the sinful pit into which the fall from pristine excellence brought him. Luther may be justified in conjecturing that Adam's "powers of vision exceeded those of the lynx" and his strength enabled him to manage lions and bears.[2] Robert South, in his famous sermon on "Man Created in God's Image," was probably right in saying that an Aristotle was the "rubbish" of an Adam (because the natural ability of newly created man must have been greater than that of fallen man), but probably not right in saying that Athens was but the "rudiment" of Paradise (because the acquired culture of the first man could not have been so great as that of the experience of a race).

(3) *Male and Female.* Genesis 1:27 teaches that man was created male and female: "Male and female created he them." Woman was not a separate creation, although the Bible presents her as differentiated from the male by being drawn from his side, made of him. It is so universally agreed today that woman, as well as man, was created in the divine image that it seems almost quaint to find Dr. Franz Pieper lining up four or five formidable biblical arguments to prove the point.[3]

(4) *Body and Soul.* That man was made a composite creature—a

---

[1] K. Barth: *Die kirchliche Dogmatik*, III, 2, p. 187.
[2] H.T. Kerr: *Compendium of Luther's Theology*, p. 79.
[3] F. Pieper: *Christliche Dogmatik*, p. 261.

body and a soul—is taught in the first chapter of Genesis. He is made as the other creatures before him were made, though later and evidently more complex,[4] but in addition, and distinguishingly, God breathes into him (not into the others) and he becomes a living soul.[5] So, though the body is good and divinely made and therefore never to be despised or downgraded, not to mention charged with being evil, it is still inferior to the soul which God breathed into man exclusively.

Of course, if man was created body and soul, it goes without saying that Adam was an historical being. He was not merely "man," he was a particular man. He was not everyman, but one individual. It is fashionable in our time to take Genesis 1-3 as *Urgeschichte*, or primal history, and Adam as "*Urmensch*," or primal man. We will save ourselves the labor of a positive exposition of this difficult idea and make but one observation: whatever this does mean, it denies that Adam was a person as we are persons and that his history is history as our history is history. But the Bible teaches that Adam was a person as we are persons and that his history is a history as ours is. First, on the surface of it, these three chapters, as the other chapters of Genesis, purport to be genuine history (*Historie*, not *Geschichte*). Second, the Church universal has so understood these chapters up to this very time, with the exception of the dialectical theologians and their converts. Third, it is extraneous factors (geological and anthropological theories) and not biblical exegesis that have produced this deviation. Fourth, Genesis 1-3 is integrated with the rest of Genesis, which is typical history (virtually everyone admits this of Genesis 12-50, at least). Fifth, Genesis 5:1-5 specifically mentions Adam, as does I Chronicles 1:1, in an indisputably historical sense. Sixth, the New Testament also mentions Adam in historical genealogy in Jude 14 and Luke 3:38. Seventh, Paul compares and contrasts Adam with Jesus Christ as the first and second Adam. There is a dualism here, as the demythologizers contend, but not a cosmic dualism—simply the dualism of two historical persons in representative roles. Eighth, if Adam can be "demythologized," we see no reason to stop Bultmann from demythologizing the entire Bible, as he seems intent on doing. Ninth, if we were to demythologize, then not only can Bultmann do it to the entire Bible, but he or anyone else can interpret the demythologized Bible as he pleases.

(5) *The Image of God*. But without question, the most significant aspect of the nature of man is the *imago Dei*. Genesis 1:26 ("let us make

---

[4] Gen. 1:26.   [5] Gen. 2:7.

man in our image, after our likeness") reveals the nature of man. As created or made, he is a dependent being. As created in the image of God, he is rational, for God deliberates and plans His creation; he is social, for God made him in "our" image; he had dominion over the other creatures, for of none of these was this superior image predicated. But does this text not imply materiality in God, as the Mormons teach, and eternality in man, as the pantheists say? Should the "image" not be construed exhaustively, rather than restrictively? No, because the creation context carries vast implications that are part of the teaching of the text. God being here presented as Creator, but Himself uncreated and independent, is infinitely and eternally superior to the creature. Thus, the spiritual qualities of the *imago* are those which are consistent with the Creator-creature relationship, such as knowledge, righteousness, and holiness. The physical qualities of man are manifestly not part of the *imago*, because an eternal, independent spirit could not possess a temporal, dependent body as an essential, necessary part of His being.

What is taught didactically in Genesis 1:26 is set forth by description in "they heard the voice of the Lord God walking in the garden in the cool of the day,"[6] an anthropomorphic representation of fellowship between creature and Creator. This illustrates the ability of man's rational nature to understand, in a measure, the rational being of God, as the latter chooses to reveal it. Likewise, the assignment of "naming the animals,"[7] that is, classifying the subordinate creatures, presupposes rationality, scientific knowledge, or potentiality. Moral duty is implicit in such an assignment, but the moral nature of man is more evident still in the command and the prohibition concerning eating of the forbidden fruit.[8] The intellectual nature of man is usually designated as the image of God in the broader sense; the moral, or holy, nature is the image of God proper in the narrower sense. The former is inalienable even in hell; the latter was losable even in the paradise.

Apart from the creation narrative itself, little in the Bible is concerned with the description of man as such, but much with man as sinner. Psalm 8 is a rare passage reflecting on ideal man. Most of the post-Genesis anthropological references are oblique: to the restoration of man as sinner toward his former state of man as man. Psalm 8 does not so much add to our knowledge of the basic nature of man, as ac-

[6] Gen. 3:8. [7] Gen. 2:20.
[8] Gen. 2:16 f.

centuate his exaltedness in comparison with the other creatures and his insignificance in comparison with his Creator. Though man is little lower than the angels, to whom he is inferior in nature though superior in destiny, it is a mark of extreme condescension that God visits him. Second Corinthians 15:47, 48 shows that man as originally created was of the earth, earthy in contrast to man as re-created and resurrected, who possesses the Spirit in a manner not formerly characteristic. In Ephesians 4:24, Paul shows that the regenerated man is restored in principle to his former state of knowledge and holiness. When Paul indicates that the Thessalonian Christians should be sanctified in body, soul, and spirit,[9] I believe he is viewing the soul of man in the double aspect of animating principle (*psuche*) and imago (*pneuma*).

APPLICATION

(1) *Causal Evolutionism.* How do causal evolutionists account for the origin of man? Ultimately, it is not by natural selection; that is merely a proximate cause. Ultimately, it is by chance. G.G. Simpson, in his *The Meaning of Evolution*,[10] seems to think that man was an un-intentional accident. Bertrand Russell says: "... even if it is enormously improbable that the laws of chance ... will produce an organism capable of intelligence out of a causal selection of atoms, it is nevertheless probable that there will be in the universe that very small number of such organisms that we do in fact find."[11] A still-more recent statement by William S. Beck in *Modern Science and the Nature of Life*[12] is to the same effect: "When the time scale is long enough, the improbable becomes the inevitable." But this probability thinking and the dice analogy used by Russell do not fit the case before us. With dice, any number from two to twelve may occur, and the law of averages says that all possibilities will occur in certain proportions. But what does the law of averages have to say about getting blood from a turnip or a silk purse from a sow's ear or, to stay with the original analogy, about getting a "one" or a "thirteen" out of a pair of dice? *Emergent* evolution, *epi*phenomenalism, and *creative* evolution are merely quasi-scientific, question-begging terms, no more acceptable than "spontaneous generation," of which they are indeed merely sophisticated modern variations.

9 I Thess. 5:23.   10 1951.
11 B. Russell: *Why I Am Not a Christian*, p. 24.
12 W.S. Beck: *Modern Science and the Nature of Life*, p. 252.

(2) *"Psychologism."* Much psychology has become very deterministic in our time and philosophy, at least in its existentialist varieties
extremely voluntaristic. M.B. Arnold[13] regards Jung and Adler, as well
as Freud, as necessitarian; Reinhold Niebuhr notes that Sartre is voluntaristic to the point of denying human nature.[14] The truth lies between them, as we shall see. Against the view that man is as he eats or
as he secretes or as he is stimulated, is the biblical view that man's
choices are influenced by these, but not "determined" in the sense of
constrained or coerced by these factors. God commanded the ideal
man, the "first" and the "second" Adam. The Bible does not accept the
doctrine that man's choices belong not to him but to his glands. Nor
does the God of the Bible become angry with man's nerves when sin is
committed. Nor are the organs of a man—in distinction from the man—
sentenced to judgment.

(3) *Existentialism.* Existentialism moves to the other pole: from
cause without voluntary action, to voluntary action without cause.
Reasons, motives, causes do not determine the actions of men, but the
actions of men determine the reasons, motives, causes. Existentially
speaking, man is absolutely free, his actions altogether contingent; his
decisions are in the moment of crisis. Man does not act because of
such and such reasons. But the "reasons" are given substance by the
decisions. Free actions involve a crucifixion of the intellect. Existentialist
theologians sometimes think that they have the Bible to father, inasmuch as it says that out of the heart are the issues of life[15] and every
man does what is right in his own eyes.[16] This is the type of thing
which has led some Roman Catholic theologians to think themselves,
and even Thomas Aquinas, existential. The notion is effectively
scotched by F.H. Heinemann in his "Existentialism, Religion and Theology,"[17] not to mention Pius XII in *Humani Generis.*[18] Protestant
scholars have been even more susceptible.

While existentialism has hold of an important truth (it seems to
me that ninety percent of existential writing could come under the
title, "On the Importance of Being Earnest"), it is badly out of focus.
Genesis represents the creature, man, as being given reasons for following virtue, avoiding sin. If man eats of a certain tree, he dies; if not, he

---

[13] M.B. Arnold: *Religious Education,* "Psychology and the Image of Man."
[14] *A Handbook of Christian Theology,* "The Self."
[15] Prov. 4:23.   [16] Judges 27:35.
[17] *Hibbert Journal,* July, 1960.   [18] 1950.

lives. His decision is called for (which puts the Bible against the determinist), but the decision is motivated by reasons (which puts the Bible against the paradoxical existentialist).

(4) *Neo-orthodoxy.* There are at least three fundamental neo-orthodox deviations from the biblical doctrine of man. First, Adam is presented not as one historical individual, but as the eternal non-historical symbol of every historical individual. "Adam is Everyman."[19] Second, there is no original righteousness or created goodness, but mere potentiality. Third, the natural and moral image tend to be confused and both eradicated by the Fall. "Barth goes far beyond Calvin," who sets forth the biblical view, "in holding that Imago Dei is effaced, not defaced, so that our human nature is not only incapable of spiritual good, but can neither retain nor pass on a divine gift."[20]

BIBLIOGRAPHY

J. Edwards: *Freedom of the Will* [P. Ramsey, ed.]
H. Heppe: *Reformed Dogmatics*
J.G. Machen: *The Christian View of Man*
R. Mixter, ed.: *Evolution and Christian Thought Today*
J. Orr: *God's Image in Man*, 2nd edition

[19] A. Richardson, ed.: *A Theological Word Book of the Bible*, p. 14.
[20] A.M. Fairweather: *The Word of Truth*, p. 1.

15

THE COVENANT OF WORKS

✝

OSWALD T. ALLIS

Oswald T. Allis, formerly Professor of Old Testament History
and Exegesis at Princeton Theological Seminary, received his
general and theological education at the University of Pennsylvania (B.A., 1901), Princeton Theological Seminary (B.D.,
1905), Princeton University (M.A., 1907), University of Berlin
(Ph.D., 1913), and Hampden Sydney College (D.D., 1927).
He is the author of *The Five Books of Moses, Prophecy and
the Church, Revision or New Translation?*, and *The Unity of
Isaiah*, among other works.

Whatever else the statesmen and economists of today may report to
us, they cannot say, "We have walked to and fro, through the earth,
and, behold, all the earth sitteth still and is at rest." The earth is not
sitting still; it is not at rest. Recent years have been marked by constant change, accompanied by turmoil and confusion. Many foundations have been destroyed; and the question is asked anxiously: what
can the righteous do? What of the future?

As we look out on the world, we can hardly fail to see that the
great problem which confronts us is that of *authority* and *obedience*.
It faces us at every level: personal, domestic, social, religious. Is man

an autonomous anarch? Or is he a responsible being; and if responsible, to whom?

The Bible has a simple but comprehensive answer to this question. Briefly stated it is this: man was created by God and in the image of God, and the duty which God requires of man is "obedience to his revealed will." The authority of God, implied in His Creatorship, has as its correlate the obedience of man; and God's will is revealed in the Bible.

That this is so is the Bible's constant claim. It is plainly set forth in the account of the creation of man. Five imperatives are at once laid upon man,[1] and three times the word "commanded" is used of God's dealings with Adam and Eve. The story is briefly and simply told. God commanded; Adam and Eve disobeyed; the penalty or sanction attached to the command was invoked; and the guilty pair, under sentence of death, were driven forth from the presence of God.

The relationship established in Eden has been properly called the covenant of works. That it promised life as the reward of obedience is not immediately stated. But it is made abundantly clear elsewhere, notably in Deuteronomy.[2] The First Psalm is a poetical expounding of this covenant, and it has its counterpart in Romans 2:7-9. The penalty of disobedience is shown in the mournful cadence in Genesis 5, "and he died," and in the terrible judgment of the Flood which destroyed "the old world of unrighteousness." The consistent teaching of the Bible is that "the wages of sin is death."

The covenant was made with Adam in a state of innocence, and almost his first recorded act was the breaking of it; and human history from that day to this is a tragic record of man's failure to keep it. Consequently, in the plan and purpose of God, the covenant of works was immediately followed by the covenant of grace. This covenant is first set forth cryptically in the words of the protevangel,[3] which promised Eve ultimate triumph over the enemy of her race. In this covenant, the emphasis is on faith. This is made clear in the wonderful words that are said of Abram: "And he believed in the LORD, and he accounted it to him for righteousness,"[4] to which Paul appeals to show that Abraham was justified by faith and not by the works of the law. He also appeals to the words of the prophet, "the just shall live by faith."[5]

---

[1] Gen. 1:28.   [2] Deut. 6:5, 10–12 f.; 30:15–20.
[3] Gen. 3:15.   [4] Gen. 15:6.
[5] Hab. 2:4.

The New Testament abounds in statements which justify Luther's challenge to Rome—"justification by faith alone." John 3:16, Acts 16:31, Romans 2:8 are a few of them.

Since these two covenants are often contrasted rather sharply as works *versus* faith, it is important to remember that the basic requirement of both is exactly the same. They both require *obedience* to the revealed will of God. This is made especially clear in the life of Abraham. Abraham is Paul's great example of salvation by faith. But no mere man was ever more severely tried and tested in the school of obedience.[6] In the great faith chapter in Hebrews we read that when Abraham was called to go forth to the unknown country, he "obeyed; and he went out, not knowing whither he went." This whole chapter should not be called "the faith chapter," but the chapter of "the obedience of faith."[7] For, of all its examples of faith, it can be said, "They climbed the steep ascent of heaven through peril, toil, and pain."

By the covenant of grace the Christian is not offered faith as an easy substitute for works of righteousness. It offers him an unmerited and unearned righteousness, the righteousness of Christ received by faith, which challenges him and demands that he walk worthy of his high calling, that he learn to say as Paul did, "the love of Christ constraineth us."[8] The fact that he is not under the law as a basis of works-salvation does not set before the Christian a lower standard than that of the Mosaic law, but a far higher one; and this for at least four reasons: (1) Being made free from the curse and bondage of the law as a covenant of works, he ceases to be a servant (slave) and becomes a son, a member of the household of God. (2) He has set before him the perfect pattern of obedience in the person and work of Christ. (3) He is given the strongest motive for loving and obedient service, gratitude to Him Who died that he might live. (4) He has received the indwelling of the Holy Spirit to illumine, sanctify, and energize him for the willing and obedient service of God. When Jesus gave His disciples a new commandment, "As I have loved you that ye also love one another," He set them a standard of obedience that surpassed the commandment of the Law, "Thou shalt love thy neighbor as thyself." Little wonder then that Paul answers the question, "Do we then make void the law through faith?" with the emphatic words, "God forbid: yea, we establish the law." And the great catechisms of Protestantism—Luther,

[6] Gen. 22:18, 26:5.   [7] Rom. 16:26.
[8] II Cor. 5:14.

Heidelberg, Westminster—devote much space to delineation of the meaning of the Decalogue as setting forth what Tyndale called "the obedience of the Christian man."

Since, then, it is clear that the Gospel does not abrogate the moral law as a standard of life and conduct but raises it to a higher level both by example and precept, it is not surprising that various efforts have been made from New Testament times until now, by carnally-minded Christians—and none are wholly dead unto sin—to set aside the covenant of works as of obligation to the Christian or to modify its demands. Space will permit only brief discussion of the most important of them.

ANTINOMIANISM

This heresy was met with already by Paul. Stating the antithesis between faith and works in the most absolute fashion, "Shall we continue in sin that grace may abound?" Paul gave it the conclusive answer, "God forbid. How shall we that are dead to sin, live any longer therein?" The whole teaching of the New Testament is that justification has as its objective sanctification, redemption from all iniquity. A faith which does not bring forth fruit unto righteousness is not a living faith. The bandit who comes secretly to the priest for confession and absolution only that he may with a quieted conscience return to his life of thievery and violence is like the Jews of old who made the Temple "a den of robbers," a refuge against the consequences of their evil deeds.

PERFECTIONISM

This is the opposite extreme. It not merely recognizes the duty of man to do the will of God, but insists that he is able to do it. It has its familiar illustration in the Pharisee who thanked God that he was not as other men and took pride in his good works. And the lesson of the parable is that all self-righteousness is an offence in the sight of God. This teaching must either lower the standard of obedience or minimize the corruption of man and his consequent inability to obey God perfectly. This is illustrated most clearly in the doctrine of the church of Rome. It teaches that baptism removes the guilt and corruption of man's nature and that prevenient grace is given him to enable him to do the will of God. The extreme form of this teaching is supererogation, that man can do not merely all that God requires but more, that by special acts of obedience (celibacy, poverty, austerity), he can lay up additional merit, which the church can administer, for the benefit of sinful members of the body of Christ. This teaching makes the super-righteousness of the saints, the few, the means of saving sinners, the many, from the torments of purgatory. It has no warrant in Scripture.

Perfectionism is taught in various forms in Christian churches to-day. It is biblical and sound when it recognizes and stresses the de-mands of Scripture for perfect obedience to the will of God. It is mistaken and dangerous when it fails to recognize that "no mere man since the fall is able in this life perfectly to keep the commandments of God, but doth daily break them, in thought, word, and deed." The Apostle Paul confessed that he had not "already attained." But he said, "I press to the mark the prize of the high calling of God in Christ Jesus." Anyone who thinks he has *attained* deceives himself. Everyone who does not *press toward the mark* fails to realize the obli-gation of his high calling.

DISPENSATIONALISM

This popular teaching is characterized by the dividing of biblical history into a series of distinct and contrasted dispensations. The most important are: *promise, law,* and *grace*. It teaches that the dispensation of promise was introduced by the Abrahamic covenant, the sole re-quirement of which was faith; that obedience was not required until at Sinai Israel "rashly accepted the law."[9] The fallacy of this teaching can be shown in several ways: (1) Abraham's faith was proved by his obedience when he was called upon to offer up Isaac,[10] and the blessings promised him and his seed were given "because thou hast obeyed my voice."[11] (2) Dispensationalists admit that the promise to Abraham was conditional when they tell us that to be or to remain in the land was a *condition* of blessing. (3) Refusal to accept the law at Sinai with its promise of blessing would have been an act of disobedi-ence, which would have been dealt with as severely as was the re-fusal to go up to possess the land.[12]

BARTHIANISM

The primary emphasis in the crisis theology, of which Karl Barth is the most distinguished representative, is placed on the transcendence

[9] Scofield.
[11] Cf. Gen. 26:5.

[10] Gen. 22:1–18.
[12] Num. 14:26–38.

of God. This was the natural reaction to the immanentism of the old liberalism. It holds the separation between God and man to be utter and absolute. God must break through to man, if man is to know God redemptively. This breakthrough or "crisis" is an act of revelation, and it is made in and through the Scriptures. But according to Barth, the Bible is not a divine and infallible book but a very human and fallible book. It is not the Word of God; it contains it. It is only as God speaks through it to the human soul that the written word becomes God's Word to the individual man; only if the word "finds" him is it God's Word for him. Let us illustrate from the Decalogue. Suppose the command, "Honor thy father and thy mother," does not "find" the adolescent of today. What power has Barthianism to require him to obey it? The great peril in Barthianism is its subjectivism. If man's knowledge of God and His will comes only through the Bible, then only a fully dependable Bible can give man the clear and certain knowledge which he needs. But the Barthian must first decide for himself what the will of God for him is, before he is under any obligation to accept it. Thus, every man makes for himself his own "covenant of works" and does that which is right in his own eyes.

EXISTENTIALISM

Like Barthianism, existentialism, despite its great popularity, is a relatively new teaching. It is traced back to Kierkegaard who, in revolt against the spiritual coldness and lethargy of the Danish State Church, placed the emphasis on personal decision as against what has been aptly called the "spectator attitude" toward life.

This has developed into a tendency to reject the authority of all external standards and codes. It involves such familiar ideas as that of the sophists that "man is the measure of all things." It may be atheistic or theistic.

An extreme form of it is found in the attempt of Bultmann to demythologize the Bible. Since the supernatural does not appeal to the "scientific" man of today, does not *find* him, it is treated as myth and eliminated, which means, of course, the denial and rejection of any divine authority or sanction in the Bible or elsewhere.

Centuries ago, in a time of distress in Israel, a prophet of the Lord promised the people deliverance from Shishak. But he added these impressive words in the name of the Lord: "Nevertheless, they shall be his servants; that they may know my service, and the service of the kingdoms of the countries." Freedom is a great word today, a word to conjure with. The Bible speaks in terms of service—service to God, servitude to man. It pictures the glory of the one, the misery of the other. Let us hope and pray that the trials through which men are passing today, in their struggles for self-expression and for liberty, may lead them to submit themselves in loving obedience to Him of Whom alone it can be said that His service is perfect freedom.

BIBLIOGRAPHY

Westminster Confession and Catechisms
H. Witsius: *The Economy of the Covenants*
General works on systematic theology, such as those of C. Hodge, A.A. Hodge, A.H. Strong
Of recent works, *see:*
C.F.H. Henry: *Christian Personal Ethics*
———— ed.: *Contemporary Evangelical Thought*
Scofield Reference Bible
O.T. Allis: *Prophecy and the Church*
A. Reese: *The Approaching Advent of Christ*
Monographs in the *Modern Thinkers Series:* A.D.R. Polman, "Barth"; S.U. Zuidema, "Kierkegaard" and "Sartre"; H. Ridderbos: "Bultmann"

16

THE ORIGIN AND

NATURE OF SIN

✚

J. OLIVER BUSWELL, JR.

J. Oliver Buswell, Jr., Dean of the Graduate Faculty at Covenant College and Seminary, St. Louis, Missouri, received his general and theological education at the University of Minnesota (B.A., 1917), the University of Chicago (M.A., 1924), McCormick Theological Seminary (B.D., 1923), Dallas Theological Seminary (D.D., 1927), Houghton College (LL.D., 1936), New York University (Ph.D., 1949). He is the author of *Problems in the Prayer Life, The Philosophies of F.R. Tennant and John Dewey, Thomas and the Bible,* and *Being and Knowing: An Introduction to Philosophy,* among other works.

"When He comes He will convict the world of sin...." This was Jesus' promise as He told of the ministry of the Holy Spirit. The world of our day is strangely unconvicted, unconvinced, and unconcerned, yet where Spirit-filled men faithfully present the Spirit-inspired Word of God, conviction of sin comes. The great need of the world today is for consecrated channels for the convicting work of the

Holy Spirit. Only so can there be a genuine turning to the Lord and acceptance of the Gospel.

THE NATURE OF SIN

There is very wide divergence of opinion among philosophers as to the criterion of what ought, or ought not, to be. Thus, when it comes to the question of what is good and what is evil, we come across several major schools of thought.

The Christian answer is that God has given us the sense of *oughtness*, and that He has revealed the criterion and the substance of what is good and what is evil. The mere fact that we have a sense of what ought, or ought not, to be, a sense quite different from the sense of pleasure or desire, is inexplicable on a merely naturalistic basis. Let us turn then to the Christian view.

"Sin is any want of conformity unto or transgression of the law of God." These words from the *Westminster Shorter Catechism* are based upon I John 3:4, "missing the mark [that is, want of conformity] is breaking the law."[1] The biblical view of sin, however, does not depend wholly upon the concept of law, for the biblical writers appeal to the holy character of God as the basis of the law. "Ye shall be holy for I, Jehovah, your God, am holy"[2] is the constant presupposition. It was the revelation of the holy character of God[3] which caused Isaiah to recognize his own sinful corruption. Thus, sin is not only violation of the divine law, which is an expression of God's will; more profoundly, it is violation of the expression of God's holy character. It is corruption of the goodness which the Creator originally imparted to His creatures; and, especially, it is the corruption of the godliness with which God originally endowed man when He created him in His own image.

The divine character is expressed by the divine will in the divine law. Christians generally understand that the Ten Commandments and the law of love[4] constitute a brief summary of God's holy moral law for man. And this is all based upon God's holy character.

Sin may then be defined ultimately as anything in the creature

[1] Bible quotations, when not from the King James Version, are the author's own translation.
[2] Lev. 19:2.   [3] Isa. 6:1–6.
[4] Cf. Exod. 20:1–17 and Luke 10:27.

which does not express, or which is contrary to, the holy character of the Creator.

THE ORIGIN OF SIN

The origin of human sin, according to the Bible, is very simply ascribed to the willful self-corruption of the creature under temptation. The record is given in the third chapter of Genesis, and the fact of the original human sin is expounded in Romans 5:12-21 and elsewhere.

According to the account of Genesis 3, man was created with a holy nature, in fellowship with God, and placed in an environment which was "all very good"; but man was tempted to sin by a personal being of another kind, or order, who had previously sinned against God. This fact indicates that the record of the original sin of man is not intended as an account of the absolute origin of sin in the universe.

The record of the original human sin is of more value to us because this sin was induced by the tempter. Aside from the doctrine that Adam was our representative, the "federal" head of the human race, and we, representatively, sinned in him, the fact is that in our common experience, sin is induced by previous sin. We are in Adam and individually guilty and corrupt sinners; but no human being has brought about the absolute origin of sin in the universe. We must therefore search for the origin of sin in the tempter.

The tempter in the Genesis record is an evil personal intelligence. The words "the Serpent," I suggest, should be read as a proper name.[5] The Genesis account has nothing to say about a biological reptile. "The Serpent" is not said to be one of the "beasts of the field" but to be more subtle than any of them,[6] and destined for a greater curse than any.[7] Snakes do not literally eat dirt,[8] but to be prostrated and to eat dust constitute an ancient metaphor for the humiliation of an enemy. There is no natural antipathy between human beings and snakes,[9] not as much as between humans and insects. Children have to be taught to avoid poisonous reptiles. The whole meaning of the "enmity" of verse 15 is the enmity between "the Serpent" and the promised Redeemer. "The Serpent" is Satan, and figures throughout the Bible as the archenemy of God and man, the instigator of all kinds of evil.

What does the Bible say about the primeval origin of sin, before the

[5] Cf. Isa. 65:25 and Rev. 12:9, where the "Serpent" is a person.
[6] Gen. 3:1.   [7] Gen. 3:14.
[8] Gen. 3:14; Isa. 65:25.   [9] Gen. 3:15.

fall of man? There is definite indication in the Bible that mankind is not the only order of created personal beings among whom sin has become an actuality. In Jude, verse 6, there is reference to "the angels that did not keep their own realm [arche] but left their proper dwelling." The parallel verse, II Peter 2:4, speaks of "the angels that sinned." The biblical writers assume that Satan is the chief of the fallen angels. In I John 3:8, we read, "the devil sins from the beginning." From I Timothy 3:6, it is suggested that Satan's root or basic sin was pride. The words of Jesus are more explicit: "He [the devil] was a murderer from the beginning. He did not take his stand in the truth. [This is evident] because truth is not in him. When he speak falsehood he speaks out of his own things, for he is a falsifier and the father of falsehood."[10]

Jesus' statement that the devil is, from the beginning, a murderer and a falsifier is probably based upon the fact that by falsehood Satan brought about the fall of man, in which man (1) became liable to physical death, (2) became liable to eternal punishment, "the second death," and (3) became spiritually dead, that is, alienated from fellowship with God.

There are expositors who hold that, aside from the rather clear references given above to the fall of Satan, the prophetic denunciations of Babylon[11] and of the king of Tyre[12] contain references to Satan's original status and his fall. It is not unreasonable to hold that certain sentences in these prophecies may contain analogies which would throw light upon Satan's probable original status and his fall.

The statements are not very full, yet the biblical account of the primeval origin of sin is clear enough: sin first became actual in an order of personal beings who are not a race.[13] They do not have racial solidarity or racial representative responsibility. This order of beings, presumably having fully adequate understanding of the holy character of God and of God's impartation of His holy character to his creatures, was endowed with the power of ethical spiritual choice. Some of these beings, including Satan as the chief, deliberately chose to corrupt their God-given holy character, and chose further to spread their corruption as widely as possible in God's creation. Their sin was the act of a group of individuals as individuals, and does not involve the "federal" or representative principle. Since their sin was, we suppose, a

---

[10] John 8:44.   [11] Isa. 13 and 14, especially 14:12–14.
[12] Ezek. 28:1–19, especially vv. 12–19.
[13] Matt. 22:30; Mark 12:25; Luke 20:35, 36.

deliberate act, with fully adequate understanding, it is analogous to the fully conscious and responsible act subsequent to conviction by the Holy Spirit, in which act Jesus said that the sinner is "guilty of eternal sin."[14] In other words, they sinned without remedy. (For a penetrating study in the psychology of a determinative act and a permanent attitude of sin, compare Milton's soliloquy of Satan in the early part of *Paradise Lost*. Satan is represented as refusing the very thought of repentance, and settling in the attitude, "Evil, be thou my good!")

According to the Bible, then, sin originated in an act of free will in which the creature deliberately, responsibly, and with adequate understanding of the issues chose to corrupt the holy character of godliness with which God had endowed His creation.

QUESTIONS THAT REMAIN

Two philosophical questions remain: (1) How could there be a free responsible act from the cosmic point of view? (2) How could a holy God permit sin?

The Christian determinist is usually driven to an inscrutable paradox. He may accept all that the Bible says about primeval sin as factually true, but the biblical statements afford no philosophical explanation. Satan sinned necessarily. God is rightly angry with all sin. So be it!

As for this writer's opinion, the denial of free will seems to be purely arbitrary philosophical dogmatism, contrary to the biblical view. If God is rightly angry with sin, then it follows that the sinner is blameworthy—cosmically, ultimately, absolutely.

We come now to the question: How could a good God permit sin?

Calvin and Calvinists generally (with the exception of certain supralapsarians) agree in denying that God is in any sense the author of sin.[15] Nevertheless, we find that God "worketh all things after the counsel of his own will."[16] We cannot deny that "whatever comes to pass" is within the eternal decrees of God. Sin must be within God's eternal decrees in some sense in which He is not the author of it.

In the ninth chapter of Romans, Paul gives two answers to the problem: "You will say to me, then, 'Why does He still blame anybody? Who ever stood up against His will?'

14 Mark 3:29.
15 *Westminster Confession of Faith*, I, i.
16 Eph. 1:11.

"Well now then, O man, you, who are you, answering back to God? Will the thing which is moulded say to the one who moulded it, 'Why did you make me this way?' Or does not the potter have a right to make from the same mass of clay a valuable dish, and one of no value?"[17]

Many persons never go beyond Paul's first, or preliminary, answer. God has a right to do what He chooses with His creation. Some devout minds still cling to the paradox. On the one hand, it is assumed that what ought not to be ought not to be permitted. On the other hand, God "worketh all things after the counsel of his own will."[18]

Some have even taken refuge in Pope's couplet:

> Wrong is not wrong if rightly understood
> And partial evil, universal good.

But the Christian answer cannot question "the exceeding sinfulness of sin." To do so would be to question the necessity of the atonement of Christ for the salvation of sinners.

Paul's answer clearly breaks one horn of the dilemma and does not leave us in a paradox; but Paul does not accomplish this by questioning the fact that sin absolutely ought not to be. The fallacy which leaves some minds in a state of contradiction is *the false assumption that what ought not to be, ought not to be permitted.* Those who have studied modern educational methods should be the last to criticize God's permission of sin. As parents, we must, within the limits of our finite understanding, permit our children to experience the trying but inevitable assortment of bumps and bruises if they are ever to learn to walk.

Paul does not merely leave the question with his reference to the potter and the clay. In previous verses,[19] he had pointed out that by allowing Pharaoh to be born, to come to the throne of Egypt, and to resist the salvation of Israel, and by forcing the issue with Pharaoh, God had demonstrated His *power* and caused His *name* to be reported in all the earth. "For this purpose I stirred you up."[20]

After presenting God's rights, Paul continues. "What if God endured [Pharaoh] with much longsuffering," in order to demonstrate His *wrath* and make known His *ability* and the wealth of His *glory* in saving His people?

---

[17] Rom. 9:19-21.   [18] Eph. 1:11.
[19] Rom. 9:17-18.   [20] *Exegeira se*, Alford's suggestion.

In the word "endured," we certainly have the suggestion of God's permission. We must conclude, then, that within the decrees of God, there are decrees of the permission of those things of which God Himself is not the author.

This is not *mere* permission of the unavoidable, a view against which Calvin often protests. It is God's permissive decrees for His own purposes of revelation. What would the history of God's redemptive program be without the revelation of God's "power," "name," "wrath," "ability," and "glory," as these were revealed by the events included in the decree in which he permitted Pharaoh's sin?

In the light of the ninth chapter of Romans, we may assume that God's decree permitting the primeval sin may be justified, even to our finite minds, on the analogy of Paul's justification of the permission of Pharaoh's sin. In terms of Joseph's words to his brethren,[21] we may say to every sinner in cosmic history, "As for you, ye thought evil ... but God meant it [that is, permitted it] for good."

The purpose of this study in the nature and origin of sin is to magnify the "amazing grace" of God in His redemptive program, as that program includes "even me," "the chief of sinners."

BIBLIOGRAPHY

J.O. Buswell, Jr.: *Sin and Atonement*
F.R. Tennant: *Origin and Propagation of Sin*
————: *The Concept of Sin*
K. Barth: *Die kirchliche Dogmatik*, III, 1, 3, Secs. 50, 51
E.M. Adams: *Ethical Naturalism and the Modern World View*

[21] Gen. 50:20.

17

ORIGINAL SIN,

IMPUTATION, AND INABILITY

✛

CORNELIUS VAN TIL

Cornelius Van Til, Professor of Apologetics at Westminster Theological Seminary, Philadelphia, Pennsylvania, received his general and theological education at Calvin College (B.A., 1922), Princeton University (M.A., 1924; Ph.D., 1927), and Princeton Theological Seminary (Th.B., 1924; Th.M., 1925). He is the author of *The New Modernism*, *The Defense of the Faith*, and *The Theology of James Duane*.

Socrates was, as usual, after definitions. In particular, he wanted definitions of the good, the true, and the beautiful. This business of finding definitions was, for him, an existential question. His life, and even the state of the "life hereafter," depended upon it. He was being tried for corrupting the youth of Athens and death might be the penalty.

When Socrates met Euthyphro, it seemed as though the end of his quest had come. Euthyphro knew all the definitions that men and gods had given. But Socrates wanted a definition of holiness, *regardless of what men or gods say about it*. So he died without the desired definitions. For him, the good is good in itself, and god or the gods must look up to it as such. For him, man was the center and final reference point of all predication.

Paul, the Apostle, was also in search of definitions. He, too, wanted definitions of the true, the good, and the beautiful. For him, too, the finding of definitions was a matter of life and death. When Paul met Christ, the end of his search had really come. Christ was God. In the Scriptures, as the Word of Christ his Lord, Paul found himself defined by God. Henceforth, his mind was subject to the mind of Christ. Paul had found, or rather had been found, of God. For him, the true, the good, and the beautiful are what they are by his Creator's and his Redeemer's ordinance. The holy is holy, because God says it is holy.

At this point, a new search for a new kind of definition began for Paul. His chief concern was now to learn how great was the grace of Christ to him; how great was the love of God that sent His Son into the world to save not only him, but also a numberless host of others with him, to be members of the body of Christ. Here was corporate salvation.

Here "the gift of grace, which is by one man, Jesus Christ, hath abounded unto many" and here "they which receive abundance of grace and of the gift of righteousness shall reign in life by one, Jesus Christ."[1] "For he hath made him to be sin for us, who knew no sin; that we might be made the righteousness of God in him."[2]

Sinners are *constituted righteous* by the righteousness of one, even Jesus Christ. Here was imputed righteousness. And on its basis, Paul knew, he had true ability to serve his Saviour.

THE ANALOGY

Having seen the vision of corporate salvation in Christ, Paul also sees the vision of corporate sin. All men have sinned in Adam. Through the "offense of one many be dead." Judgment was "by one to condemnation." By "one man's offence death reigned by one." "For as by one man's disobedience many were constituted sinners, so by the obedience of one shall many be constituted righteous."[3]

(1) *Original Sin.* So deep, says Paul, is the nature of our sin that, as death comes to Adam for his sin, death comes also to all men "for that all have sinned." Thus, Paul speaks of "the one sin and the sin

[1] Rom. 5:15, 17.   [2] II Cor. 5:21.
[3] Rom. 5:19.

of all." "We must not tone down either the singularity or the universality."[4]

We cannot ask: When does the individual *become* a sinner? "For the truth is that each person never exists as other than sinful. He is eternally contemplated by God as sinful by reason of the solidarity with Adam, and, whenever the person comes to be *actually* he comes to be as sinful."[5]

Paul's sense of guilt is deepened, not reduced, because of this, his view of original sin.

(2) *Imputed Sin*. Paul says that all men were in Adam "constituted sinners," as believers are in Christ "constituted righteous."[6] There is "as truly an imputation of the disobedience of Adam as there is of the obedience of Christ."[7] God contemplates all men as actually one with Adam in his sin. There is "as truly an imputation of the disobedience of Adam as there is of the obedience of Christ. As the latter imputation is not that of the benefit accruing follows upon the imputation, so the former must not be conceived as the liability entailed but the liability as flowing from the imputation."[8] Thus "the kind of relationship which Adam sustains to men is after the pattern of the relationship which Christ sustains to men."[9]

(3) *Inability*. Only when the Church, with Paul, confesses its sin as being corporate and imputed does it sense its spiritual inability. Due to the fall in Adam "we are utterly indisposed, disabled, and made opposite to all good and wholly inclined to all evil."[10] The natural man is able to perform moral acts, good as well as evil" which are "as to the matter of them" prescribed by the moral law.[11] But the natural man, due to his false motivation and aim, cannot "perform any act in such a way as to merit the approbation of God."[12] Man cannot regenerate himself, and as unregenerate, he is under the wrath of God.

THE CONTRADICTION

What would Socrates have said about all this: definitions of grace and sin given to man by sheer authority, original sin, imputed sin, and spiritual inability? Out with one and all of them!

[4] J. Murray: *Epistle to the Romans*, Volume I, p. 186.
[5] J. Murray: *The Imputation of Adam's Sin*, p. 90.
[6] *Ibid.*, p. 88.   [7] *Ibid.*
[8] *Ibid.*   [9] *Ibid.*, p. 39; cf. I Cor. 51:22, 45–49.
[10] *Westminster Confession*.
[11] C. Hodge: *Systematic Theology*, II, p. 261.
[12] *Ibid.*, p. 264.

In modern times, no one has expressed the Socratic attitude more pointedly than did Immanuel Kant. For Kant, human personality is altogether a law unto itself. Its autonomy is its freedom.

Kant's moral consciousness is, for him, the ultimate source of the distinction between good and evil. Kant, as well as Socrates, wants to discover the nature of sin regardless of what God says about it.

THE SYNTHESIS

(1) *Pelagius.* In addition to open opposition to its confession of sin, the church has always faced the problem of synthesizers. Holding to an essentially Socratic view, Pelagius insisted that sin "consists only in the deliberate choice of evil. It presupposes knowledge of what is evil, as well as the full power of choosing or rejecting it."[13] Away then with solidaric sin, with imputed sin, and with spiritual inability.

The Pelagian view was too obviously anti-Christian to be tolerated as such in the Christian church. But soon the process of synthesis began again. The semi-Pelagians sought for a compromise between the Socratic and the Pauline views.

(2) *Roman Catholicism.* Then, in terms of a framework of theology itself taken in part from Aristotle and in part from the Scripture, the Roman Catholic church developed a further refinement of synthesis in its view of sin. Since man, as first created, was in part composed of matter, this fact implied an inherent defect in man as such. God, therefore, gave man at the outset a superadded gift. Conceivably, man could exist without this gift. And even without this gift he would, though defective, not be, properly speaking, sinful.

Accordingly, in the course of time, Romanist theology, while teaching original sin, imputation, and inability, toned down the meaning of these doctrines in terms of the Aristotelian notion of negation.[14]

(3) *The Reformation.* Over against this Roman Catholic view, the Protestant Reformation recovered and developed the scriptural view of grace, and with it the scriptural view of sin. Instead of viewing sin as, even in part, due to any limitation of being, the Reformers thought of Adam as created without any defect and of his sin as a willful transgression of the known will of God. The deep sense of guilt expressed in the Protestant confessions rests upon this truly ethical concept of the relation of man to God.

(4) *Modern Theologians.* But within the Protestant churches, a

---

[13] *Ibid.,* p. 153.
[14] H. Bavinck: *Gereformeerde Dogmatiek,* Volume III, pp. 84–85.

contest has broken out. This time the dispute concerns the question of what constitutes a truly ethical relation of man to God. Building on Kant's view of the autonomous moral self, modern theologians hold that the historic Protestant view of sin and grace is anything but ethical.

To be truly ethical, these modern theologians contend, man must be thought of as truly free. And how can he be truly free unless autonomous?

With his "ethical" view of man and God, the modern theologian re-interprets the biblical view of original sin, of imputation, and of inability. The modern theologian seeks, to be sure, to be biblical and Christological in his view of sin. But the Christ in terms of Whom grace and sin are interpreted is Himself first reinterpreted according to the demands of an independent moral consciousness.

(5) *Friedrich Schleiermacher.* It is well known that Schleiermacher, the father of modern theology, violently rejects as unethical the idea that God should have made "the destiny of the whole human race contingent upon a single moment, the fortunes of which rested with two inexperienced individuals, who, moreover, never dreamt of its having such importance."[15] For Schleiermacher, "what is now innate sinfulness was something native also to the first pair."[16] Thus, finite being is, as such, assumed to be inherently defective. Schleiermacher's supposedly ethical view of man thus appears to be more fully controlled by a nonbiblical metaphysic than does the Romanist view.

(6) *Albrecht Ritschl.* Albrecht Ritschl seeks to be more truly Christological in his theology than Schleiermacher. In reality, the framework of Ritschl's theology is more obviously patterned after the requirements of Kant's autonomous moral consciousness than is that of Schleiermacher. The ideas of solidaric, imputed sin and inability in the biblical sense are ruled out, together with Adam as the first man through whom sin came into the world.

(7) *Karl Barth.* Much more complicated is the question of Karl Barth's concept of original sin, imputation, and inability. Barth's aim is to offer a *Theology of the World.* He wants to build on Reformation "principles." But the Kantian idea of free personality rules supreme in Barth's theology.

Barth seeks to be far more truly Christological in his approach to all questions of theology than were Schleiermacher and Ritschl. But he

[15] F. Schleiermacher: *The Christian Faith,* p. 301.
[16] *Ibid.,* p. 301.

will not submit his thinking to the Christ Who died for sinners once for all in history. And Barth will not submit his thinking to this Christ as He speaks once for all in Scripture.

Barth has no room for the imputation of the righteousness of Christ to sinners on the basis of His finished work on Calvary. Barth's view of substitutionary atonement rests on the idea that all men have from all eternity been participant in the being of God through Christ. Thus, in his case, it is once again a non-Christian metaphysic that chokes the biblical view of grace.

And Barth's view of sin is patterned after his view of grace. When we deal with a passage such as we find in Romans 5, Barth avers, we must not speak of Adam and Christ, but of Christ and Adam. Paul is primarily speaking of the righteousness of God.

The original relationship of every man is to Christ. "*Jesus Christ is the secret truth about the essential nature of man, and even sinful man is still essentially related to Him.*"[17] "In Christ the relationship between the one and the many is original, in Adam it is only a copy of that original. Our relationship to Adam depends for its reality on our relationship to Christ."[18]

This primacy of Christ over Adam, according to Barth, involves this: that "sin is subordinate to grace, and that it is grace that has the last word about the true nature of man."[19] Human nature appears in both Adam and Christ, but "the humanity of Adam is only real and genuine insofar as it reflects and corresponds to the humanity of Christ."[20] "We are real men in our relationship to Adam, only because Adam is not our head and we are not his members, because above Adam and before Adam is Christ. Our relationship to Christ has an essential priority and superiority over our relationship to Adam."[21] It is because of this basic priority of Christ that "human existence as constituted by our relationship with Adam in our unhappy past as weak, sinners, godless, enemies, has no independent reality, status, or importance of its own."[22]

Barth has, therefore, no more room for the biblical teachings on original sin, imputation, and spiritual inability than do Schleiermacher and Ritschl. The supposedly ethical view of human personality pre-

[17] K. Barth: *Christ and Adam*, 1st edition, p. 86.
[18] *Ibid.*, 58–59.   [19] *Ibid.*, p. 43.
[20] *Ibid.*, p. 34.   [21] *Ibid.*
[22] *Ibid.*, p. 30.

cludes, in the case of all three of these typically modern theologians, the truly biblical and therefore truly ethical view of sin and its effects. For on the nonbiblical view, human personality must act in a vacuum.

Modern theologians either reinterpret or openly reject the biblical view of sin. So, for example, Paul Tillich speaks of the "literalistic absurdities" of the traditional Protestant view.[23] But what is the foundation on the basis of which Tillich makes this charge? He makes it on the basis of his idea of Christ as the New Being. But he knows very well that "the quest for the New Being presupposes the presence of the New Being as the search for truth presupposes the presence of truth."[24] Tillich cannot identify his New Being with a Christ that is really present to man. Thus, it appears again that unless we take our definition of sin from the Christ as speaking directly in Scripture, we have no intelligible foundation even for our basic hostilities.

BIBLIOGRAPHY

K. Barth: *Die kirchliche Dogmatik*
———: *Christ and Adam*
H. Bavinck: *Gereformeerde Dogmatiek*
G.C. Berkouwer: *De Zonde*, I and II
C. Hodge: *Systematic Theology*
J. Murray: *The Imputation of Adam's Sin*
A. Ritschl: *Justification and Reconciliation*
F. Schleiermacher: *The Christian Faith*

[23] P. Tillich: *Systematic Theology*, Volume II, p. 40.
[24] *Ibid.*, p. 80.

18

THE COVENANT OF GRACE

✤

HERBERT M. CARSON

The Rev. Herbert M. Carson, Vicar of St. Paul's Church, Cambridge, England, received his general and theological education at Trinity College, Dublin, Eire (B.A., 1943; B.D., 1946). He is the author of *The Christian and the State,* and *Commentary on Colossians and Philemon.*

The concept of the covenant might well be described as the normative idea of biblical revelation. It does justice to two important elements in that revelation, namely its unity and its progressive character. There is in Scripture a divine unfolding of the eternal purposes of God; but amid all the diverse modes by which that revelation is made, there is an inner coherence, so that the complete revelation is the Word of God, the one perfect and fully coherent utterance of the Most High. Yet it is probably a fairly safe generalization to say that even in evangelical thought, which claims to be biblical, this normative concept has tended to become a peripheral idea.

A covenant is essentially a pledged and defined relationship. There are three main elements in it: the parties contracting together, the promises involved, and the conditions imposed. It is clearly possible to have a covenant between equals or one which is imposed unilaterally by a superior. It is obvious, however, that any covenant between God and man can never be as between equals, but must be imposed from above. The LXX translators clearly saw this point when they translated *berith* not by *suntheke* but by *diatheke*, which still retained something of its original connotation of a sovereign disposition.

GRACE AFTER THE FALL

In God's dealings with man, the Fall presents a clearly defined line of demarcation. Prior to that point, it is with man in a state of innocence that God deals. Afterward, it is to man as a guilty rebel that God extends His free and undeserved favor. Hence, the distinction has been drawn between the covenant of works and the covenant of grace. The former, in so far as it is still a gracious act of condescension, might be better described in Matthew Henry's phrase as "the covenant of innocency." It is true, of course, that the term covenant is not explicitly mentioned, but the elements of a covenant relationship—contracting parties, promises, and conditions—are all present.

With the Fall, a completely new situation emerges. Man is now a sinner under God's wrath and condemnation. The fellowship between the creature and his Creator has been severed, and he is estranged. Yet, his changed condition is seen not only in his alienation from God, but in the corruption of his nature. Thus, he is not only out of touch with God, but is utterly displeasing to God, and, further, is incapable of restoring the relationship. This means that if there is to be a renewed relationship, it will be entirely due to the grace of God. God must take the initiative, for man in his rebellious state will not of his own accord turn Godward. But God must also enable him to return; for, because of his sin, he is in such a state of bondage that he cannot turn. The covenant then, if it is to be established, is inevitably a covenant of grace. It is one in which God freely, and without any constraint outside Himself, brings men who are wholly without merit into fellowship with Himself. The promises made are gracious ones, for man deserves not blessing but condemnation. The conditions imposed are also gracious, for it is only by the enabling grace of God that man can fulfill them. The guarantee of the blessings of the covenant, which is to be found in God's own character, is a further token of His gracious activity. That God the sovereign Judge should pledge Himself to guilty men in such a way that they should have claims upon Him is the supreme demonstration of His grace.

THE ONE AND THE MANY

The further question now arises: in what sense can it be valid to speak of the covenant of grace as if there were only one covenant when in Scripture there are a number of covenants? But it is surely at this very point that we find how essential the covenant idea is to an understanding of the structure of biblical revelation, for it is in terms of the oneness of the covenant of grace that we can trace the unity which is a fundamental characteristic of Scripture. And it is because of the diversity of administration of the one covenant, as seen in the successive covenants, that we do justice to the progressive nature of God's self-disclosure in His Word.

THE COVENANT WITH ABRAHAM

Turning first to the diversity of covenants, we find a succession of these culminating in the one sealed by the blood of Christ. Prior to Abraham, there are elements of a covenant relationship, but the terms are not explicitly formulated, unless one includes the covenant with Noah which does not, however, seem to fall within the main stream. But for the precise formulation of the covenant, we must wait until the call of Abraham. Here, the covenant is rooted in the electing grace of God, who takes the initiative in calling Abraham. In the relationship established by God in Genesis 17, He pledges himself to Abraham to be His God. He promises blessing to him and through his seed to the nations of the earth. He gives to him as a seal of the covenant the rite of circumcision, and Abraham's acceptance of this rite and of the promises of God is his fulfillment of the demand of the covenant, namely, faith in the God of the covenant.

THE COVENANT ON SINAI

That the covenant with Israel on Sinai is still a covenant of grace is seen in various ways. It is because of what God has done, rather than what they will do, that God establishes His covenant with them. Thus, in Exodus 19:4, it is the redemption from Egypt which is the basis of the covenant. But this redemption from Egypt is itself the outcome of the covenant with Abraham. It is because God had pledged Himself to be their God that He delivered them.[1] Hence, the law of Sinai must not be interpreted apart from the covenant of grace, for it is itself embedded in that covenant. Indeed, it was this separation of the law,

[1] Exod. 2:34; 3:16, 17.

in an attempt to make it a means of salvation, which was the error of of the bulk of the Jews and which was the target of the great polemic of the Apostle Paul. The law in isolation becomes a system of bondage. The law viewed within the covenant becomes itself an expression of grace, for, by intensifying the awareness of sin and leading God's people to self-despair, it intensifies also their longing for the promised deliverer and leads them to cast themselves upon the mercy of God. Obedience to the law, then, is not a means of establishing the covenant, but of enjoying and retaining its blessings.

FURTHER COVENANTS

This Sinaitic dispensation of the covenant really embraces the period from Moses to Christ. There are in this period further covenants, but while they fall within the terms of the one made with Moses, there is more of the Messianic element in them. Thus, in the Davidic covenant,[2] the promise given is primarily in terms of the coming Davidic king.[3] So it is with the covenant with Israel after the exile. While it looks back to God's past mercies and while it insists on obedience as a condition for enjoying the fruits of this gracious covenant, it also looks forward to culmination of God's mercies in the coming of the Messiah.[4]

THE NEW TESTAMENT CULMINATION

The new covenant, inaugurated by the Messiah and sealed in his blood, is thus the culmination of the gracious activity of God already manifested in the covenants made with Israel. In it, the blessings promised, and already received by faith, are fully realized. The prophecy of Jeremiah 31:31 is fulfilled. Thus, in Luke 1:72, the coming of the Saviour is viewed as the outcome of the promises of God to the fathers. The law written on tables of stone is now written on the heart. The blood of the sacrifice by which forgiveness is effected is no longer in terms of a mere prefiguring by means of animal sacrifice, for the blood of the Saviour Himself is shed that He might become the mediator of the covenant.[5] The central affirmation of the covenant, so often declared in the Old Testament, is again declared; but now it is accompanied by a deeper assurance rooted in the full and final revelation of God in Christ, and imparted to the believer by the Spirit of God, so

[2] II Sam. 7:12–17; Ps. 89:3–4, 26.   [3] See also Isa. 55:3–4.
[4] See Hag. 1:13, 2:4–9; Zech. 12–14; Mal. 3:1–4, 4:4–6.
[5] Matt. 26:28; Mark 14:24; I Cor. 11:25.

that it is with a deeper awareness of its wonder that believers now listen to the gracious word: "I . . . will be your God, and ye shall be my people."[6]

There is a development also in the character of the community with whom the covenant is made. Formerly, it was with a particular family, the offspring of Abraham, and then with the nation of Israel. To participate in the blessings of the covenant involved membership of this nation. Of course, not all those who were outwardly numbered among the covenant people were partakers of the inward and spiritual blessings of the covenant. But the new covenant breaks forth from this Jewish limitation. Now the promises of the Gospel extend to every nation. The covenant people in its visible aspect is now the Church of Christ dispersed throughout the world, while in its inward aspect it remains what it has always been, the elect of God.

THE UNITY OF THE COVENANTS

The attempt has been made in this brief survey of the various covenants within Scripture to stress the common element throughout, namely the gracious activity of God. But the unity of the covenants may be demonstrated in other ways. In the New Testament, the men of the Old Testament are always reckoned as true believers, and the Church of God is continuous throughout both dispensations.[7] Nor is this some artificial reconstruction based on a romantic estimate of Old Testament religion, for it corresponds to what is apparent within the Old Testament itself. Believers there are promised not just material blessings, but spiritual; Canaan, for example, is clearly not their final goal.[8] Indeed, one could scarcely read the Psalms, with their passionate aspirations for God and their exuberant delight in Him, without discarding the notion that such men were laboring under the bondage of a covenant of works. They are surely recipients of the rich blessings of the covenant of grace. That which distinguishes the covenants of the period before the Messiah and the new covenant inaugurated by His coming is not a difference of essential character, but rather a diversity of administration. The former are administered in terms of promise, prophecy, and type; the later in terms of fulfillment. The privileged position of the New Testament believer is not that he lives by faith, in

[6] Lev. 26:12; cf. Gen. 17:7; Exod. 19:5, chapter 21; Jer. 31:33; Heb. 8:10.
[7] Rom. 4, 11:17; Heb. 11; *see also* John 10:16; Acts 7:38; Gal. 3:29, 6:16.
[8] Cf. Heb. 11:13.

contrast to those who tried to live by works. It is rather that while they rejoiced in the signs of the dawning day, he stands in the full blaze of the noonday of revelation, with a fuller knowledge, a deeper assurance, and a richer experience of the Spirit, yet at the same time sharing with them a common faith in Christ, the mediator of the covenant.

THE MEDIATOR OF THE COVENANT

From the foregoing it may be seen that when we say the covenant of grace is the unifying theme of Scripture, we are not saying anything different from the assertion that Christ is the one who gives Scripture its unity. For Christ is at the heart of the covenant of which He is the mediator. We may view this from two different standpoints. We may speak of the covenant of redemption between the Father and the Son, which is the basis of the covenant of grace between the triune God and the elect. Or we may speak throughout of the covenant of grace made with the Son, as the head and representative of His people. In either case, Christ is the mediator in that His work is the foundation of the covenant and union with Him is the effectual means of membership. The Old Testament believer thus looked forward in hope to the Christ Who was yet to come. We look back to the Christ Who has already come. All alike are justified by faith in the one Saviour, Whose blood brings to us the blessings of the covenant.

SUMMARY OF THE ELEMENTS

We may well follow Pierre Marcel in summarizing the essential elements of the covenant of grace. It is freely given by God Himself, and in this gracious activity the three persons of the Trinity are at work. The Father chooses those whom He will call into covenant relationship. It is with the Son that the covenant is made, and it is His blood which establishes its basis. It is the Spirit who realizes the covenant in the life of the believer. It is an eternal and, thus, an unbreakable covenant. It is made with a particular people, formerly with Israel and now with God's elect in every nation. Throughout God's dealings, the covenant, while differently administered, remains essentially the same.

PRIVILEGE AND RESPONSIBILITY

A firm grasp of this truth is not only vital to a clear understanding of the unity of the biblical revelation; it is also an essential element in a healthy spiritual experience. So we study it, not merely to have a neat theological system, but as the great means of strengthening faith in the God of the covenant. Has He pledged Himself to be our God? Then we can face whatever life may send with calm assurance. Indeed, death itself can hold no terrors, for this is an everlasting covenant. But while it is a source of encouragement, it also brings a challenge and often a rebuke. It speaks of privilege, but also of responsibility. It promises blessing, but demands obedience. The inevitable corollary of the gracious promise, "I will be your God," is the call to holy living implicit in the searching words, "and ye shall be my people."

BIBLIOGRAPHY

J. Calvin: *Institutes*, II, x–xii
C. Hodge: *Systematic Theology*
P. Marcel: *The Biblical Doctrine of Infant Baptism*
J. Murray: *The Covenant of Grace*
G. Vos: *Biblical Theology*

19

THE PERSON OF CHRIST:

INCARNATION AND

VIRGIN BIRTH

✝

F.F. BRUCE

F.F. Bruce, Rylands Professor of Biblical Criticism and Exegesis, University of Manchester, Manchester, England, received his general and theological education at the University of Aberdeen (M.A., 1932; D.D., 1957) and the University of Cambridge, England (B.A., 1934; M.A., 1945). He is the author of *The New Testament Documents: Are They Reliable?*, *Biblical Exegesis in the Qumran Texts*, *Second Thoughts on the Dead Sea Scrolls*, and *The Acts of The Apostles: Greek Text with Introduction and Commentary*, among other works. He is also the Editor of *The Evangelical Quarterly* and the *Palestine Exploration Quarterly*.

If there is, among the distinctive articles of the Christian faith, one which is basic to all the others, it is this: that our Lord Jesus Christ, the eternal Son of God, became man for our salvation. This is the affirmation that we have in mind when we speak of the doctrine of the incarnation.

While "incarnation" (a term of Latin origin, meaning "becoming-in-flesh") is not itself a biblical word, it conveys a biblical truth, the truth which finds classic expression in John 1:14, "the Word became flesh."

The incarnation of Christ implies His deity and humanity alike. To assert that any of us "became flesh" or "came in the flesh" would be a truism; it is no mere truism that John voices when he insists that "Jesus Christ has come in the flesh," and makes this confession the crucial test of truth.[1] He means, rather, that one Who had His being eternally within the unity of the Godhead became man at a point in time, without relinquishing His oneness with God. And by the word "flesh," he does not mean a physical body only, but a complete human personality.

Nor is John the only New Testament writer so to speak. Paul speaks of God as "sending his own Son in the likeness of sinful flesh"[2] where "likeness" does not suggest that His manhood was less than real, but that His human nature was like our sinful nature except that *His* nature was unstained by sin. Again, in the early Christian confession reproduced in I Timothy 3:16, the "mystery of our religion" (that is, Christ himself, the "mystery of God," as He is called in Col. 2:2) is said to have been "manifested in the flesh." The writer to the Hebrews bears the same witness when he says of the Son of God, through Whom the world were made,[3] that since those whom He came to deliver "are sharers in flesh and blood, he also himself in like manner partook of the same"—in order that He might accomplish his saving purpose through death, which He could not otherwise have undergone.[4]

The doctrine of our Lord's incarnation, then, is broadly based throughout the New Testament. When John, Paul, and the writer to the Hebrews present such agreement as this, it is usually safe to trace their agreement back to a germinal principle in the life and teaching of Christ.

THE FACT OF THE INCARNATION

That Jesus of Nazareth was a real man none of His companions doubted. But sometimes it came home to them with special force that there was something extraordinary about Him: "Who then is this?"

[1] I John 4:2.
[3] Heb. 1:2.
[2] Rom. 8:3.
[4] Heb. 2.14 ff.

they asked, when He stilled the tempest with a word.[5] Even when they came to acclaim Him as the Messiah, they did not immediately appreciate all that was involved in Messiahship as He accepted and fulfilled it. Fuller apprehension followed His death and exaltation, however, and nothing is more eloquent in this regard than the spontaneous and unself-conscious way in which New Testament writers take Old Testament passages which refer to the God of Israel and apply them to Jesus, whom they all knew to be a real man. In Jesus, they claimed, God had drawn near to man for his redemption; in Him, indeed, God had *become* man. "The Word became flesh"; in the man Christ Jesus, they recognized the crowning revelation of God.

These simple affirmations, however, called for more precise definition. The relation of Christ as Son to God the Father raised questions to which conflicting answers were given; so did the relation of Christ's divine Sonship to His manhood. Some answers offered to these questions might seem adequate at first blush, but they were quickly seen to create more difficulties than they claimed to solve, if indeed they did not positively undermine the Christian faith. There was the problem of vocabulary, too. Greek and Latin terms had to be used in new and specialized senses to fit a set of data with which these languages had not been called upon to deal before. And one thinker might use a term in a completely adequate sense, while another would use it in a sense which did much less than justice to the data of biblical revelation and Christian experience.

In the first three or four centuries, the major obstacle in the way of doing full justice to these data was the dualistic presupposition of much contemporary Gentile thought. This dualism involved a complete antinomy between spirit and matter, spirit being essentially good, and matter essentially evil. This meant that any direct contact between the spirit world and the material world was impossible. In consequence, people whose thinking was based on this kind of dualism could not accept, in its proper sense, the biblical doctrine of the incarnation of the Son of God, nor yet the biblical account of His death and resurrection. They had to present alternative interpretations of these events. One of these interpretations, which began to emerge as early as the apostolic age (for New Testament writers are at pains to refute it), was Docetism, which considered our Lord's humanity to be only apparent and

[5] Mark 4:41.

not real. A later interpretation was Arianism, which thought of Him as neither fully God nor fully man, but as a being of intermediate status. It is a matter of more than historical interest that such knowledge of Christianity as Muhammad had was derived from one of these defective interpretations. This accounts for those statements in the Koran which deny that Jesus was the Son of God and also that He was really crucified.

It was only slowly and painstakingly that the early Church achieved a statement of our Lord's incarnation which has commended itself ever since as satisfying all the data. Before this happened, we can watch the tripartite baptismal confessions of the first three Christian centuries (tripartite because they affirmed faith in the Father, the Son, and the Holy Spirit), having their central section—that which affirmed faith in the Son—expanded so as to make a fuller statement of the doctrine of Christ. The familiar Apostles' and Nicene creeds provide sufficient examples of this. But the statement which the historic church has adopted as definitive is that approved by the Council of Chalcedon in 451 A.D. This statement acknowledges "one and the same Son, our Lord Jesus Christ, at once complete in Godhead and complete in manhood, truly God and truly man, consisting also of a reasonable soul and body; of one substance with the Father as regards his Godhead, and at the same time of one substance with us as regards his manhood; like us in all respects, apart from sin; as regards his Godhead, begotten of the Father before the ages, but yet as regards his manhood begotten, for us men and for our salvation, of Mary the Virgin. . . ."

The wording of this Chalcedonian definition may seem remote from the modes of expression with which we are familiar today. Yet, according to so able a theologian as B.B. Warfield, it has well deserved to remain the authoritative statement of the church's Christology (although it does not mitigate the difficulty of the conception to which it gives expression) because it "does justice at once to the data of Scripture, to the implicates of an Incarnation, to the needs of Redemption, to the demands of the religious emotions, and to the logic of a tenable doctrine of our Lord's Person."[6]

We have in our day a vocabulary for expressing the various concepts and problems associated with personality which was not available in the fifth century. It would be an exciting and rewarding task to use

[6] B.B. Warfield: *The Person and Work of Christ*, p. 189.

this vocabulary to restate the doctrine of the incarnation in a form which would correct defective views held today, as defective views of an earlier age were corrected at Chalcedon. But such a restatement ought to pass the same stringent tests as Warfield applied to the Chalcedonian statement.

THE MEANS OF THE INCARNATION

The church's confession, as we trace it back to primitive times, sets alongside the fact of our Lord's incarnation the claim that He became incarnate through being conceived by the power of the Holy Spirit in the womb of the Virgin Mary.

There are those, indeed, who acknowledge our Lord's incarnation without believing in His virgin birth, just as others, Muslims for example, believe in His virgin birth but not in His incarnation. But it is undeniable that His incarnation and virgin birth are intimately bound together in the historic faith of the church. Nor is this surprising. The incarnation was a supernatural event—an unprecedented and unrepeated act of God. The more we appreciate the uniqueness of the incarnation, the more may we recognize how fitting—indeed, how inevitable—it is that the means by which it was brought about should also be unique. Our Lord's virginal conception must certainly be understood as a pure miracle; attempts to explain it by analogies drawn from parthenogenesis in lower forms of life are worse than useless.

Only two New Testament writers, Matthew and Luke, record the virgin birth of Christ; but they are the only two who record His birth at all. Their birth narratives are independent of each other; all the more impressive, therefore, are the features on which they agree: not only that Christ was born in Bethlehem, the son of Mary, who was affianced to Joseph, a descendant of David; but more particularly that Mary conceived Him by the Spirit of God while she was still a virgin. One of these two birth narratives, moreover, Luke's, has claims to be regarded as one of the most archaic elements in the New Testament.

These two narratives do not exhaust the evidence for the virgin birth, although they command the special respect due to their canonical status. Ignatius (c. 115 A.D.) also bears testimony to the virgin birth, which to some extent reflects a distinct tradition—preserved probably in the church of Antioch.

Whether other New Testament writers knew anything about the

virgin birth or not, they say nothing to contradict it. Indeed, in one or two places some of them seem to betray some acquaintance with it. However, these are not definite enough to have evidential value.

The argument that if the chief characters in the birth narratives had known about the virgin birth, they would not have acted or spoken as they did on certain later occasions, makes insufficient allowance for the changing moods of human beings; besides, how can we make confident generalizations about the psychological effects of a unique event? The argument that our Lord would not have been perfectly man had he been virgin-born is hypothetical and undemonstrable; that He was indeed perfectly man is certain in any case.

The fact that He was publicly known as "Jesus of Nazareth, the son of Joseph"[7] is irrelevant to the question of His virgin birth. There are other expressions in the Gospels which have been supposed to be inconsistent with it, but these are commoner in the two Gospels which exclude any misunderstanding by recording His virgin birth at the outset. Thus, Luke, toward the end of his infancy narrative, refers to Jesus' "father and mother" or His "parents,"[8] and reports His mother as saying to Him, "thy father and I have sought thee sorrowing."[9] But the earlier part of his narrative shows how these expressions are to be understood. Later, he reports the people of Nazareth as saying, "Is not this the carpenter's son? Is not his mother called Mary?"[10] Whether these Nazarenes knew anything of the circumstances of His birth is doubtful; but the reader of Matthew and Luke is already acquainted with the real circumstances and is not misled by their question. Mark, on the other hand, who has no nativity narrative, reports them as saying: "Is not this the carpenter, the son of Mary?"[11]

The conception and birth of Christ could not and cannot be susceptible to the laws of evidence in the same way as His resurrection, for which eyewitnesses were not lacking. But God did a new thing in the earth when his Son became incarnate, and the virginal conception was part and parcel of that new thing. In this way, for once, the entail of sin was broken within the human family. No one will suspect Dr. W.R. Matthews of obscurantism, but there is substance in his statement that, "though we may still believe in the Incarnation without the Virgin Birth, it will not be precisely the same kind of Incarnation, and the

[7] John 1:45.   [8] Luke 2:33, 41.
[9] Luke 2:48.   [10] Matt. 13:55.
[11] Mark 6:3.

conception of God's act of redemption in Christ will be subtly but definitely changed."[12]

RICHES FOR POVERTY

In the light of the further revelation of the New Testament, this Old Testament affirmation acquires a deeper significance. It is because God made man in His own image that He could accurately reveal Himself in a human life. So when, in the fullness of time, "God sent forth his Son, born of a woman," it was in the form of man that He sent Him, the form which He had from the beginning intended man to have. Thus, the Son of God became partaker of our nature so that we in Him might become "partakers of the divine nature."[13]

He deigns in flesh to appear,
Widest extremes to join,
To bring our vileness near
And make us all divine;
And we the life of God shall know,
Since God is manifest below.[14]

BIBLIOGRAPHY

C. Gore: *The Incarnation of the Son of God*
E.H. Gifford: *The Incarnation*
W. Sanday: *Christologies Ancient and Modern*
J.G. Machen: *The Virgin Birth of Christ*
D.M. Baillie: *God Was in Christ*
H.E.W. Turner: *Jesus, Master and Lord*
O. Cullmann: *The Christology of the New Testament*

[12] W.R. Matthews: *Essays in Construction*, pp. 128 f.
[13] II Pet. 1:4.　　　　　　　　　　[14] C. Wesley.

20

THE PERSON OF CHRIST:

THE KENOTIC THEORY

WAYNE E. WARD

Wayne E. Ward, Associate Professor of Theology, Southern
Baptist Theological Seminary, Louisville, Kentucky, received his
general and theological education at Ouachita College, Ouachita,
Arkansas (B.A., 1943) and Southern Baptist Theological Seminary (B.D., 1949; Th.D., 1953).

In the nineteenth century, the rise of new scientific theories, including
the biological theory of evolution as well as the rapid development of
biblical criticism, contributed to the formation of some new viewpoints concerning the person of Christ. Usually these interpretations
were intended to make the miracle of the incarnation more reasonable
or more acceptable to the scientific mind of that century. One theory,
which received widespread emphasis and acceptance in the late nineteenth century and whose influence is still felt today, is the so-called
"kenotic theory" of the person of Christ. The name "kenotic" comes
from the Greek word *kenoō*, used by Paul in Philippians 2:7 to describe the action by which Christ "emptied" Himself, taking the form
of a servant, when He came incarnate into the world. In order to un-

derstand the tremendous importance of this theory and its widespread influence even today, it will be necessary to survey briefly the historical background and then concentrate upon a biblical exposition of those passages which have been crucial in the discussion of kenosis.

HISTORICAL BACKGROUND AND DEVELOPMENT

Apparently, Theodotion[1] is the first to use "kenosis" as a theological term in his translation of Isaiah 34:11. However, both Gregory Nazianzus[2] and Cyril of Alexandria[3] use the term in the technical theological sense to express the action in Philippians 2:7 by which Christ "emptied himself."[4] The Latin Vulgate renders this phrase "*semetipsum exinanivit*,"[5] while Tertullian used the phrase "*exhausit semetipsum*"[6] in his *Adversus Marcionem*. The real point of concern for each of these thinkers, as for us today, was this: "Of what did Christ empty Himself?"

A secondary question for these early Christian writers, and a question which came to the fore in the Reformation period, was this: "Exactly *who* is the subject of the verb *emptied?*" Is it the pre-existent Son of God, Who by sovereign choice divested Himself of some of the prerogatives of deity in order to become incarnate; or is it the incarnate Son, Who, in the days of His flesh, was involved in a kind of repeated or continual emptying of Himself in order to fulfill His mission as the Servant of God and submit even to death on the cross?

The Synod of Antioch (341 A.D.) had spoken suggestively and pointedly on both questions with these words: *kenosas heauton apo tou einai isa Theo* (emptying himself of "the being equal with God"). It was stoutly maintained that Christ was fully divine, having given up temporarily not some portion of His deity, but rather the status or position at the right hand of God, which was His by right, in order to become the suffering Servant.

Medieval theology was concerned with the attempt to define more explicitly what attributes of deity were laid aside in the incarnation, or what actual limitations were experienced by Christ *during* His incarnate life. During the Reformation period, the discussion centered upon the divine attributes of omnipotence, omniscience, and omnipres-

---

[1] Second century.   [2] Fourth century.
[3] Fifth century.   [4] Greek, *heauton hekenosen.*
[5] He emptied, i.e., *desolated*, his very self.
[6] He exhausted, i.e., *completely emptied*, his very self.

ence. Much of this discussion was rather barren, because it often degenerated into an exercise in imagining certain characteristics of deity which might be laid aside without seriously impairing essential deity.

The discussion moved on into the seventeenth century with bold assertions that Christ certainly was, according to the Scriptures, less than divine. Some tried to soften this heresy by maintaining that Jesus actually possessed the divine powers all the time, but kept them under a conscious restraint. Others supposed that He actually had the divine attributes in all their fullness, but that He was unaware of the extent of these powers and therefore lived His incarnate life within the limits imposed upon any creature.

With such an unfortunate pilgrimage throughout Christian history, the whole idea of kenosis might have been summarily dropped as a dangerous and confusing concept for Christian faith, except for something which happened in the nineteenth century. This great century of scientific discovery, historical investigation, and biblical criticism brought about a rediscovery of the real humanity of Jesus. Against the background of the Darwinian theory of evolution, the Graf-Wellhausen school of Old Testament history, and the radical Tübingen school of New Testament criticism, a group of English theologians fought valiantly to save the central dogma of the unique divine humanity of Jesus Christ. Bishop Gore, along with many other scholars, published the symposium on incarnation theology entitled *Lux Mundi,* which went through twelve editions between 1889 and 1891. This book did much to popularize the concept of the divine kenosis. This zenith of the doctrine in the whole history of Christian thought can best be understood by turning to the biblical evidence which they were attempting to expound.

THE BIBLICAL DATA

The Bible certainly does not elaborate a doctrine of kenosis, but it does set forth the data with which serious biblical theologians have developed the doctrine of the divine "self-emptying." Basic elements of the scriptural evidence are easily categorized:

(1) The divine relationship or unity between Father and Son.[7]

(2) Closely connected with this explicit claim of unity with God is the expression of limitations upon this relationship.[8]

[7] John 1:1–18, 10:30; Heb. 1:1–4.   [8] John 5:19, 30; Matt. 27:46.

(3) Also, there are specific statements of Jesus in regard to limitations upon His knowledge and pre-incarnate glory.[9]

(4) The emphasis of New Testament writers upon the real humanity of Jesus can be seen in the account of His temptations,[10] His growth and development in wisdom and stature,[11] and His learning by the suffering which He endured.[12]

(5) Finally, the most important passage of all, the one which actually contains the term which carries the central idea of the doctrine of kenosis is Philippians 2:5-11. This is further amplified by the Pauline statement in II Corinthians 8:9, which Albrecht Oepke calls "the best commentary" on the Philippian passage.

THE CENTRAL PASSAGE: PHILIPPIANS 2:7

In the Philippian context, Paul is urging the Christians to practice unselfishness and humility. In order to illustrate this, he turns to the supreme example: "Have this mind among yourselves, which you have in Christ Jesus, who, though he was in the form of God, did not count equality with God a thing to be grasped, but emptied himself, taking the form of a servant, being born in the likeness of men."[13]

While most commentators have agreed on the subject of the verb "emptied," that is, the pre-incarnate Christ who emptied Himself, they have had differing ideas as to *what* He emptied or *of what* He divested himself. In 1880, H. Crosby set forth the idea in *The True Humanity of Christ* that during the whole period of the incarnation, although the essential deity must have necessarily existed without interruption, yet His conscious and active deity was entirely quiescent. Only at the Resurrection did He reassume the full power of deity.

Bishop Charles Gore in *The Incarnation*, 1891, maintained that the Son of God voluntarily surrendered or abandoned certain natural prerogatives of external attributes of God, while He yet retained the essential, ethical attributes of truth, holiness, and love. A similar idea was advanced by A.M. Fairbairn, *The Place of Christ in Modern Thought*, 1893, and by a host of others in the last decade of the nineteenth century.

Other kenotic theologians carried the speculation to even more extreme lengths. W.N. Clarke in *An Outline of Christian Theology*,

---

[9] Mark 13:22; John 17:5.   [10] Matt. 4:1-11.
[11] Luke 2:52.   [12] Heb. 4:15; 5:7, 8.
[13] Phil. 2:5-7.

1898, suggested that on the basis of an original kinship between God and man, God became man in the incarnation by self-limitation. Henry Van Dyke in *The Gospel for an Age of Doubt: The Human Life of God*, 1897, also sought to make the incarnation more acceptable to human reason upon the assumption of an original kinship between God and man. This would suggest that the incarnation was the most perfectly natural thing in the world, offering no affront to human reason. Modern psychology was called to the aid of the theory by R.H. Hutton in *Essays Theological and Literary*. He recalled the capacity of the conscious mind to deposit a portion of its contents in the subconscious mind, suggesting a pattern by which conscious deity may have become unconscious deity.

Perhaps the most constructive suggestion in all this period of kenotic speculation came from D.W. Simon in his *Reconciliation through Incarnation*, 1898, which states: in the creation God certainly limited Himself with reference to future choices and deeds of free moral beings. If men have any true freedom, it must be because of divine self-limitation which chooses not to determine every action of His creatures but, rather, gives them the responsibility of making real choices. The incarnation then becomes a further and supreme example by which God limits Himself in relation to His creation—He actually comes into His creation, accepting the limits of creaturehood.

EVALUATION

In all this theological speculation, which often rambled far from the Pauline passage, the commentators seemed compelled by some hidden force to interpret the passage only in one way: What did Christ give up? Of what was He divested when He became incarnate? The Greek scholar William Hersey Davis cut through this Gordian knot by suggesting in his lectures that Paul is not talking about what the Son gave up, but what He gained; not the royal status He forsook, but the role of the Servant which He chose. This is certainly the point of emphasis Paul is making to the Philippians; they are to have the mind of the Servant of God; they are to be filled with humility rather than lording it over one another. Davis even went so far as to suggest that *kenoō* should be understood in the sense of emptying the contents of one vessel into another vessel, so that it was a matter of pouring the same content into another form: Christ emptied Himself (i.e., poured Himself) into the form of a servant. Whether Greek grammar requires, or even permits, this interpretation, it is clear that the context emphasizes the change of *form*, not the change of *content*, of the Divine Being. He did not give up deity, but He gained *humanity*. There was no attrition of the divine nature in the incarnation; His life incarnate, containing the fullness of the Godhead bodily, was offered for man's redemption.

Although the main thrust of the kenotic theory led into some barren speculation, it is well to note positive contributions which the theory has made to the doctrine of the incarnation:

(1) Kenosis does emphasize the divine initiative. With the few exceptions indicated, the kenotic theologians have proclaimed a salvation which comes from above rather than from below, from God rather than man.

(2) Kenosis emphasizes the free, voluntary act of the pre-incarnate Son in choosing the path of humiliation. Not of necessity, but out of the sovereign choice of love, He gave up heaven's glory for the way of the cross.

(3) Closely related to this is the emphasis laid upon Christ's conscious restraint in the use of divine powers during the days of His flesh. Surely, as the Gospels testify, Jesus had powers upon which He could have called to deliver Himself, but He refused to use them. We must admit that this continuing voluntary element is of supreme importance in our understanding of the person of Christ. Without it, Christ would become the helpless victim of the incarnation, once the original decision was made; and the significant, repeated, voluntary submission of Christ to suffering and death would be destroyed.

(4) Kenosis emphatically preserved the doctrine of the real humanity of Christ against all Docetic attempts to undermine it. The basic motivation behind most kenotic interpretations is clearly to provide a pattern of thought in which one must take seriously the actual lowliness, condescension, and humiliation of Christ.

The most serious criticism of the kenotic theory is the one which may be leveled at Arius, Eutyches, Nestorius, and the long line of theologians who were rejected by the main stream of the Christian community: all of these made the fatal mistake of trying to rationalize the supreme miracle of the incarnation, to make intelligible by analogy and illustration that event which is absolutely without parallel, the coming of the Divine Being into the world as a real man.

Closely connected with this criticism is another: kenotic thinkers often fell into the hopelessly negative position of trying to define the divine nature in less and less essential terms, until they might at last squeeze the residue into a human personality with no strain at all.

While we can be grateful for the kenotic defense of the humanity of Christ, we can be just as thankful that we are not required to defend this doctrine on such misleading grounds. We can proclaim the humanity He gained, without attempting to define certain aspects of deity which He could have given up; we can certainly bow before that throne to which He was exalted by the way of the cross.

BIBLIOGRAPHY

Athanasius: *De Incarnatione*

H. Crosby: *The True Humanity of Christ*

H. Van Dyke: *The Gospel for an Age of Doubt*

A.M. Fairbairn: *The Place of Christ in Modern Thought*

C. Gore: *The Incarnation of the Son of God*

————: *Belief in Christ*

———— ed.: *Lux Mundi*

G. Kittel, ed.: *Theologisches Wörterbuch zum Neuen Testament*, article "Kenosis" by A. Oepke

J. Orr: *The Christian View of God and the World*

21

THE PERSON OF CHRIST:

DEATH, RESURRECTION,

ASCENSION

✠

RALPH EARLE

Ralph Earle, Professor of New Testament at Nazarene Theological Seminary, Kansas City, Missouri, received his general and theological education at Eastern Nazarene College (B.A., 1933), Boston University (M.A., 1937), and Gordon Divinity School (B.D., 1935; Th.D., 1941). He is the author of *The Story of the New Testament, Meet the Minor Prophets,* and *Meet the Apostles.*

It was the world's blackest hour. It was the world's brightest hour. This is the paradox of the cross.

It was the blackest hour because human hate came to its fiercest focus. It was the brightest hour because divine love came to its fullest flower. There, hate was seen in all its heinous horror. But there also, love revealed the heart of God.

Calvary stands at the crossroads of human history. All the divine paths of the past led to it. All the divine paths of the present and future lead from it.

At the cross, all the sin of the ages was placed on the heart of the sinless Son of God, as He became the racial representative of all humanity. From the cross, salvation flows to every believing soul. This is the Gospel, the greatest good news the world has ever heard.

THE DEPARTURE

On the Mount of Transfiguration, Moses and Elijah appeared to the praying Christ and "spake of his decease which he should accomplish at Jerusalem."[1] To us, "decease" means death. But the Greek word is *exodos*—exodus, departure. Precisely, it means here the death, resurrection, and ascension of Jesus Christ, by which three events He made His departure from this world back to the heavenly glory.

THE DEATH

The death of Jesus differed from that of every other man. He "dismissed his spirit."[2] His was a completely voluntary decease—"No man taketh it from me, but I lay it down of myself."[3] Death was not forced upon Him. He accepted it as the will of God for the salvation of man.

What did Jesus' death mean for Him? The answer is best suggested by His prayer in Gethsemane. There He cried out in agony of soul, "O my Father, if it be possible, let this cup pass from me." Then, He bowed his head in humble submission and said: "Nevertheless not as I will, but as thou wilt."[4]

What was this cup from which He prayed to be delivered? Carping critics have said that Jesus cringed with cowardly fear at the thought of death. But such cavilers are utterly ignorant of the true significance of that hour. Jesus was not afraid to die!

What was it, then, from which He shrank in anguish of spirit? It was His Father's face turned away from Him in the awful hour when "Him who knew no sin he made to be sin on our behalf; that we might become the righteousness of God in him."[5] Our Substitute took the torturous trail of a lost soul, walking out into the labyrinthine depths of outer darkness. He tasted death for every man.[6] That means more

---

1 Luke 9:31.   2 Matt. 27:50.
3 John 10:18.   4 Matt. 26:39.
5 II Cor. 5:21, ASV.   6 Heb. 2:9.

than physical death. When Christ cried out on the cross, "My God, my God, why hast thou forsaken me?"[7] He was experiencing something far deeper. He was paying the penalty for sin—not His, but ours. The penalty for sin is separation from God. This was the price that Jesus had to pay for our salvation. There was no alternative. The final words of Christ in the Garden were these: "The cup which my Father hath given me, shall I not drink it?"[8] To secure man's salvation, the Son of God let the blow of divine justice fall on Himself. He who could say, "I do always those things that please him"[9] had to endure the displeasure of the one He delighted to serve.

In those few but fateful hours on the cross Jesus tasted the unspeakable horror of eternal death. Spiritual darkness shrouded His soul. His cry of dereliction is the measure of His sacrifice. Olin A. Curtis has well expressed it thus: "And so, there alone, our Lord opens his mind, his heart, his personal consciousness, to the whole inflow of the horror of sin—the endless history of it, from the first choice of selfishness on, on to the eternity of hell; the boundless ocean and desolation he allows, wave upon wave, to overwhelm his soul."[10] This terrific cost reveals God's moral concern for sin. His holiness forbade Him to treat it lightly. That He would forsake His Son shows the ethical intensity of the redemptive deed.

We have noted what Jesus' death meant for Him. What does it mean to us?

First, it means that a guilty sinner has access to a holy God. The writer of Hebrews speaks thus: "Having therefore, brethren, boldness to enter into the holiest by the blood of Jesus, by a new and living way, which he hath consecrated for us, through the veil, that is to say, his flesh..."[11] This was symbolized by the fact that at Jesus' death the inner veil, which closed off the Holy of Holies, was torn in two.

Secondly, it means the forgiveness of sins. At the Last Supper, Jesus spoke these symbolic words: "This is my blood of the new testament, which is shed for many for the remission of sins."[12] In the same vein, Paul writes: "In whom we have redemption through his blood, the forgiveness of sins."[13] Both "remission" and "forgiveness" are translations of the same Greek word, *aphesis*. It comes from *aphiemi*, which

[7] Mark 15:34.   [8] John 18:11.
[9] John 8:29.
[10] O.A. Curtis: *The Christian Faith*, p. 325.
[11] Heb. 10:19, 20.   [12] Matt. 26:28.
[13] Eph. 1:7.

is used for the canceling of debts, the remitting of a penalty, the pardon of the guilty. All these ideas are wrapped up in the thought of divine forgiveness. The essential thing in forgiveness is the separation of the sinner from his sin. This required Calvary. Only the cross could meet the moral crisis.

Thirdly, it involves the crucifixion of self. Paul declared: "I have been crucified with Christ; and it is no longer I that live, but Christ liveth in me: and that life which I now live in the flesh I live in faith, the faith which is in the Son of God, who loved me, and gave himself up for me."[14] His crucifixion must become *our* crucifixion. What was potential and provisional at Calvary must become actual and experimental in our own lives.

The death of Christ seemed to be stark tragedy. But in it, He triumphed over sin. The cross, symbol of shame, has become the sign of victory. Ethelbert Stauffer states it thus: "The ignominious raising on the cross is really a majestic elevation to glory."[15]

THE RESURRECTION

"Biblical theology finds its clearest starting point and interpreting clue in the resurrection of Jesus Christ." Thus Floyd Filson asserts the importance of this event.[16] Alan Richardson makes a similarly emphatic statement: "Christianity is a religion of miracle, and the miracle of Christ's resurrection is the living centre and object of Christian faith."[17] The doctrine of the resurrection is not peripheral, but central. It is not secondary, but primary. Brunner asserts: "On the resurrection everything else depends."[18]

Without the resurrection the crucifixion would have been in vain. It was the resurrection which validated the atoning death of Jesus and gave it value. Paul describes it strikingly this way: "Who was delivered for our offences, and was raised again for our justification."[19] The resurrection of Jesus proved that His sacrifice for sins had been accepted. The whole redemptive scheme would have fallen apart with-

---

[14] Gal. 2:20, ASV.
[15] E. Stauffer: *New Testament Theology,* p. 130.
[15] F. Filson: *Jesus Christ the Risen Lord,* p. 25.
[17] A. Richardson: *An Introduction to the Theology of the New Testament,* p. 197.
[18] E. Brunner: *Letter to the Romans,* p. 131.
[19] Rom. 4:25.

out it. For by his resurrection Jesus Christ became the first fruits of a new race, a new humanity.

It is no wonder, then, that the fact of the resurrection has been vigorously attacked. A generation ago most liberal theologians scoffed at the idea of a literal, bodily resurrection of Jesus. But the theological climate has changed a great deal in recent years. One need only note that the witness to the resurrection is strong and incontrovertible.

Paul gives a brief summary, with some additions, in I Corinthians 15:4–8. In this same chapter he points out the importance of the resurrection of Jesus. He declares, "And if Christ be not risen, then is our preaching vain, and your faith is also vain";[20] "And if Christ be not raised, your faith is vain; ye are yet in your sins."[21] Thus, he affirms clearly that the resurrection is essential to our salvation.

The resurrection bulked larger in the earliest apostolic preaching than it does today. It was at times, at least, the central emphasis of the church's *kerygma*. This is demonstrated abundantly in Acts. In the very first chapter we discover its primary importance. To take the place of Judas Iscariot, Peter proposed the selection of one who would "be ordained to be a witness with us of his resurrection."[22] It would appear that an essential, if not *the* essential, function of an Apostle was to witness to the resurrection of Jesus.

In the first recorded sermon in Acts, that of Peter on the day of Pentecost, considerable space is given to the resurrection.[23] Peter also asserted it in his second sermon.[24] The first persecution of the believers was due to their preaching of the resurrection.[25] When again arraigned, the Apostles once more declared their faith in this doctrine.[26] So on it goes.

In fact, one can say that the resurrection holds a more prominent place in the New Testament as a whole than in modern preaching, even that of evangelicals. This obvious fact provoked Dr. Merrill Tenney to write his excellent little volume, *Resurrection Realities*. Alan Richardson asserts: "Every book in the New Testament declares or assumes that Christ rose from the dead."[27] And Floyd Filson writes: "The entire New Testament was written in the light of the resurrection fact."[28]

20 I Cor. 15:14. 21 I Cor. 15:17.
22 Acts 1:22. 23 Acts 2:24-32.
24 Acts 3:15. 25 Acts 4:2.
26 Acts 5:30.
27 A. Richardson: *A Theological Word Book of the Bible*, p. 193.
28 Filson, *op. cit.*, p. 31.

One striking feature of early apostolic preaching is the emphasis not only on Christ's rising from the dead but on the fact that God raised Him. The resurrection was a divine act. This is stated over and over again in Acts: "whom God hath raised up";[29] "That Jesus hath God raised up, whereof we all are witnesses";[30] "The God of our Fathers raised up Jesus."[31] Paul asserts the same thing. He says we should "believe on him that raised up Jesus our Lord from the dead."[32] Because of this emphasis, Arthur Ramsey writes: "Christian theism is Resurrection-theism."[33]

The resurrection is the keystone of the Christian faith. Without it, we have no salvation from sin and no hope of our own resurrection.[34] It is one of the main proofs of the deity of Jesus. Paul says He was "declared to be the Son of God...by the resurrection from the dead."[35] William J. S. Simpson rightly asserts: "All distinctively Christian belief in Jesus has been founded on a knowledge of His Resurrection."[36]

THE ASCENSION

Actual descriptions of the Ascension are very limited in number and scope. Only two specific passages can be cited, both written by Luke.[37] But, as Filson notes, "...eleven New Testament books, by at least seven different writers, refer clearly to this Exaltation. It obviously was a constant feature of early Christian preaching and teaching."[38]

It should be noted in this connection that the resurrection and ascension are very closely united in the apostolic *kerygma*.[39] Together, they constitute the exaltation of the crucified Christ.

Because of the paucity of description of the ascension, some have questioned its historicity. Even such a moderate scholar as Alan Richardson can say: "The ascension need not be thought of as an historical event."[40]

Of course, Bultmann calls for a demythologizing of much of the Gospel narrative, including the resurrection. For him, it is simply a

[29] Acts 2:24.
[30] Acts 2:32; cf. Acts 3:15; 4:10.
[31] Acts 5:30.
[32] Rom. 4:24; cf. Rom. 8:11.
[33] A. Ramsey: *The Resurrection of Christ*, p. 8.
[34] I Cor. 15:17, 18.
[35] Rom. 1:4.
[36] J. Hastings, ed.: *A Dictionary of Christ and the Gospels*, Volume II, p. 514.
[37] Luke 24:50, 51; Acts 1:9–11.
[38] Filson, *op. cit.*, p. 50.
[39] E.g., Acts 2:32–35; Eph. 1:20; I Pet. 3:21, 22.
[40] Richardson, *op. cit.*, p. 199.

doctrine rising out of subjective experience. It is not an historical event. But Barth warns: "We must not transmute the Resurrection into a spiritual event."[41]

To us, it seems inconsistent to insist, as some others do, on the historical reality of the bodily resurrection of Jesus, and yet deny the historicity of the ascension simply because one does not accept the three-story concept of the universe held long ago. The cosmic import of the death, resurrection, and ascension of Christ is not affected by differing cosmologies.

The significance of the ascension is clear. It means that Jesus Christ was exalted to the right hand of the Father, there to receive His proper place as Sovereign Lord.[42]

But it also suggests that He carried His humanity with Him back to heaven. This idea is emphasized in Hebrews, where it is stated that since He shared our human experiences, He is able to be a merciful and faithful High Priest.[43] To know that we have an Elder Brother in heaven is a great comfort.

OUR IDENTIFICATION WITH CHRIST

The death, resurrection, ascension—these were epochal events in human history. But have they become epoch-making experiences in our individual lives? Do we know Christ in the forgiveness of our sins, in identification with Him on the cross, in the crucifixion of self? Do we know Him in the power of His resurrection? Have we accepted Him as Sovereign Lord of our lives?

BIBLIOGRAPHY

J. Denney: *The Death of Christ* [The classic in the field]
F.W. Dillistone: *The Significance of the Cross*
W. Milligan: *The Resurrection of Our Lord*
R.R. Niebuhr: *Resurrection and Historical Reason*
J.S. Simpson: *The Resurrection and Modern Thought*
B.F. Westcott: *The Gospel of the Resurrection*

[41] K. Barth: *Dogmatics in Outline*, 1949, p. 123.
[42] Acts 2:33–36; 5:31; Eph. 1:19–23.
[43] Heb. 2:14–18; 4:14–16.

22

THE MEDIATORIAL OFFICES

OF CHRIST:

PROPHET, PRIEST, KING

✛

SAMUEL J. MIKOLASKI

Samuel J. Mikolaski, Associate Professor of Theology at New Orleans Baptist Theological Seminary, New Orleans, Louisiana, received his general and theological education at the University of Western Ontario, London, Ontario, Canada (B.A., 1952; M.A., 1954), the University of London, England (B.D., 1955), and the University of Oxford, England (D.Phil., 1958).

Christ is prophet. Christ is priest. Christ is king. This three-fold division of the mediatorial work of Jesus Christ has become traditional in Protestant theology. The offices declare the righteousness of God in Christ, the mediation of God for our salvation, and the sovereignty of God in the world.

One of the earliest clear references to the offices in the patristic literature occurs in Eusebius (though the work of Christ in each role was evident to the church from apostolic days): "We have also received the tradition that some of the prophets themselves had by anointing already become Christs in type, seeing that they all refer to the true Christ, the divine and heavenly Logos, of the world the only High Priest, of all creation the only king, of the prophets the only archprophet of the Father. The proof of this is that no one of those symbolically anointed of old, whether priests or kings or prophets, obtained such power of divine virtue as our Saviour and Lord, Jesus, the only real Christ, has exhibited . . . that until this present day he is honoured by his worshippers throughout the world as king, wondered at more than a prophet, and glorified as the true and only High Priest of God . . ."[1]

John Calvin made the offices a point of special attention in the *Institutes*, where his discussion, though brief, is characteristically lucid.[2] He remarks that while the concept was not unknown to the papists of his time, they used it frigidly without the accompanying knowledge of the end of the offices, nor their use in the exposition of the Gospel. Succeeding theologians, especially of the Reformed tradition, have used it with varying emphasis. For example, Charles Hodge, A.H. Strong, and Louis Berkhof devote but scanty space to the prophetic and kingly offices (the substance of the latter doctrine is usually reserved for elucidation in eschatology), but each expands the priestly role to include a comprehensive statement of the doctrine of the atonement.

The idea of the offices also figures in Eastern theology. For example, in answer to the question: "Why, then, is Jesus, the Son of God, called *The Anointed?*" *The Longer Catechism of the Orthodox, Catholic, Eastern Church*[3] says, "Because to his manhood were imparted without measure all the gifts of the Holy Ghost; and so he possesses in the highest degree the *knowledge* of a prophet; the *holiness* of a high priest; and the *power* of a *king*." The offices set forward the divine-human nature of the Mediator, proclaiming thus not only His uniqueness, but also His prerogatives.[4]

CHRIST, THE ANOINTED ONE

In the early stages of biblical history, the three offices seem to have been joined in the role the patriarch assumed in the family. Each was in effect prophet, priest, and king to his own household, but under God.

[1] Eusebius: *Historia Ecclesiastica*, I, 3.   [2] J. Calvin: *Institutes,* II, XV.
[3] 1839.   [4] I Tim. 2:5.

Later, the division of these roles seems clear, but whether earlier or later, the idea generic to each is that of divine anointing to the office. This was as true of prophets and kings as of priests.[5] Further, Israel's hope was that, in the Messiah, all three offices would be fulfilled perfectly and joined harmoniously for the inauguration of the kingly-redemptive rule of God. The claim of our Lord upon such prophetic anticipations is both authoritative and revealing.[6] Prominent figures in the Old Testament point to Christ, whether they were anointed prophets, priests, or kings. The Coming One was to be both Jehovah's anointed and a personal deliverer. The revelation at each point of history was revelation discrete, concrete, actual, and saving; but, together, the words and events heralded the antitype Jesus Christ.

For this reason, sight must not be lost of the fact that the offices interpenetrate. Christ fills them all at once and yet successively in the achievement of His mission for the world in history. His proclamation of the righteousness of God[7] was fulfilled when He purged our sins (God's justifying the sinner justly, as Paul says), and then sat down upon the throne of heaven in regal glory;[8] and this trilogy has been seen by Christians everywhere in Scripture, for example, Isaiah 53. Christ comes as the personal word of God, the personal redeemer of the world, and the personal center of the kingdom of God.

THE THEOLOGICAL FOOTING

Mediation raises the question of its rationale. This should be seen jointly in terms of righteousness and grace, wrath and love, judgment and mercy. Now, the revelation of the divine love in Jesus Christ is an important emphasis in contemporary theology, but, not infrequently, judgment and wrath are reduced to a definition of love that evacuates them of their common meaning. The love of Christ is God's self-giving,[9] and sight must not be lost of its recreating and reconciling power. Certainly the loving concern of God in Jesus Christ for wayward man and an evil-infected world is the dominant note of the Christian revelation. But that note is no monotone; rather, it is the harmonious chord that sin deserves wrath, that grace is in view of impending judgment, and that the divine love is revealed redemptively active, not over but through judgment.

[5] I Sam. 16:3; I Kings 19:16; Ps. 105:15.
[6] Isa. 61:1, 2; Luke 4:18, 19.   [7] Rom. 3:21–26; Matt. 11:27; John 3:34.
[8] Heb. 1:3.   [9] John 3:16.

The relations between God and man are personal, and to say this is to say that they are moral. Both of these realities bear upon the mediatorial offices of Christ. To say that God loves sinners without saying that God will judge unatoned for and unforgiven sin is a saccharine conception of the divine love that squares neither with the biblical revelation of God's character nor the plain facts of human experience. The judgment of God is real, and He claims this both as His prerogative and duty. Personal and moral categories are the highest we know. Here, the freedom of God and man is preserved and righteousness vindicated in the judgment of evil. The work of Christ is addressed to these two sides of the issue, and we ignore either one at our peril. The theology of the offices takes account of both, and this is a salutary corrective of certain contemporary trends.

CHRIST AS PROPHET

It has been said popularly that the prophet spoke for God to men, while the priest acted on behalf of men before God. As the prophets of old, Jesus Christ did proclaim the Word of the Lord, but more than that, He Himself was the living embodiment of that Word. The idea of *the* prophet to come, who would sum up both the prophetic ideal and the prophetic message, dominated Israelitish thinking from the time of Moses.[10] Our Lord clearly identified Himself with the prophetic office in its preaching, teaching, and revelatory functions, as well as with the rejection borne by and sufferings inflicted upon the ancient men of God.[11] He called Himself a prophet;[12] He claimed to bring a message from the Father;[13] and people recognized him to be a prophet.[14]

Primarily, He epitomized the righteousness of God which He proclaimed, and His presence, as incarnate, joins together mysteriously the working of righteousness and grace for our salvation. A poignant manner of expressing His prophetic role as both proclaiming and being the righteousness of God is the figure of the pierced ear in both testaments of Scripture.[15] His humanity sums up the perfection of the divine ideal for men, and in His righteousness and obedience our response is taken up and made actual. He is the true *sui generis:* the One Who loves righteousness because He is righteous. The Scriptures forever

---

[10] Deut. 18:15.   [11] Matt. 23:29 f.; Luke 4:24 ff.; 13:33, 34.
[12] Luke 13:33.   [13] John 8:26–28; 14:10–24; 17:8, 26.
[14] Matt. 21:11, 46; Luke 7:16; 24:19; John 3:2; 4:19.
[15] Exod. 21:5–6; Ps. 40:6–10; Heb. 10:5–7.

join the noetic and moral elements of human experience, which contemporary positivism and naturalism perpetually try to bifurcate. What a man knows and what he does depend upon what he is, and this moral judgment is what Christ brings to bear upon the race. He can say, "Lo! in the volume of the book it is written of me I come to do thy will, O God" and "I have preached righteousness in the great congregation...I have declared thy faithfulness and thy salvation." This is precisely because the divine law is within His heart, and our calling is to the same freedom in righteousness.

CHRIST AS PRIEST

The surpassing worth of Christ's priestly work over the Aaronic priesthood is the theme of the Epistle to the Hebrews. The forgiveness of sins in Scripture is peculiarly attached to sacrifice for sin,[16] and, as the prophetic word is the word of righteousness, Christ's priestly act is the fulfillment of righteousness, under judgment, for the world's salvation. The conception of His life given for our lives dominates the biblical revelation.[17]

The analogies and contrasts between the Aaronic priesthood and Christ's priesthood are clear. He, as sinless, needed not to offer up sacrifice first for Himself as the other priests did; His blood could take away sin, whereas the blood of bulls and goats could not; His work was final while theirs must be repeated.[18] Christ is both priest and victim, both punisher and punished, and herein lies the profoundest mystery of Christianity touching the doctrines of the Trinity, incarnation and atonement. The fact is that Christ's sacrifice does not buy divine love, but is the gift of that love where He submits to the judgment of our sin. The relation we sustained to God because of sin was death, and Christ entered fully into that.[19] This atoning act is His high priesthood, where He joins Himself to us and makes reconciliation for sin,[20] and, now having entered into heaven, He continues His intercessory ministry for us.[21] He is a kingly priest, glorified with the full splendor of the throne of God and by the distinctive glory of a finished saving work.[22] He bore our judgment and He died our death; He carried our sorrows and He lives now to succor us.

[16] John 1:29.
[17] Mark 8:31; 9:31; 10:33, 34, 35.   [18] Heb. 7; 9; 10.
[19] I Cor. 15:3; Rom. 4:25; Gal. 1:4; 3:13.
[20] Heb. 2:17; 3:1.
[21] Heb. 4:4, 15; 9:11–15, 24–28; 10:19–22.
[22] Heb. 10:10–14; Rev. 1:13; 5:6, 9, 12.

But a further analogy is drawn, namely, between the Melchizedec priesthood and Christ's, in contrast to the Aaronic, because Melchizedec typifies the eternal and kingly character of Christ's work.[23] The work Christ did had to do not with sprinkling animal blood in an earthly tabernacle, where the priest passed beyond the embroidered veil shielding the holiest place, but with presenting His own sacrifice in the very "temple" of heaven, the antitype of the earthly.[24] This priestly order, priestly service, and sacrifice are celestial, eternal, supranational, and final. It is the prerogative of God in Christ not to receive but to make sacrifice. What God demanded, He provided. This is grace not over but through judgment.

CHRIST AS KING

The reign of God among His people was the ideal of the theocratic kingdom, witnessed to continually even in the failings of the Israelitish monarchy. The promise of Messianic kingship is clear in the Davidic covenant,[25] in the expectation of the prophets,[26] in the ejaculation of Nathaniel,[27] in the care with which our Lord guarded Himself from the impetuous crowd,[28] and in the ironic superscription of the cross.[29] He was thought of as a king,[30] declared a king,[31] and expected to return in regal power and splendor.[32]

This kingship has been taken commonly to be spiritual over the hearts of men, in the manner of our Lord's speaking to Pilate, and many theologians have held that the Sermon on the Mount is the declaration of the Kingdom principles and its institution. No ministry, no administration of ordinance or sacrament, no work or gift of the Spirit can be conceived of as operating under less than the suzerainty of Jesus Christ.[33] The Great Commission proclaims not only the standing orders of the church, but the lordship of its author. Indeed, Paul, led by the Holy Spirit, advances from the truth that "Jesus is Lord" for every Christian to the declaration of Christ's sovereignty in the universe.[34]

Thus, the Christian hope moves along two planes of comprehension: Christ's kingdom is the kingdom of truth and righteousness bought by

23 Heb. 7.   24 Heb. 8:2.
25 II Sam. 7:12–29.   26 Isa. 9:6–7; 11:1–10; 42:1–4.
27 John 1:49.   28 John 6:15.
29 John 18:37; 19:19.   30 Matt. 2:2; Acts 17:7.
31 Heb. 1:8; Rev. 1:5.   32 I Tim. 6:14–16; Rev. 11:15; 19:16.
33 Matt. 28:19–20; John 16:13–14.   34 Col. 1:16, 17; Heb. 1–3.

His own blood, and the prerogatives He possessed and vindicated in the cross and resurrection and now exercises in the church and the world point to His final assumption of power. His enemies *will* become His footstool;[35] he *will yet* judge the world.[36]

Upon the cross, as at His temptation, He could not be corrupted by evil. "The prince of this world comes," He remarked in the night of His passion, "and hath nothing in me." Evil is borne and overcome, and the finality of Christ's prophetic, priestly, and kingly work becomes translated into an actual victory in life for the Christian. Sin "shall not have dominion over us," because it "can not" do so any longer. Who shall lay anything to the charge of God's elect? It is God that justifieth.

This is our priesthood, our prophetic ministry, and our victory. As He was in the world, so are we. There is, for the Christian, the suffering *for* Christ and the suffering *with* Christ. And the certainty of the Christian is this: that he is the only soldier in history who enters the field of battle with the victory already behind his back.

BIBLIOGRAPHY

J. Orr, ed.: *International Standard Bible Encyclopedia*, Volume I, article "Offices of Christ" by L.D. Bevan

J. Hastings, ed.: *Dictionary of the Bible*, Volume II, article "The Incarnation" by R.L. Ottley

E. Brunner: *Dogmatics*, Volume II

T. Watson: *A Body of Divinity*

————: *The Larger Catechism of the Westminster Confession*

[35] Heb. 10:13. [36] Matt. 25:31.

23

THE ATONEMENT

✛

LEON MORRIS

Leon Morris, Warden at Tyndale House, Cambridge, England, received his general and theological education at the University of Sydney, Australia (B.Sc., 1934), the University of London, England (B.D., 1943; M.Th., 1946), and the University of Cambridge, England (Ph.D., 1952). He is the author of *The Wages of Sin: Tyndale Commentary on I, II Thessalonians*, *The Biblical Doctrine of Judgment*, and *The Dead Sea Scrolls and St. John's Gospel*, among other works.

When R.C. Moberley spoke of the incarnation as "the crucial doctrine" of Christianity, his adjective completely gave his case away. "Crucial" is from the Latin *crux*, "a cross." So, whenever we say, "this is the crucial point" or "the crux of the matter is this," our language means "just the cross is central to Christianity, so the point I am making is central to the present discussion." The centrality of the cross to the Christian faith has shaped the language we use.

Right at the heart of Christianity there is a cross, and on that cross the Son of God wrought man's salvation. Put simply, the atonement means that Jesus Christ in His death dealt completely with the problem that man's sin had set. Whatever had to be done, He did it, and now those who come in faith may enter into full salvation. Throughout the centuries there have been many theories current in the church as to how this was done, and none of them has been able to command universal acceptance. This leads us to the conclusion that there is an essential mystery about the atonement, so that men cannot know completely how it works. But there are some points that the Bible makes very clear, and any satisfactory understanding of the atonement must reckon with them.

THE LOVE OF GOD

The first point to notice is that the atonement proceeds from the loving heart of God. In the best-known text in the whole Bible, we read that "God so loved the world, that he gave his only begotten Son, that whosoever believeth in him should not perish, but have everlasting life."[1] With this, accord the words of Paul: "God commendeth his love toward us, in that, while we were yet sinners, Christ died for us."[2] This line of teaching could be traced through the whole of Scripture, for it is fundamental that the atonement takes place only because God's love leads to it.

Notice that the passages we have cited do not speak of the love of Christ, which we would perhaps think more natural. It is the love of the Father that is seen in the cross (the love of the Son is, of course, seen too, but that is not the point in the passages under discussion). This is important in that it shows us that our salvation comes to us with all the majesty of God the Father behind it. It is a divine work in the fullest sense. It is important also in that it shows us that in this work of salvation the Father and the Son are completely at one. Sometimes, with the very best motives in the world, theologians have given the impression that God the Father is a stern judge; just, it is true, but stern. He lays down His requirements, and when men do not reach them, insists on punishment. Into that situation comes the loving Son who intervenes in such a way as to save men from their judge. This is not the scriptural teaching at all, and must unhesitatingly be dismissed as a caricature. The atonement takes place because God the Father loves us and makes provision in His Son for our salvation.

THE SIN OF MAN

Paul gives as one of the fundamental pieces of the church's teaching (it had been given to him; he did not originate it), that "Christ died

[1] John 3:16   [2] Rom. 5:8.

for our sins according to the Scriptures."[3] This, too, is teaching that could be widely documented, for the early church was sure that Christ's death and man's sin were closely connected. So frequently do we find the two linked that it is more or less a commonplace of New Testament teaching on the subject, and it could be passed over quickly were it not for the fact that in modern times the church has often lost sight of this altogether. Many think of Christ as a martyr and of His death as taking place because He was not understood or because His teaching was rejected or for political reasons or the like. "Explanations" of this type are legion, and they make a strong appeal to many in our day. But they are out of keeping with the New Testament. There, it is clear that, humanly speaking, Jesus could have avoided the cross had He so chosen. But He did not so choose, for this was the divine way of dealing with sin.

Sometimes the New Testament speaks of Christ's blood as shed "for the remission of sins."[4] This same blood "cleanseth us from all sin."[5] Christ "purged our sins;"[6] He "bare our sins in his own body on a tree."[7] And there are other expressions. Whatever had to be done about sin, He did it. And He did it perfectly and finally, for "where remission of these is, there is no more offering for sin."[8]

The New Testament witness is clear. The death of Jesus was connected with the sin of man. And the death of Jesus was the perfect atonement for man's sin.

PENAL SUBSTITUTION

The way this is effected in the traditional evangelical statement of the position is by Christ's bearing the penalty that sinners had incurred, by His taking their place. It is true that the New Testament never uses this term, but it is difficult to explain such a passage as Romans 3:21-26 any other way. Here, Paul says that the cross shows us the righteousness of God. His point is that the truth that God is righteous was in danger of being obscured, because in earlier days God had not always exacted the penalty for sin. "Remission" in verse 25[9] is better "passing over"; the meaning is that God had passed over men's sins without punishing them; therefore He might appear not to be just. But in the light of the cross, such an accusation can never be

---

[3] I Cor. 15:3.   [4] Matt. 26:28.
[5] I John 1:7.   [6] Heb. 1:3.
[7] I Pet. 2:24.   [8] Heb. 10:18.
[9] KJV.

leveled again. What does this mean, if it does not mean that the penalty of sin has been borne?

Substitution is to be found in many places. We see it in the saying of Mark 10:45, "The Son of man came . . . to give his life a ransom for many." The expression *lutron anti pollon* expresses a substitutionary thought, as, indeed, does the whole saying, for the meaning is "Because Christ died the many do not." Again, the agony in Gethsemane, taken with the cry of dereliction,[10] points to the same thing. Why should Jesus be in an agony as He contemplated death? He was no coward, and many lesser by far have faced death calmly, including not a few who have been inspired by Him. It was not death as such that He feared, but the death that was the death of sinners, that death in which He should experience the horror of being forsaken by Him who is of purer eyes than to behold evil.[11] Paul is surely referring to the same thing when he says that God "made him to be sin for us, who knew no sin."[12] This identifies Christ in His death in the closest manner with the sinners. He died the death of sinful men. So Paul can say, "one died for all, then were all dead."[13] And the same truth underlies his words, "Christ hath redeemed us from the curse of the law, being made a curse for us."[14] This must surely mean that Christ bore the curse that we should have borne. And this is substitution.

Twice Christ is said to have borne our sins.[15] In modern times this is sometimes understood to mean that Jesus put up with the frustrations and difficulties involved in living among sinful people. But that is not the biblical meaning of the term. It occurs often in the Old Testament in contexts showing plainly that the bearing of penalty is in mind, as when Ezekiel says, "The soul that sinneth, it shall die. The son shall not bear the iniquity of the father . . . "[16] The expression then means that Christ bore our penalty. He stood in our place.

Substitution is also in mind when John records the cynical prophecy of Caiaphas, "it is expedient for us, that one man should die for the people, and that the whole nation perish not."[17] Caiaphas spoke out of a worldly political cynicism, but John records the words because they were an unconscious prophecy of the significance of the death of the Lord.[18] His death is a substitute for that of the people. We must

[10] Mark 15:34.
[11] Hab. 1:13.
[12] II Cor. 5:21.
[13] II Cor. 5:14.
[14] Gal. 3:13.
[15] Heb. 9:28; I Pet. 2:24.
[16] Ezek. 18:20; *see also* Num. 14:33 f.; etc.
[17] John 11:50.
[18] John 11:51 f.

surely understand the references to Christ as "the propitiation for our sins"[19] in the same way.

Thus, the evidence that the New Testament regards Christ's saving work as substitutionary is considerable and varied. He took our place. This is not the whole story. His death is an example for us.[20] It is a display of God's love.[21] There are other aspects. None can be dismissed as unimportant, and all must be kept in mind, if we are to obtain the complete picture. But an emphasis which is usually overlooked in modern theological writing is this substitutionary one, which is found throughout the New Testament and which is so fundamental. Whatever it was that Christ did for us, He did by taking our place. He bore what we should have borne and we go free.

Those who deny this do not usually reflect on the consequences of their denial. But there are only two possibilities: either Christ bore the burden of our sin, or we bear it. There is no middle course. Thus, to deny that in any sense Christ took our burden means that the whole idea of Christianity as a *redemptive* religion must be abandoned. Substitution may need to be understood carefully. It is not some crude, external thing. It includes the thought that the Substitute is on the one hand, one with God and on the other, one with sinful men. Believers are not saved as detached units; they are "in Christ." But the fact that we need to understand substitution carefully does not mean that we are at liberty to abandon the concept altogether. It is too deeply rooted in the Scriptures and too imperatively demanded by the logic of the situation for that.

THE TRIUMPH OF THE CRUCIFIED

As he comes to the climax of his great treatment of the resurrection, Paul exults, "O death, where is thy sting? O grave, where is thy victory?" He answers his questions, "The sting of death is sin; and the strength of sin is the law," and immediately proceeds, "But thanks be to God, which giveth us the victory through our Lord Jesus Christ."[22] This note of victory runs through the New Testament treatment of the work of Christ. The Gospels do not finish with the cross, but go right on to speak of the resurrection. The Acts pictures the early church as living in the afterglow of the same fact, and the extent to which it dominated their thought is revealed in the speeches that Luke records.

---

19 I John 2:2; 4:10.   20 I Pet. 2:21.
21 I John 4:10; etc.   22 I Cor. 15:55-57.

In the Epistles the same triumph is depicted, and this rings on to the last book of the Bible, where the note of triumph sounds forth clear and sustained. There cannot be the slightest doubt that the New Testament writers conceived of their Christ as having won for them a complete triumph over all the forces of sin and death and hell. "We are more than conquerors through him that loved us."[23]

Throughout the New Testament it is assumed that man's salvation rests entirely and only on what God has done in Christ. The atonement is the very central doctrine. Without Christ's saving work, men are lost. In Christ they are triumphantly saved.

BIBLIOGRAPHY

J. Denney: *The Death of Christ* [revised edition by R.V.G. Tasker]
————: *The Christian Doctrine of Reconciliation*
R.W. Dale: *The Atonement*
H.E. Guillebaud: *Why the Cross?*

[23] Rom. 8:37.

24

THE INTERCESSORY WORK

OF CHRIST

✠

ROBERT PAUL ROTH

Robert Paul Roth, Professor of Systematic Theology at North-western Lutheran Theological Seminary, Minneapolis, Minnesota, received his general and theological education at the University of Illinois (M.A., 1942), Northwestern Lutheran Seminary (B.D., 1945), and the University of Chicago (Ph.D., 1947).

The intercessory work of Christ presupposes that the predicament of man is not an alleged flaw in his existence but the enmity which separates the creature from the Creator. "For if while we were enemies we were reconciled to God by the death of his Son, much more, now that we are reconciled, shall we be saved by his life."[1] Furthermore, just as no mere analysis of human existence in psychological or philosophical categories will provide an adequate anthropology, so, likewise, no definition of Christ in terms of substance or nature will properly describe His intercessory action. Much modern Protestant theology, however, exhibits such a protest against the merely physical conception of the Lord's state in heaven that the reality of Christ's work

[1] Rom. 5:10.

has been volatilized into a gaseous vacuity. A true biblical understanding will appreciate the power of Christ's personal pleading as God's Word in *action*, God in Jesus giving his life at the right time for the ungodly.

OLD TESTAMENT PRIESTLY SACRIFICE

The concept of intercession has its roots in the priestly sacrifice of the Old Testament. God was at work in the family of Israel, providing sacrifices which were acceptable for atonement before the once-for-all sacrifice of Jesus. Aaron was instructed to come once a year to the holy place with a bull, a ram, and a goat, sacrificing them with the laying on of hands and sprinkling the blood of the bull and the goat on the mercy seat and offering the ram as a burnt offering.[2] A second goat was driven into the wilderness with the laying on of hands and the confession of the sins of the people.[3] This system of sacrifices hearkened back to the experience of Abraham in which God provided a ram as a substitute for Isaac, and it projected forward to Christ in the anticipation of the Suffering Servant of Isaiah on whom was laid the iniquity of us all.[4]

The significant thrust throughout the history of sacrifice is therefore the *intercession of God* in providing the sacrifice from the ram of Abraham to Jesus, the lamb of God, Who was also caught on the branches of a tree. Precisely here is the difference between the biblical understanding of sacrifice on the one hand and both pagan and perverted Jewish notions on the other. In pagan sacrifice, a gift is offered by man in hope of gaining favor from the god. Thus, man works a change upon the god through his offering. In the practice of Judaism, a work is done by man in the hope of changing the heart of man, cleansing him so as to render him acceptable to God. But the Christian revelation in both Testaments teaches that God intercedes, providing a sacrifice which changes the wrath of God into mercy and the sinner into a saint.

Sören Kierkegaard's references, in *Fear and Trembling*, to the sacrifices of Iphigenia, Jephthah's daughter, and Abraham's son serve well to illustrate these three conceptions of sacrifice.[5] Agamemnon and Jephthah make their sacrifices for a reason: Agamemnon vows to

---

[2] Lev. 16:3–19.   [3] Lev. 16:20–22.
[4] Gen. 22:8; Isa. 53:6.
[5] S. Kierkegaard: *Fear and Trembling*, pp. 127 ff.

offer his daughter to gain a favorable wind; Jephthah vows to provide a thank offering of whoever comes to meet him from his door, after he has defeated the Ammonites. Abraham has no reason that might be justified ethically. He simply prepares to sacrifice Isaac in obedience to the Lord. What was done by Agamemnon was a supreme human effort to control the gods; what was done by Jephthah was a valiant human attempt to preserve the integrity of the heart. Abraham alone accepted the intercessory work of God by offering whatever God provided, whether it be his only beloved son or a ram caught in a bush.

CHRIST'S RECONCILING SACRIFICE

When, according to the history of salvation, the right time, *kata kairon*, had come, God's Messiah interceded by means of His sacrifice, in order to reconcile helpless and rebellious sinners with the Father.[6] Thus, as in the Old Testament the priest represented man and offered a sacrifice to God, so now Christ Jesus as man offers Himself as a "fragrant offering and sacrifice to God."[7] "For our sake he [God] made him [Christ] to be sin who knew no sin, so that in him we might become the righteousness of God."[8]

Since God in His gracious favor toward man was concerned to free us from our bondage to sin, flesh, and the power of the devil, he sent His Son "in the likeness of sinful flesh."[9] "Therefore he had to be made like his brethren in every respect, so that he might become a merciful and faithful high priest in the service of God, to make expiation for the sins of the people."[10] The Greek verb *hilaskesthai* and its substantive form *to hilasterion* in Romans 3:21 are both used in the Septuagint to render the propitiation offered to God at the mercy seat in the holy of holies.[11] The meaning is that God, in the person of Christ, acts mercifully on behalf of sinners by sacrificing His life. This suffering, which is accepted that all righteousness may be fulfilled, is well pleasing to God, because it is God's glory that He spends Himself for His creature.[12]

Intercession must be made by a mediator who can successfully represent both sides. A priest is such a mediator because he represents his

[6] Rom. 5:6.
[7] Eph. 5:2.
[8] II Cor. 5:21.
[9] Rom. 8:3.
[10] Heb. 2:17.
[11] Exod. 25:17; 31:7; 35:12; 37:6; Lev. 16:2, 13.
[12] Matt. 3:15–17.

own people, as he offers their spotless gift which is received by the holy God. But here the ineffectualness of every human intercession is manifest: the gift is never spotless and hence it is not well pleasing to God. In Christ's intercession, a pure gift is offered since He Who is sinless gives Himself.

CHRIST'S CONTINUING WORK

Christ's work is not ended with His death on the cross in the sense of *finis*, although it is certainly complete in the sense of *tetelestai*, but He *continues* to plead for sinners in heaven. Sacrifice we found to be the basic meaning of Christ's intercession, since through it God is glorified magnificently over His enemies, and His rebellious creatures are reconciled. But in the Old Testament, the central moment of sacrifice was not in the slaying of the victim but in what was done with the blood when it was released. Blood was understood to mean the *life* of the victim. When blood was shed, it signified the pouring out of the victim's life. On the Day of Atonement, the ritual sacrifice brought the priest into the holy of holies behind the veil of the temple, where he sprinkled the mercy seat with the lifeblood of the sacrificial animal. Hence, the moment of the *ephapax* of Christ's sacrifice is not the death on Golgotha alone, but also, and especially, the heavenly moment of presentation of His sacrifice to the Father at His ascension. Paul gives this emphasis to the heavenly intercession, when he says: "Is it Christ Jesus who died, yes, who was raised from the dead, who is at the right hand of God, who indeed intercedes for us?"[13] And the author of Hebrews, who is so careful to guard the once-for-all character of the sacrificial death on Golgotha, is no less concerned to declare the continuing intercession in heaven: "Consequently he is able for all time to save those who draw near to God through him, since he *always lives* to make intercession for them."[14]

Christ does not offer Himself repeatedly, as the high priest offered his sacrifices each year, but He appeared once for all in the world to be seen by all in the scandal of the cross.[15] But inasmuch as He lives now throughout all eternity in the true holy of holies in the presence of God, He continually intercedes on our behalf. Thus the cross, which was an unrepeatable historical event, becomes an effective sacrifice for every generation in history, both before it by proleptic promise in the

[13] Rom. 8:34.   [14] Heb. 7:25.
[15] Heb. 9:25.

word of prophets and after it by fulfilled faith in the word of Apostles. Our salvation is "built upon the foundation of the apostles and prophets, Christ Jesus himself being the chief cornerstone."[16]

Through this intercession of the ascended Christ, His priestly office is coupled with His kingly office. "But when Christ had offered for all time a single sacrifice for sins, he sat down at the right hand of God, then to wait until his enemies should be made a stool for his feet."[17]

It is just this paradox of Christ's sacrificial humiliation and His triumphant exaltation that Jesus reveals in His high priestly prayer of John 17. The theme of the whole prayer is *doxa*, the glory of God. He begins with the petition: "Glorify thy Son that the Son may glorify thee." Yet, He has just referred to the hour for which He came into this world, the hour of His death. The violence of the godly scandal is manifest in that God is glorified by the obscene and hateful execution of His Son. Jesus glorified God on earth through His lowly birth, through His coming in our sinful flesh, through his rejection and death. Now, He comes to the moment when He will glorify God in heaven. He has been exalted in the resurrection from the dead, and He sits at the right hand of the Father and rules over heaven and earth, bringing all things into subjection under Him."[18] But His work, as He rules in kingly power, is just this continuous intercession before God. God's glory is none other than Christ's intercessory work.

The rest of the prayer is the petition that God's glory may be given to the elect ones whose names are written in heaven, so that they may be one as Christ and the Father are one. In effect, this amounts to an invocation of the Holy Spirit who is the guide to truth,[19] and truth is revealed not as the wisdom of this world, whether abstract or operational, but the personal, active, unifying love of God suffering for His creatures and drawing them into the same active passion. It is interesting to note here the relation between the intercession of Christ and the Spirit. Paul, in Romans 8, speaks of the intercessory work of the Spirit in such a way that one could almost substitute for it the continuing work of Christ without change of meaning. This is not surprising, when we consider that God is one and any separating distinction would improperly divide the Godhead; but it is clear from the teaching in John that since the ascension, the intercessory work of Christ is God's love as seen from within the veil of the heavenly temple, whereas the in-

---

16 Eph. 2:20.   17 Heb. 10:12, 13.
18 I Cor. 15:25.   19 John 16:13.

tercessory work of the Spirit is the same gracious love as seen working in this world to draw all men to Christ. It is not that Christ is absent from this world, but that only through the Spirit can men confess Him to be Lord.[20]

OUR SHARE IN CHRIST'S INTERCESSION

The concluding application of Christ's intercessory work concerns our share in this intercession. The suffering of Christ is proclaimed as God's glory. Inasmuch as this work is done on our behalf, the Spirit calls and gathers us into the worshiping community which we call the church. Thus the author of Hebrews says: "Therefore, brethren, since we have confidence to enter the sanctuary by the blood of Jesus ... let us draw near with a true heart ... and let us consider how to stir up one another to love and good works, not neglecting to meet together ..."[21] The shape of our response to Christ's intercessory work is the sacrifice of thanksgiving, in which we offer ourselves as living sacrifices. Thus, Paul says to the Colossians: "Now I rejoice in my sufferings for your sake, and in my flesh I complete what is lacking in Christ's affliction for the sake of his body, that is the church ..."[22]

Luther makes the distinction between the sacrifice of atonement and the sacrifice of thanksgiving.[23] Christ's sacrifice is *ephapax*, the all-sufficient sacrifice of atonement. Our share in this intercession is the thankful participation of response, the eucharistic worship commemorating Christ's atoning sacrifice, in which we repeatedly plead His work before the Father and thus provide the context in which the church offers itself in union with Christ's own sacrifice to God. The offering of the church is the graceful stewardship of enacting the truth, of suffering, sacrificing, serving in the world on behalf of the neighbor. This is the true meaning also of Luther's doctrine of the priesthood of all believers. The universal priesthood has nothing to do with a polemic on church polity, but it has everything to do with our share in Christ's intercession. It means that every man in Christ becomes a priest to his neighbor. It is not that every man is his own priest, in any sense of religious individualism, but that through eucharistic oblation in the church every man is able and must be exhorted to become a little Christ (i.e., a Christian) to his neighbor.

[20] I Cor. 12:3.   [21] Heb. 10:19–24.
[22] Col. 1:24.
[23] J. Pelikan: *Luther the Expositor*, p. 238.

It should be clear, in conclusion, that the biblical proclamation of Christ's intercessory work teaches that the glorious suffering of Christ draws us into a participating fellowship, in which peace is made with God and new life is given to His fallen creatures, so that they in turn may glorify God through a joyful suffering in this world. As John says in his first letter: "My little children, I am writing this to you so that you may not sin; but if any one does sin, we have an advocate with the Father, Jesus Christ the righteous."[24] John uses the same word, *parakletos,* to designate Christ as he used in his Gospel to define the function of the Holy Spirit. Thus, whether the work is seen to be oriented to God in heaven or to man on earth, the gracious love of God is always all-sufficient for our needs. We are assured that we have an advocate, One who is called alongside to help us, whether we are strong in our works of love, or weak in our failures of sin. Jesus Christ is our interceding, comforting friend, whose suffering love is for us and the world.

BIBIOGRAPHY

G. Aulén: *Eucharist and Sacrifice*
E. Brunner: *The Mediator*
O. Cullmann: *The Christology of the New Testament*
W. Manson: *The Epistle to the Hebrews*
V. Taylor: *Jesus and His Sacrifice*
———: *The Atonement in New Testament Teaching*

[24] I John 2:1.

25

THE WORK OF

THE HOLY SPIRIT

✚

JOHN F. WALVOORD

John F. Walvoord, President of Dallas Theological Seminary,
Dallas, Texas, received his general and theological education at
Wheaton College (B.A., 1931), Texas Christian University
(M.A., 1945), and the Evangelical Theological College, Dallas,
Texas (Th.B., 1934; Th.D., 1936). He is the author of *The Doc-
trine of the Holy Spirit, The Holy Spirit, The Rapture Ques-
tion,* and *The Millennial Kingdom,* among other works.

The work of the Holy Spirit not only pervades the Scriptures from
Genesis 1 to Revelation 22, but extends to every aspect of divine creation. Abraham Kuyper, the great Dutch theologian, summarized the
work of the Holy Spirit in two significant propositions: "First, the
work of the Holy Spirit is not confined to the elect and does not begin
with their regeneration; but it touches every creation, animate and inanimate, and begins its operations in the elect at the very moment of
their origin. Second, the proper work of the Holy Spirit in every
creature consists in the quickening and sustaining of life with reference
to his being and talents, and, in its highest sense, with reference to

eternal life, which is his salvation."[1] From the standpoint of the importance of the person of the Spirit as the Third Person of the Godhead, from consideration of His extensive works as revealed in the Scriptures, and because the work of the Spirit is integral to every important undertaking of God, the work of the Holy Spirit is a pivotal doctrine of the Scriptures and of systematic theology, and its statement determines any system of theology of which it is a part.

DEFINITION

The Nicene Creed, as amended in 589 A.D., states the faith of the church on the person and work of the Spirit in these words: "And I believe in the Holy Ghost, the Lord and giver of life, who proceedeth from the Father and the Son, who with the Father and Son together is worshipped and glorified." In modern creeds, such as the *Westminster Confession of Faith*, the Spirit of God is defined as one of the three persons of the Godhead, "of one substance, power, and eternity" with the Father and Son. Even Karl Barth, who avoids the word *person* in reference to the Trinity, states of the Spirit: "The Holy Ghost is God the Lord in the fullness of Deity, in the total sovereignty and condescension, in the complete hiddenness and revealedness of God."[2] The personality, deity, procession, and divine attributes of the Holy Spirit are always affirmed in orthodox theology. As Charles Hodge expresses it: "Since the fourth century His true divinity has never been denied by those who admit His personality."[3]

The work of the Holy Spirit, therefore, is the work of God. Every important undertaking of God is related in some way to the ministry of the Holy Spirit. Among the more prominent ministries of the Spirit are those of divine revelation, the inspiration of the Scriptures, the creation of the physical world, the conception of Christ, enablement for spiritual service, the impartation of eternal life to believers, indwelling and baptizing of the saints, miraculous works, the bestowal of spiritual gifts and the revealing of prophecy.

THE HOLY SPIRIT IN THE OLD TESTAMENT

Early in the first chapter of Genesis the Spirit of God is introduced as one who moves upon the face of the waters. John Owen in his clas-

[1] A. Kuyper: *The Work of the Holy Spirit*, p. 46.
[2] K. Barth: *The Holy Ghost and the Christian Life*, p. 11.
[3] C. Hodge: *Systematic Theology*, Volume I, p. 527.

sic work, *A Discourse Concerning the Holy Spirit*, states: "Without Him, all was a dead sea; a rude inform chaos; a confused heap covered with darkness: but by the moving of the Spirit of God upon it, He communicated a quickening prolific virtue."[4] The work of the Spirit in creation seems to be related to its order, as in Genesis 1:2; its design, as in Job 26:13; its life, as in Job 33:4 and Genesis 1:26; and the glory of creation, as in Psalm 33:6 and Psalm 19:1.

The most important work of the Holy Spirit in the Old Testament, however, is in relation to divine revelation and inspiration of the Scriptures. The revelation given to the prophets, as well as that recorded in the Scriptures, is traced to the Holy Spirit.[5] Frequently, the writing of Scriptures themselves is attributed to the inspiration of the Holy Spirit.[6] The Apostle Peter spoke of the Spirit of God as the origin of all prophecy in these words: "For no prophecy ever came by the will of man: but men spake from God, being moved by the Holy Spirit."[7]

Important also in the Old Testament was the ministry of the Holy Spirit to man. In numerous cases, specific enablement for some divine services is attributed to the Holy Spirit.[8] The indwelling ministry of the Holy Spirit in the Old Testament in contrast to the New Testament, however, does not seem to be especially related to spiritual qualities, nor is it necessarily a gift to every believer. In some cases, the indwelling of the Spirit was temporary.[9] The Spirit of God was the source of wisdom, special skills, unusual physical strength, of miracles, and of divine revelation in the Old Testament.

THE HOLY SPIRIT'S RELATION TO CHRIST

The introduction of the ministry of the Holy Spirit in the New Testament is found in His relationship to the virgin birth of Christ. According to Luke 1:35, Christ was begotten of the Holy Spirit and filled with the Holy Spirit from the moment of conception.[10] The ministry of the Holy Spirit to Christ at His baptism by John was not the beginning of this relationship, but rather its declaration. The pub-

[4] J. Owen: *A Discourse Concerning the Holy Spirit*, p. 56.
[5] II Pet. 1:21; cf. II Sam. 23:2; Mic. 3:8.
[6] II Sam. 23:2; Isa. 59:21; Matt. 22:42, 43; cf. Ps. 110:1; Mark 12:36; Acts 1:16; cf. Ps. 41:9; Acts 28:25; cf. Isa. 6:9, 10; Heb. 3:7; 10:15, 16.
[7] II Pet. 1:21.
[8] Gen. 41:38; Exod. 28:3; 31:3; 35:30-35; Num. 11:17, 25; Judges 3:10; 6:34; 11:29; 13:25; 14:6, 19; 15:14; I Sam. 10:9, 10; 16:13; Dan. 4:8; 5:11-14.
[9] I Sam. 16:14; Ps. 51:11.
[10] Isa. 11:2, 3; 42:1-4; 61:1, 2; John 3:34; cf. Luke 1:15.

lic works of Christ, such as His miracles, were attributed to the Holy Spirit in Matthew 12:28 and Luke 4:14, 15, 18. By the Spirit, Christ was anointed to preach.[11] Some evidence may be adduced that the Holy Spirit ministered to Christ in His sufferings and trials leading up to His crucifixion.

THE WORK OF THE HOLY SPIRIT IN SALVATION

One of the major ministries of the Holy Spirit is related to the salvation of the lost. According to John 16:8, the Holy Spirit "when he is come, will convict the world in respect of sin, and of righteousness, and of judgment." The work of the Spirit enters inscrutably in the act of faith in Christ. When a soul enters into the sphere of salvation, he is born of the Spirit or regenerated.[12] The regeneration effected by the Holy Spirit results in the believer's possessing a new nature, a new experience, and also a new safety in Christ.

THE INDWELLING OF THE SPIRIT

Prominent in the New Testament is the doctrine of the indwelling of the Holy Spirit. Christ had predicted in John 14:17 concerning the spirit of truth, "ye know him; for he abideth with you, and shall be in you." This promise of the indwelling of the Spirit was fulfilled on Pentecost, when the indwelling presence of the Spirit became the common possession of all believers. Hence, the possession of the Spirit is essential to salvation.[13] The presence of the Spirit is the seal of God until the day of redemption.[14]

THE BAPTISM OF THE SPIRIT

Prophesied in the Gospels and occurring for the first time on the Day of Pentecost,[15] the baptism of the Spirit is defined in I Corinthians 12:13 as placing the new believer in the body of Christ. It should, herefore, not be confused with regeneration, the indwelling of the Spirit, or the filling of the Spirit.

THE FILLING OF THE SPIRIT

Important and vital is the ministry of the Spirit, decribed as the filling of the Spirit. This important work is given to those who fulfill the

[11] Matt. 12:18–21; cf. Isa. 42:1–4; Luke 4:18–21; cf. Isa. 61:1, 2.
[12] John 1:13; 3:3–7; Rom. 6:13; II Cor. 5:17; Eph. 2:5, 10; Titus 3:5; Jas. 1:18.
[13] Rom. 8:9; Jude 19. [14] Eph. 4:30; cf. Eph. 1:13; II Cor. 1:22.
[15] Acts 1:5; cf. Acts 11:15–17.

the conditions, and is not to be confused with the ministries of the Spirit which are found in every Christian, such as those of regeneration, indwelling, baptism, and sealing of the Spirit. It is a work of the Spirit which may be bestowed repeatedly and also withdrawn. Practically all spiritual experience is related to this aspect of the work of the Spirit.

The basic requirement for the filling of the Spirit is given in Galatians 5:16: "Walk by the Spirit, and ye shall not fulfill the lust of the flesh." The power to overcome the sinfulness of human nature is therefore attributed to the Holy Spirit. Walking by the Spirit implies a constant dependence upon and faith in the delivering power of the Spirit. Though sinless perfection is not promised the one filled by the Spirit, the control and divine grace represented by the experience transforms the life of the recipient. Instead of manifesting the works of the flesh, he produces the fruit of the Spirit: "Love, joy, peace, long-suffering, kindness, goodness, faithfulness, meekness, self-control."[16]

Related to this satisfying experience are the commands: "Quench not the Spirit,"[17] meaning not to resist the Spirit of God; and: "Grieve not the Holy Spirit of God,"[18] referring to a state of disobedience to God and failure to confess sin. The filling of the Spirit is characterized by an unhindering ministry of the Spirit of God to the believer, permitting the work of the Holy Spirit in sanctifying,[19] teaching,[20] guiding,[21] giving assurance,[22] inspiring worship,[23] leading in prayer,[24] and empowering for service.[25] The varied gifts of the Spirit upon individual believers can be used to the full only when empowered by the Spirit of God.

APPLICATION

The secret of all spiritual power for the child of God lies in a proper relationship to the Holy Spirit of God. This is true for the novice as well as the mature saint, for those unusually gifted as well as those with moderate abilities. In the words of Paul: "We received, not the spirit of the world, but the spirit which is from God; that we might know the things that were freely given to us of God. Which things also we speak, not in words which man's wisdom teacheth, but which the Spirit teacheth; combining spiritual things with spiritual words.

16 Gal. 5:22, 23.
17 I Thess. 5:19.
18 Eph. 4:30.
19 Rom. 15:16.
20 John 16:12, 13; I Cor. 2:9; 3:2.
21 Rom. 8:14.
22 Rom. 8:16.
23 Eph. 5:18–20.
24 Rom. 8:26.
25 John 7:38, 39.

Now the natural man receiveth not the things of the Spirit of God: for they are foolishness unto him; and he cannot know them, because they are spiritually judged."[26] In our modern sophisticated world, just as in its counterpart in Corinth, the power of the Spirit working in the heart of man is the difference between human wisdom and divine revelation, human weakness and divine power, carnality and spirituality. Every soul that is saved is born of the Spirit; every revival is a work of the Spirit; every spiritual truth is taught by the Spirit; every holy character is sanctified by the Spirit.

BIBLIOGRAPHY

K. Barth: *The Holy Ghost and the Christian Life*
L.S. Chafer: *Systematic Theology*, Volume VI
L. Gaussen: *Theopneustia*
A. Kuyper: *The Work of the Holy Spirit*
F.E. Marsh: *Emblems of the Holy Spirit*
J. Owen: *A Discourse Concerning the Holy Spirit* [from *The Works of John Owen*, edited by W.H. Goold in four volumes]
R. Pache: *La Personne et l'Oeuvre de Saint-Esprit*
W.H.G. Thomas: *The Holy Spirit of God*
J.F. Walvoord: *The Holy Spirit*

[26] I Cor. 2:12–14.

26

COMMON GRACE

✚

M. EUGENE OSTERHAVEN

M. Eugene Osterhaven, Professor of Systematic Theology at Western Theological Seminary, Holland, Michigan, received his general and theological education at Hope College (B.A., 1937), Western Theological Seminary (B.D., 1941), and Princeton Theological Seminary (Th.D., 1948). He is the author of *Our Knowledge of God According to John Calvin* and *What Is Christian Baptism?*.

In a surprising remark, our Lord once told a group of His disciples that "the children of this world are in their generation wiser than the children of light."[1] Although the latter might wish to dispute that judgment, it is too often only too true. But how can it be, if we assume the truth of the biblical doctrines of sin and of salvation? The "children of this world," Scripture teaches, have had their minds blinded by "the god of this world," whereas the children of light have received "the light of the knowledge of God in the face of Jesus Christ."[2] How then can worldlings carry on so admirably, sometimes, by canons of common sense and decency, and appear to be superior to those whose God is the Lord? This is the question to which the doctrine of common grace addresses itself. It seeks a rationale for the phenomenon of

[1] Luke 16:8.   [2] II Cor. 4:4 ff.

heathen, afar or in our midst, being such "nice people." For if sin is the corrupting influence which Scripture portrays it to be, there must be some explanation for the curbing of its devastating effects where the Gospel of salvation is unknown.

Augustine, that intellectual giant whose influence has been so long felt in the Church, saw the problem when his Pelagian adversaries reminded him of the virtues of the heathen. He had struck gold in his exploration of the Scriptures when he wrought out the evangelical doctrines of sin and saving grace. The laudable deeds of the heathen, however, were an enigma to him, unless they were understood to be nothing other than splendid vices motivated by love of glory and praise or a desire to avoid difficulty.[3] After Augustine, medieval theology substituted the antithesis of *nature* and grace for that of *sin* and grace, with a resulting minimization of the exceeding sinfulness of sin. Man's nature was considered to be still largely intact. There was then no theological problem in the virtues of the heathen or in the accomplishments of the "natural man." Such men do good deeds because their nature is not vitiated by sin, as Augustine had believed it to be, and because considerable health remains in them. The recovery of the biblical doctrine of sin brought the problem back to the Reformers of the sixteenth century. John Calvin, in particular, dealt with it frequently in his writings, and the answer that he gave has entered the broad stream of Reformed theology to become a permanent part of its *corpus* of the faith.

DEFINITION

Common grace is understood to be the unmerited favor of God toward all men whereby (1) He restrains sin so that order is maintained, and culture and civil righteousness are promoted; and (2) He gives them rain and fruitful seasons, food and gladness, and other blessings in the measure that seems to Him to be good. It is evident from this definition that the doctrine of common grace is closely related to a number of other important matters of theological interest. It is directly related to the doctrine of God, for it is concerned with His attitude toward all men, sinners outside His saving grace as well as those within. It is concerned with the problems of philosophy of history and of culture, for it addresses itself to the progress of history and

[3] Augustine: *The City of God*, V, 12–20; *On Marriage and Concupiscence*, I, 4.

the personal and social development of mankind. It is a part of the
broader problem of revelation, for it has to do with God's communication of Himself to mankind and the relation of special to general revelation. Moreover, it is interested in the knotty problem of the relation
of the Christian to the world about him, and of God's general blessings
to mankind in relation to saving grace. Most of these intriguing areas of
investigation can only be mentioned here without elaboration.

A prime consideration in the doctrine of common grace is the
restraint of sin in the lives of individuals and of society. Augustine had
failed to perceive this truth in spite of his usual perceptiveness. "Sins
are not really restrained," he writes, "but some sins are overpowered
by other sins."[4] With clearer insight, Calvin wrote that history demonstrates there have been persons in all ages who have lived laudably
by the guidance of nature (*natura duce*). This, in view of the corruption of humanity through sin, he avers, is a question which must
be resolved. The answer, he adds, is to be found in the fact that human
nature is not totally corrupt (*in totum vitiosam*), because in the midst
of the corruption of nature "there is some room for Divine grace, not
to purify it, but internally to restrain its operations (*intus cohibeat*).
For should the Lord permit the minds of all men to give up the reins
to every lawless passion, there certainly would not be an individual in
the world, whose actions would not evince all the crimes, for which
Paul condemns human nature in general, to be most truly applicable
to him. . . . Some by shame, and some by fear of the laws, are prevented
from running into many kinds of pollutions, though they cannot in any
great degree dissemble their impurity; others, because they think that
a virtuous course of life is advantageous, entertain some languid desires
after it; others go further, and display more than common excellence,
that by their majesty they may confine the vulgar to their duty. Thus
God by his providence restrains the perverseness of our nature from
breaking out into external acts, but does not purify it within."[5] In a
variety of ways, internally and externally, God checks human sin.[6]
In some instances, He ceases His restraining activity and gives men
over to a reprobate mind in order that their sin may work itself out in
its utter godlessness and corruption.[7] Even this, however, shows that

[4] Augustine, *On Marriage and Concupiscence,* I, 4.
[5] J. Calvin: *Institutes,* II, iii, 3.
[6] I Sam. 16:14; II Kings 19:27 f.; Acts 7:42; Rom. 13:1-4; II Thess. 2:6 f.
[7] Rom. 1:24, 26, 28.

previously He had prevented their sin from running its natural course and that He had held it in abeyance.

In their description of fallen man in the state of corruption, the *Canons of the Synod of Dort* read: "There remain, however, in man since the fall, the glimmerings of natural light, whereby he retains some knowledge of God, of natural things, and of the difference between good and evil, and discovers some regard for virtue, good order in society, and for maintaining an orderly deportment."[8] Herein is described a second characteristic of the grace which God gives all men. Although they are "dead in trespasses and sins ... by nature the children of wrath ... aliens ... strangers from the covenants of promise, having no hope, and without God in the world,"[9] they are not utterly forsaken by Him. God continues to give them abundant evidence of His compassion and benignity. By His restraint of sin, He enables science, government, and human culture to develop and flourish. Moreover, He gives men an appreciation for the good, the true, and the beautiful, and a desire to live meaningfully. He enables them to desire and to perform works of civil righteousness. The *Heidelberg Catechism*, like other Reformation statements of faith, declares the natural man to be unable to do any good and inclined to all wickedness,[10] but in his commentaries on the same, its chief author allows for "some traces and remains of moral virtues" and for a "civic" good whose works "promote our temporal welfare."[11] The *Westminster Confession* declares that conversion enables the sinner to will and to do that which is *spiritually* good, with the implication that the unconverted can do good of an inferior quality.[12] This *justitia civilis* does not spring from faith, is not performed with respect to the law or will of God, and is not done to His glory. Hence, it falls short of the scriptural requirement of that which is pleasing to God. Yet it is good of a kind, and it is possible because of the general benevolence and blessing of God toward all men. Even sinners can do *good*, says Jesus,[13] and the sin-

---

[8] *Canons of the Synod of Dort*, III–IV, 4.
[9] Eph. 2:1, 3, 12.   [10] *Heidelberg Catechism*, questions 8, 91.
[11] Z. Ursinus: *Commentary on the Heidelberg Catechism*, question 6; *Schat-Boeck*, Lord's Day III; in the latter, he distinguishes a threefold good the last of which, "spiritual and supernatural good," he declares is meant in the catechism, "In the other an unconverted man can even far excell a regenerated person although he has these [as a common gift] from God."
[12] *Westminster Confession*, chapter IX, 4; cf. *The Canons of Dort*, III–IV, 3: "All men are ... by nature ... incapable of any saving good."
[13] Luke 6:33.

cursed world yet retains something of the *goodness* of Him Whom it should, even though it refuses to, acknowledge as its rightful Lord.

A third evidence of common grace is the natural blessings which God showers on all men.[14] Every good gift is from the Father above[15] and is an evident token of His constant faithfulness and goodness toward all creatures. Not only believers but all men receive and benefit from these gifts from day to day. God means them as blessings, which men should recognize as such, so that the goodness of God will lead them to repentance.[16] That they are not received as such is not due to any lack in gift or giver, but because of impenitent and hard-hearted men who are treasuring up for themselves wrath against the day of wrath and revelation of the righteous judgment of God.[17]

RELATION TO SPECIAL GRACE

The relation of common grace to special grace requires treatment, inasmuch as there are those who claim for both essential similarity, with difference only in degree. Both, it is said, are a part of the saving intention of God; common grace enables a man to repent and believe if he only will, while special grace, working with the will, constrains him to do so. It appears, however, that common grace and special grace are not to be understood as essentially similar; rather, there is essential difference between them. The one merely restrains sin and promotes outward order and righteousness; the other renews the heart and sets man free from sin, to know and to serve the living God. The one retards the destructive power of evil and gives men and society the semblance of moral respectability, goodness, and beatitude; the other is profoundly spiritual in nature and is a resurrection from death to life. Common grace, God's benevolence toward all mankind in spite of sin, does not bring a person to faith in Jesus Christ. As God commanded the light to shine out of darkness, He must sovereignly illumine human hearts, if they are to have the light of the knowledge of the glory of God in the face of Jesus Christ. Such illumination is one aspect of what theology knows as special grace.

In spite of their essential difference, common grace and special grace are related to each other. Both flow from the bountiful loving kindness of God; both come to men through the only mediator between God

---

[14] Ps. 145:9; Matt. 5:44 f.; Luke 6:35 f.; Acts 14–16 f.; Rom. 2:4; I Tim. 4:10.
[15] Jas. 1:17.   [16] Rom. 2:4.
[17] Rom. 2:5 ff.

and men, the man Christ Jesus. Moreover, there is a sense in which common grace is related to the saving work of Christ, for God's gift of salvation is of such magnitude that its blessed effects reach far and wide into human society. This is another way of saying that the beneficent effects of special revelation are not limited to the elect. All in the community of men to whom the message is given benefit from it in some measure. An eminent Scottish divine has rightly said that "important benefits have accrued to the whole human race from the death of Christ, and that in these benefits those who are finally impenitent and unbelieving partake." These benefits, he avers, come from Christ even to unbelieving men "collaterally and incidentally, in consequence of the relation in which men, viewed collectively, stand to each other."[18] There is a general reference—to all men—as well as a particular reference—to the elect alone—in the scriptural teachings concerning the benefits of the atonement of Jesus Christ.

THE CHURCH AND THE WORLD

In their attitude toward the world and its culture the early Christians were, in general, pessimistic. They could expect little from it but persecution and scorn. This attitude gradually changed, however, when the thinking of the church matured. It has been said that this change demonstrates the defection of the early church from the simplicity and glory of the original Gospel. Rather, it should be said that the church had learned that "the earth is the Lord's, and the fullness thereof," and that His children were to try all things and to "hold fast that which is good."

What the early church discovered when it adopted what Herman Bavinck calls the "eclectic procedure in its valuation and assimilation of the existing culture,"[19] the church of today adopts as the legitimate and biblical position. In full recognition of the reality and power of evil, it remains confident of Christ's presence in its midst and of the assurance of final victory over the powers of darkness. The world in which it lives may be no friend to grace, but it is heartened by the apostolic assurance: "All things are yours; and ye are Christ's; and Christ is God's."[20] God has not left the world, even in its lostness, with-

[18] W. Cunningham: *Historical Theology*, volume II, pp. 331 ff.; cf. L. Berkhof: *Reformed Dogmatics*, p. 483; A.A. Hodge: *The Atonement*, p. 358.
[19] H. Bavinck: *Calvin and the Reformation*, "Calvin and Common Grace," p. 101; cf. C. N. Cochrane: *Christianity and Classical Culture*, pp. 213 ff.
[20] I Cor. 3:22 f.

out witness. He is still in it and with it, and He offers as proof of His benevolence the manifold evidence of His common grace.

BIBLIOGRAPHY

H. Bavinck: *De Algemeene Genade*

W.P. Armstrong, ed.: *Calvin and the Reformation: Four Studies by Emile Doumergue and Others*, article "Calvin and Common Grace"

L. Berkhof: *Reformed Dogmatics*

J. Calvin: *Institutes*

C. Hodge: *Systematic Theology*

H. Kuiper: *Calvin on Common Grace*

A. Kuyper: *De Gemeene Gratie*

C. Van Til: *Common Grace*

27

EFFECTUAL CALLING

✛

J. NORVAL GELDENHUYS

J. Norval Geldenhuys, Director of Publications, Dutch Reformed Church, Cape Town, South Africa, received his general and theological education at Pretoria University, South Africa (B.A., 1937; B.D., 1943) and Princeton Theological Seminary (Th.M., 1945). He is the author of *Commentary on the Gospel of St. Luke* and *Supreme Authority*, in addition to works in Dutch and Afrikaans.

God calls every normal human being. He does this through the *vocatio realis*—*realis* because this general call comes not through words but through *res* (things), namely, nature, history (of individuals and nations), and conscience.[1]

However great and important the influence of this *vocatio realis* is, no one can ever come to a saving knowledge of the triune God through this general, external call. Through the *vocatio realis* man is rendered without excuse[2] if he does not worship and obey Him Whose majesty, eternal power, and divinity speak to all through his mighty works in nature, in history, and in human life and conscience. But the *vocatio realis* does not proclaim the good tidings of great joy[3] for all who believe in Jesus Christ as the Son of God and as the divine Saviour.

[1] Cf. Rom. 1:20; 2:14, 15; Job 37:14; 38:1–42:6; Ps. 8:2, 4; 19:1–4; 46:11; 104.
[2] Rom. 1:20.   [3] Luke 2:10.

For the salvation of sinners there is an urgent need for much more than the *vocatio realis* can offer. And now it is the glory of the Christian faith that it unequivocally proclaims that Almighty God, who through the *vocatio realis* has called and is continually calling all to a realization of His divine majesty and omnipotence, through His Word calls sinners to repentance and to salvation. This calling to a saving faith in Jesus Christ, the Lord, through the authoritative Word of God is designated the *vocatio verbalis*. This external calling through the Gospel is to be proclaimed to all nations[4] as an earnest invitation and urgent summons that everyone should repent and believe in Him Who is the all-sufficient Saviour.

But to have practical effect in the life of man, the *vocatio verbalis* must, as it were, break through into the mind, will and heart—the innermost being—of man. For this is needed the "effectual calling," *vocatio efficax.*

DEFINITION

The effectual calling must be clearly differentiated not only from the *vocatio realis* but also from the *vocatio verbalis*. God as the Lord of nature, of man, and of history most decidedly can and does use the *vocatio realis* and in a very special sense the *vocatio verbalis* in the life of men. The proclamation of the Gospel is used by Him as a glorious means to bring us to a true faith in and knowledge of the triune God. The *vocatio verbalis* is, however, in itself not sufficient to achieve this. It cannot bring the spiritually dead to true life in communion with God.

For the lost sinner to become the reborn child of God, the effectual calling is needed, that calling of the living, sovereign, and almighty God which makes us partakers of the life eternal which Jesus Christ has earned for us.

By effectual calling we thus understand that mysterious, divine, and humanly inexplicable act of God through the Holy Spirit, which brings us into living fellowship with Jesus Christ, our Lord.

EXPOSITION

Scripture and practical experience leave no doubt about the fact that of the many to whom the Gospel is proclaimed, only a small minority accept Jesus Christ as personal Saviour.

Our Lord Himself said, "Many are called but few are chosen."[5]

---

4 Matt. 28:19; 24:14; Mark 16:15.　　5 Matt. 22:14.

Scriptures teaches that all mankind is guilty before the holy, right-eous God and that we are totally incapable of saving ourselves. Un-redeemed man is spiritually blind and dead and unable to regenerate or truly to convert himself.

In this sense, the teaching of the Bible is the most pessimistic and realistic teaching in the world. Fallen, sinning man *is* spiritually lost and completely incompetent to save himself.

How, then, can we, who are in ourselves helplessly lost sinners, ever be united to Christ in saving communion?

The New Testament leaves no doubt regarding the reply to this question. It clearly and consistently teaches us that through the sov-ereign and omnipotent power and grace of God, we are effectually called to become the inheritors of the salvation wrought by God through Jesus Christ. Thus, for instance, Paul writes the following: "... the power of God; who saved us, and called us with a holy calling, not according to our works, but according to his own purpose and grace."[6] Compare also I Peter 1:3. And in I Corinthians 1:26-30, Paul emphatically dismisses any idea that Christians themselves deserved to become the children of God. He writes: "For behold your calling, brethren, how that not many wise after the flesh, not many mighty, not many noble, *are called* ... that no flesh should glory before God."

From these and other New Testament declarations, it is clear that by "calling" in these cases is meant not merely an invitation, but that mysterious, glorious, and efficacious act of God through the Holy Spirit which brings man into true, dynamic fellowship with Jesus Christ. Therefore, it is rightly called "a heavenly calling"[7]—God is the all-sufficient cause, origin, and executor of the calling. How God ac-complishes this is beyond human comprehension, and why He acts thus only in the case of some to whom the *vocatio verbalis* comes is not within the limited sphere of human understanding. "The wind bloweth where it listeth, and thou hearest the voice thereof, but knowest not whence it cometh, and whither it goeth: so is every one that is born of the Spirit."[8]

In the Gospels, "call" is often used merely in the sense of "invite." But in the Epistles, the word is mostly used in the sense of "summon-ing, commanding" and at the same time "effecting, causing to be, prevailing." To call ($\kappa\alpha\lambda\epsilon\iota\nu$), in the Epistles means in substance "to appoint one to salvation."

[6] II Tim. 1:9.   [7] Heb. 3:1.
[8] John 3:8.

When considering the teaching of the Word of God regarding the effectual calling of sinners by the power and grace of God, we are in a field where we stand with awe before the mystery of the eternal love, holiness, grace, and wisdom of God. We cannot precisely define or describe the work of the Creator which makes possible the existence of life even in the mere physical sphere. How much less can we explain or express in human words the wonder of that effectual calling of God, through which He in His omnipotent grace and love makes us partakers of His eternal salvation in Jesus Christ! It is futile and even misplaced to try to analyze or describe this divine act. We must confess our total inability to understand this great, divine mystery. But as a tree is known by its fruit, we can also learn much regarding the divine act of God through which He calls lost and helpless sinners effectually to true life, by looking at the fruits of this divine calling.

Sin broke the bond of fellowship between the sinner and God. But through the divine act of God, we are "called into the fellowship of his Son Jesus Christ our Lord."[9] The effectual calling is thus that divine act by which the spiritual blindness of the unredeemed is removed, so that Jesus Christ is seen and embraced as the true Saviour and Son of God. The intellect of man is freed from the bondage of sin and spiritual ignorance, which formed an impenetrable barrier between him and Jesus Christ, and with renewed heart and will the called Christian is united with the Saviour in intimate fellowship. Before God called us, we wandered on our own way and revolted against Christ; but through His effectual calling, we are enabled to obey willfully and gladly Him who as of old still calls every Christian: "Follow Me!" Through the divine calling, which is not a mere invitation but an act of God that makes us listen to and obey Christ, we thus become true disciples of the Son of God. And so the broken fellowship between us and the triune God is gloriously restored. Through His calling, we are effectually drawn truly and freely by faith to accept, to love, and to serve Christ as our personal Saviour and Lord.

So intimate is the fellowship between those thus effectually called and God, that they are designated as people "beloved in God the Father, and kept for Jesus Christ,"[10] as "holy,"[11] "beloved of the Lord,"[12] "a holy nation, a people for God's own possession."[13]

This wonderful privilege of being so intimately united to God in

[9] I Cor. 1:9; cf. I Cor. 1:23, 24.   [10] Jude 1.
[11] Heb. 3:1.   [12] II Thess. 2:13.
[13] I Pet. 2:9.

His Son is in no sense our own doing or a right that we deserve. We do not achieve it ourselves. God bestows it. It is given to us unmerited through His grace, and solely because "God is faithful, through whom ye were called into the fellowship of his Son Jesus Christ our Lord."[14]

Through the effectual calling, God enlightens our minds to see and accept the truth of the Gospel,[15] changes our defiled hearts so that we come to Him with sincere repentance and conviction of sin, and gives to our erring, sinful wills a new and Godward direction. Through the effectual calling, man is not dehumanized, but his whole personality is freed and energized to enable him to live a new, sanctified life. Old inabilities are abolished, and new abilities to love and serve God are given. The blinding effects of sin on our minds are removed, so that our intellect no longer leads us astray but is recreated to be a trustworthy instrument for apprehending truth[16] and believing the Gospel.[17] Thus, through the effectual calling, our mind, heart, and will are regenerated to true holiness. And for this cause is Jesus Christ "the mediator of a new covenant, that ... they that have been called, may receive the promise of the eternal inheritance."[18]

The purpose of God with this effectual calling is, however, not merely to enlighten, renovate, enrich, and eternally save the lives of believers, but is in highest instance meant to proclaim the glory of God in Christ. Or to say it in the words of Peter: "that ye **may** shew forth the excellencies of him who called you out of the darkness into his marvelous light."[19]

We cannot know how or when God calls us in such an effectual way, nor can we exactly define the connection between the *vocatio verbalis* and this *vocatio efficax*, or the relationship between effectual calling and regeneration, but the New Testament leaves no doubt as to the fact that God is in no way, regarding the effectual calling, dependent on the merits, preparedness, or worthiness of man or of any human instrument. God "called us by his own glory and virtue."[20] The triune God Himself is the sole cause of and instrument in this calling.

For this reason the effectual calling has such a rich and wonderful meaning for time and eternity and gives believers the necessary as-

---

[14] I Cor. 1:9.   [15] Eph. 1:18.
[16] Cf. I Cor. 1:23, 24.   [17] II Thess. 2:14.
[18] Heb. 9:15.   [19] I Pet. 2:9, 10.
[20] I Pet. 1:3.

surance for the future, for "faithful is he that calleth you, who will also do it."[21]

The effectual calling of God is not an afterthought of the Almighty, but is grounded in His eternal purpose. Paul gives classic expression to this truth in his well-known words: "all things work together for good, *even* to them that are called according to *his* purpose. For whom he foreknew, he also foreordained *to be* conformed to the image of of his Son, ... and whom he foreordained, them he also called, and whom he called, them he also justified ..."[22]

The salvation of believers is "not of works, but of him that calleth; ... that he might make known the riches of his glory upon vessels of mercy, which he afore prepared unto glory, *even* us, whom he also calleth ..."[23]

That the effectual, irresistible calling of God, however, does not annul or abrogate the personal responsibility of believers is clearly and consistently taught by the Word of God. Thus, Paul writes to Timothy: "Fight the good fight of faith, lay hold on the life eternal, whereunto thou wast called ..."[24] And Jesus said: "Enter ye in by the narrow gate."[25]

Belief that the effectual calling is grounded in the eternal purpose of God is not a pagan fatalism nor does it cause moral laxity, spiritual pride, or religious apathy. On the contrary, as Paul says of himself: "Not that I have already obtained or am already made perfect: but I press on, if so be that I may apprehend that for which also I was apprehended by Christ Jesus. . . . I press on toward the goal unto the prize of the high [or upward] calling of God in Christ Jesus."[26]

Because the calling of God in Christ through the Holy Spirit imparts such glorious gifts to the elect,[27] Christians are earnestly called upon "to walk worthy of the calling wherewith ye were called."[28]

CONCLUSION

Thus Scripture teaches that the effectual calling is the sovereign, free, and irresistible act of God in Christ, through his Spirit, by which guilty, lost sinners without merit of their own are brought into living and saving fellowship with Jesus Christ, our Lord. It proclaims equally

21 I Thess. 5:24.
23 Rom. 9:11, 23, 24.
25 Matt. 7:13.
27 Cf. Rev. 17:14.

22 Rom. 8:28–30; cf. John 10:27–30.
24 I Tim. 6:12.
26 Phil. 3:12–14.
28 Eph. 4:1; cf. II Pet. 1:10, 11.

clearly our grave, inescapable, personal responsibility to cling in faith to and to obey Him, who alone is the Author of our salvation.

We cannot explain the mystery of divine calling and human responsibility, but with Peter we rejoice that "the God of all grace, who called you ... shall himself perfect, stablish, strengthen you."[29] And with Paul we "give thanks ... for you, brethren beloved of the Lord, that God chose you from the beginning unto salvation in sanctification of the Spirit and belief of the truth: whereunto he called you through our Gospel, to the obtaining of the glory of our Lord Jesus Christ."[30]

And they that are, through the effectual calling, united to Him, the Lord of lords and the King of kings, shall finally triumph because they are "with him, called and chosen and faithful."[31]

BIBLIOGRAPHY

K. Barth: *Die kirchliche Dogmatik*
J. Calvin: *Institutes*
C. Hodge: *Systematic Theology*

[29] I Pet. 5:10, 11.   [30] II Thess. 2:13, 14; cf. John 10:27–29.
[31] Rev. 17:14.

28

REGENERATION

✦

OTTO MICHEL

Otto Michel, Professor of New Testament at Tübingen University, Germany, received his general and theological education at the universities of Halle and Tübingen. He is the author of *Prophet und Märtyrer, Kommentar zum Hebräerbrief, Die christliche Hoffnung,* and *Kommentar zum Römerbrief,* among other works.

The New Testament idea of God's begetting, which has anticipations in the Qumran sect and in the baptismal movements of the Jordan area, incorporates a familiar Jewish term. John 3:3, 7, for example, speaks of begetting "from above" (thus paraphrasing the name of God which the Jews piously avoided). Christians of the Johannine type believed that thereby the living God Himself had entered into history, had encountered man in his innermost being, and had recreated him. This concept, which neither orthodox Jews nor Gnostics could understand, is a unique feature of Christianity.

By repeating the initial word, Jesus gives special significance to His statement in John 3:3: "Amen, amen, I say to you; unless one is begotten from above, he cannot see the kingdom of God." Jesus is here demanding from Nicodemus a thoroughgoing change of life, a "turning around," as the precondition of seeing the kingdom of God—

the very thing that Nicodemus, the teacher of Israel, found it difficult to do.

According to John 3:5, a second "amen" word, God's begetting is effected by water and spirit. John attaches most weight to the gift of the Spirit, which brought enlightenment and understanding.

Mysticism, philosophy, and sacramental traditions have always misunderstood the mystery of the Spirit of God, and we should not allow ourselves to be guided by them. Jesus Himself shows what is meant, for He is the one Who actually possessed the Spirit, was conceived by Him, lived in His power, and by Him was made perfect. Thus, the Johannine proclamation of God's begetting is exclusively centered in Jesus Christ. John shows how life led by the power of the Spirit is life lived in simple obedience to the word of the Father:[1] the way of faith, love, righteousness, and of turning from evil.

The full implication of the Johannine position is seen when compared with that of the Teacher of Righteousness, who had previously established in Qumran a religious community which set itself off sharply against its environment. Here, the disciples of Jesus remain in the profane world without being able to protect themselves, but sustained by an invisible reality and by their communion with God. God's begetting in John is related to the apostolic idea of "re-begetting" which appears in a hellenistic tradition. There is the same emphasis on a new beginning: "Blessed be the God . . . who . . . begat us again unto a living hope by the resurrection of Jesus Christ from the dead."[2]

Here, apparently, is a vivid picture which had its setting in Christian baptism and depicts the salvation which, granted to the church by the Word, can set the individual and the church in a new existence. The latter is, however, secondary to the Word and to the salvation which determine it. Easter is now presupposed. The church is sheltered by its steadfast faith in the resurrection of Jesus Christ.

But the church must not declare the Word and the salvation otherwise than it occurred within the scope of the apostolic tradition. The language may vary, the course of history may require other forms of expressing the proclamation, but the power of the Spirit remains to preserve the historic ground of revelation from false claims and dangerous reconstructions. The preservation of the new existence is at stake. In New Testament times, the church was still neither old nor worldly.

The Pauline conception of salvation as justification presupposes that

[1] John 4:34.   [2] I Pet. 1:3; cf. I Pet. 1:23.

the sinner is pardoned. With that promise, God created a new cosmic situation for mankind. But Paul accepted also the principle: "Therefore, if any one is in Christ, he is a new creation..."[3]—a sentence with a doxological note.

The concept of God's begetting in the thought of John, however, is the strongest way to emphasize the spiritual source, power, and objective of the Christian status, and to delimit it from other possibilities, for the two opposites—begetting by God and descent from the devil—are possible, and run right through the middle of the church. The individual's attitude toward sin determines his position.[4] Thus, the church is not closed off from the evil one: it must prove itself in and through struggle to be "children of the light." Thus, Johannine thought presupposes a tremendous power within the church to detach itself from everything contrary to the Spirit of God, not in order to disengage the church from the world,[5] but to testify to the Spirit of God in the decisions of earthly life.

While justification tends to stress the solidarity of men under the cross, and to praise exclusively the grace of God, God's begetting underscores the contrast between spirit and flesh. That, finally, only God Himself can distinguish the "children of light" from the "children of darkness" is basic to the New Testament.

THE DEVELOPMENT OF THE DOGMATIC TRADITION

For Martin Luther, the center of the New Testament was justification; upon it the preaching of the Gospel converged; by it was shaped the life of the church. Rebirth was nothing other than this very justification. In Jesus' conversation with Nicodemus, said Luther, He imposed no new law upon men; His concern was that man should become new.

Fundamentally, the various Lutheran creeds rest upon these insights of Luther. It is notable, however, that the *Formula of Concord* admits another view, which extends rebirth beyond justification to include the renewal subsequently worked by the Holy Spirit in those justified by faith. Thus, rebirth is conceived as a consequence of justification.

That brings with it the danger of subjectivizing the concept of rebirth, until it no longer describes the act of God upon man, but

[3] II Cor. 5:17.   [4] I John 3:4-12.
[5] Bultmann.

rather what happens in man. The question then rises whether one can take seriously the close relation of rebirth and justification in Titus 3:5 f. Some scholars, considering that the grace in baptism must be something other than the grace in justification, seek a way to reinterpret it sacramentally—a dangerous step dictated by practical exigency, but fraught with difficulty. Even those movements which want to help the church, such as Pietism, shift the main importance from justification to conversion and rebirth, a shift evident also in the theology of Erlangen.

The creeds of the Reformed church are less troubled by these problems. In them, the development of faith in man stood, from the beginning, more in the center of dogmatic consideration. In view of concern, moreover, to make divine election certain, rebirth helps in the understanding of salvation. Further, the justification of Jesus Christ is imparted to an individual. Thus, both rebirth and justification are interdependent corollaries. Methodism, with its insistence on an authentic experience of conversion and rebirth, is nearer to the Reformed than to the Lutheran tradition.

However, in nineteenth-century Lutheranism, the question of the assurance of faith took on theological urgency. Upon my answer to the question, Have I been born again?, depends the confidence with which I may call myself a Christian. When doubt assails, says Frank, a man can appeal to the experience of his rebirth. His new "ego" finds assurance within his own self.

Again and again, voices have registered their misgivings about subjectivizing faith, and have recalled the church to the objectivity of God's saving acts in history. But their concept of objectivity often hurried too quickly over unrest arising from the rethinking of theological statements, from scientific and philosophical knowledge, and from life's own problems with faith. Therefore, it is to be regarded with as much reservation as the struggle of pious people for subjective assurance.

In the apostolic message, God's begetting, rebirth, and the new creation were referred back to a "turning around" and to the gift of the Spirit of God. But these doctrines were largely left out of consideration in the development of dogmatic theology and of church history. Fear of enthusiastic fanaticism was a restraining factor, from the outset of the Reformation, and only after revival movements accentuating conversion and the gift of the Holy Spirit let a new sense of reality break forth were these decisive concepts of the Bible grasped anew.

J.T. Beck of Tübingen renewed interest in such biblical concepts as repentance, conversion, rebirth, and justification. He stressed the new creation of man, and spoke of reception of and begetting by the Spirit. A man does not get a new soul in rebirth; his soul is recreated by the Spirit. Philosophical motives dominated for the most part in Beck's day, but he relied on the Bible and tried to relate its individual themes to the total picture. He knew that a coherent view of biblical grace was represented in every biblical concept.

Emil Brunner, of the dialectical theology school, emphasizes that the picture of the new creation can be understood only in terms of revelation and of faith. Of himself, man suffers from "sickness unto death."[6] Sinful nature leads to despair, but sin and despair are in the last analysis the same, for we suffer from an inner contradiction which none but the Creator can overcome.

The different views of Protestant theologians show the confusion of method in which we find ourselves. We see fundamentally that only where biblical statements are acknowledged is rebirth given earnest consideration. Reformation theology has tended to push justification into the foreground and to append rebirth to it, but this distracts from the significance of Johannine theology, which speaks deliberately and insistently of God's begetting. Seldom is the revolutionary power in the contradiction between spirit and flesh, between child of God and child of the devil even taken seriously.

We should have the courage to separate justification and God's begetting, as they originally were, and to let each achieve its full significance apart from the other. Their forced and false association has hurt both.

NEW REFLECTION OF THE PRESENT

Rabbinical-Jewish existence is represented by instruction, law, and circumcision; primitive-Christian and Johannine existence, on the other hand, was characterized by the action of the Word at the end of time, which disclosed itself in "water and spirit."

While justification puts grace and forgiveness in the foreground, the connection of water and spirit expresses the power of God, which penetrates into this world of conflicting forces. That occurred prima-

[6] Kierkegaard.

rily in Jesus Himself, who was declared by the voice of God to be begotten of God.[7] Jesus' begetting by God sustained His life and constituted His messianic mission. The begotten one of God represented the concealed and future Messiah of Israel. For us, also, to be called of Jesus assigns us a destiny which we must lay hold of and follow through.

In the process, the individual is not left to himself and not merely referred back to the word of the Law of Israel, but is put under the impact of the Word, which occurred in the fullness of times.

Of course, God's begetting makes a historical start. It may pass through the most varied crises and be threatened with death. Yet, it is empowered and sustained of God, so that it can penetrate through weakness and defeat and everything that would hinder or obstruct its way.

The difficulty within theology lies in the fact that with rebirth one tends to concentrate upon the arrival of life, when the New Testament speaks of the Holy Spirit as the power of God which must make its way. The doctrine of justification cannot, therefore, substitute for the tradition of God's begetting, but the relation is one of healthy tension rather than of contradiction.

Unfortunately, the Christian church has lost the sense of God's begetting in favor of rebirth as an experience happening arbitrarily and psychologically; that misunderstands the major stress in the biblical concept. Perhaps the idea of sexuality connected with begetting is offensive to many a person, but this is an essential element of the Bible; it takes us back as nothing else can to the ground and process of life.

The concept of God's begetting stands as a radical rejection of every philosophical devaluation of the idea of God. God creates and effects reality, is not that reality itself, nor is He subordinated to it, as existential theology affirms.[8] We should not capitulate to such theology which subordinates the message of the Bible to philosophical theories, but rather examine existential contentions in terms of the Bible.

The Johannine statements concerning God's begetting are intended to make us, as Christians, strong over against all that is natural and worldly, and that does not submit itself to the claim of God. They are intended to enlighten us in opposition to those theological streams which no longer live from God, but direct their attention to the ex-

---

[7] Cf. Ps. 2:7; Mark 1:11.   [8] Tillich, Fuchs.

istence of pious or impious men. For God is the actual center of theology, upon Whom everything depends. He is not a term for that which lies beyond human limitations or a description of human transcendence.[9]

Here, we reach the sorest point in the whole of the present discussion and one which inevitably confronts us with the question, Do we still believe in a creating and begetting God?

BIBLIOGRAPHY

O. Michel: *Festschrift für Joachim Jeremias,* "Von Gott Gezeugt"

K. Barth: *Die kirchliche Dogmatik,* IV, "Die Lehre von der Versöhnung

J.T. Beck: *Vorlesungen über christliche Ethik,* I

E. Brunner: *Dogmatik,* III, "Die christliche Lehre von der Kirche vom Glauben und von der Vollendung"

[9] Bultmann.

29

REPENTANCE

AND CONVERSION

✚

JULIUS R. MANTEY

Julius R. Mantey, former Professor of New Testament at Northern Baptist Theological Seminary, Chicago, Illinois, received his general and theological education at Southern Baptist Theological Seminary, Louisville, Kentucky (Th.D., Ph.D.), William Jewell College (B.A.), and Union University, Union, Tennessee (D.D.). He is the author of *Was Peter a Pope?* and *A Manual Grammar of the Greek New Testament: A Hellenistic Greek Reader.*

The Chicago *Daily News* recently reported that Billy Graham, in talking about what Americans need most, stated: "It is absolutely impossible to change society and to reverse the moral trend unless we ourselves are changed from the inside out. Man needs transformation or conversion.... Our only way to moral reform is through repentance of our sins and a return to God."

The Old Testament in no uncertain terms reiterates the same truth over and over again. A representative and very specific statement to that effect is found in II Chronicles 7:14: "If my people, who are called by my name, shall humble themselves, and pray, and seek my face, and turn from their wicked ways; then will I hear from heaven and will forgive their sin and will heal their land."

MEANING OF REPENTANCE AND CONVERSION IN THE NEW TESTAMENT

Two Greek words are translated as repentance. *Metamelomai* has the basic connotation of feeling different, or remorse.[1] Judas repented only in the sense of remorse, not with the idea of abandoning sin. Paul used this word with such a meaning.[2] *Metanoeo* (*metanoia*, noun) is regularly used to express the requisite state of mind necessary for the forgiveness of sin. It means to think differently or to have a different attitude toward sin and God, etc.

For conversion, *strepho* (*strophe*, noun), the root word, is used twice: Matthew 18:3, "Unless you become *converted* and become as little children you will not enter into the kingdom of heaven"; John 12:40, "become *converted*, and I will heal them." The preposition prefix *epi* occurs on the word in the other passages where the sense of conversion is expressed. The basic idea of the word is to turn, and in most passages, where it denotes conversion, it is used in the active voice.

THE USAGE OF THESE WORDS IN THE NEW TESTAMENT

In two passages in the New Testament both of these words occur, and in both cases the word for repentance precedes the other. Acts 3:19, "Therefore *repent* and *turn* (be converted) in order that your sins may be blotted out, so that seasons of refreshing may come from the presence of the Lord"; Acts 26:20, "that they should *repent* and *turn* to God and perform deeds worthy [i.e., expressive] of repentance."

In the above quotations we note that both words are used to describe an experience which has two aspects, namely that of turning away from displeasing God to pleasing Him. And both words are used to denote the human volition and act by which man, convicted of sin by the Holy Spirit, determines to make his life conform to the will of God. Regeneration and justification are terms that denote God's part in transforming an individual, while the words faith, repentance, and

---

[1] Matt. 21:29, 32; 27:3.   [2] II Cor. 7:8.

conversion are used to express man's necessary response to Christ and God, if regeneration is to be experienced.

Repentance without turning one's life over to God does not obtain remission of sins, neither does turning one's life over to God without repentance, as we shall indicate, bring remission of sins. Thus, it is obvious that the two words deal with the right commitment of one's self to God, with the definite intent of doing His will as long as life lasts. But before one makes such a life-transforming and epoch-making decision, he of necessity must have faith, believing that God "rewards those who seek him."[3] An example of this is cited in Acts 11:21, "a great number that believed *turned* to the Lord."

THE EMPHASIS PLACED ON
REPENTANCE IN THE NEW TESTAMENT

Mark 1:4, 5: "John the baptizer appeared in the wilderness, preaching a baptism of repentance [i.e., a baptism expressive of repentance, genitive of description in Greek] for the forgiveness of sins. And all the country of Judea and all the people of Jerusalem were going out to him, and, confessing their sins, they were being baptized in the river Jordan."

Luke 3:7–14: "Who warned you, you serpent's brood, to escape from the wrath to come? See that you do something to show that your hearts are really changed [*metanoias*]! Don't start thinking that you can say to yourselves, 'We are Abraham's children,' for I tell you that God could produce children of Abraham out of these stones! The ax already lies at the root of the tree, and the tree that fails to produce good fruit is cut down and thrown into the fire.

"Then the crowds would ask him, 'Then what shall we do?' And his answer was, 'The man who has two shirts must share with the man who has none, and the man who has food must do the same.'

"Some of the tax collectors also came to him to be baptized, and asked him, 'Master, what are we to do?' 'You must not demand more than you are entitled to,' he replied.

"And the soldiers asked him, 'And what are we to do?' 'Don't bully people, don't bring false charges, and be content with your pay,' he replied."[4]

Matt. 3:5-12 is closely parallel to the statement in Mark and Luke, except that Luke has gone into greater detail in pointing out how the crowds, the tax collectors, and the soldiers were to demonstrate gen-

[3] Heb. 11:6.   [4] J.B. Phillips' translation.

uine repentance in their respective spheres of activity in society by using their time, talents, substance, and social position to serve others.

All three of the synoptic writers, we note, picture John the Baptist as being adamant in demanding real repentance and insisting on the expression of it in everyday living. They made it clear that being a descendant of Abraham was not enough, that fleshly descent would not abate God's wrath. Any Israelite who did not repent became subject to the severe judgment of God. But, apparently, John also preached the necessity of openly and publicly confessing sins before or at the time of baptism, for both Mark and Matthew state that the baptismal candidates were confessing their sins. Furthermore, the repentance that was demanded was not to be only personal and negative, a cessation of sinning, but it was also to be social and positive.

But we are indebted mostly to Luke for the detailed and specific spelling out of how one's repentance should and can be expressed in helpful acts of service to others. Jesus, like John, stressed the need of repentance and true conversion. "By their fruits you shall know them. Not everyone who says to me, Lord, Lord, shall enter the kingdom of heaven, but he who does the will of my Father who is in heaven."[5]

REPENTANCE A PREREQUISITE
TO BAPTISM IN THE NEW TESTAMENT

Wherever any details are given either by direct statement or by inference, repentance (also faith) was regarded as a necessary prerequisite to baptism, according to the New Testament record. In Acts 2:38, the priority of repentance to baptism is stated very definitely: "*Repent* and be baptized every one of you in the name of Jesus Christ for the forgiveness of your sins." And certainly it can be stated with less fear of contradiction that repentance was always regarded as a necessary prerequisite to forgiveness as the above passage implies. Note also Luke 13:5, 24:27; Acts 8:22, 17:30.

The Philippian jailer demonstrated his repentance before being baptized, by his washing and treating the wounds of Paul and Silas.[6] And since baptism in apostolic times was a public confession of faith in Christ, it was very unlikely that anyone who had not repented and experienced regeneration would submit to baptism. For among both Jews and Gentiles, hostility to the point of severe persecution at times was experienced by new converts to Christianity. Social pressure was

---

[5] Matt. 7:20, 21.   [6] Acts 16:33.

so intense against becoming a Christian that people would not have had the courage to break with family and community traditions and customs unless the grace of God had been experienced in their lives. And repentance was a necessary prerequisite to that.

A correct interpretation of two expressions in the Greek New Testament throws additional light on this phase of the subject. One, *baptisma metanoias*, baptism of repentance, occurs four times: Mark 1:4; Luke 3:3; Acts 13:24; 19:4. The word translated repentance in this phrase is in the genitive case and is descriptive in function. It was a *repentance* baptism, i.e., the baptism was characterized by and expressive of repentance. And, without question, the Lukan context in which the phrase occurs makes it very definite that baptism was not administered without some evidence of repentance. The Pharisees and Sadducees, the religious and political leaders at that time, who came to John for baptism, were called a "brood of vipers" and were told to "bear fruits that befit *repentance*."[7] Or in other words, John refused to baptize them on the grounds that they were not fit candidates for it. "John demands proof from these men of the new life before he administers baptism to them."[8]

The other expression is in Matthew 3:11 and is translated in the RSV, "I baptize you with (*in*, Greek) water for *repentance*." The Greek preposition, translated *for* above, is *eis*, and is used to denote cause, at times, in the Greek of the first century and in the New Testament. Our word *for* can be used to express cause; for instance, "He was arrested for stealing." In at least four modern speech translations, *eis* is translated as having causal significance in Matthew 3:11. In Weymouth, it is *on profession of*; in Goodspeed it is *in token of*; in William it is *to picture*; and in Phillips it is *as a sign of*—all of these are causal in force.[9]

REPENTANCE AND CONVERSION IN EVERYDAY LIFE

As is generally known, people do not repent and become converted until they know that they are sinners and that they need the Saviour.

[7] RSV, Luke 3:7–8.

[8] A.T. Robertson: *Word Pictures in the New Testament*, Volume I, p. 8.

[9] The most exhaustive and recent scholarly discussion on the causal use of *eis* in Matt. 3:11 and in the Greek of New Testament times is found in the *Journal of Biblical Literature*. Four articles appeared on the subject: three in 1951 in Volume LXX, and one in 1952 in Volume LXXI. Two were by Ralph Marcus of the University of Chicago, two by J. B. Mantey. Numerous examples from secular and sacred Greek were cited to illustrate how *eis* was used with causal significance.

Hence, as a precursor to salvation, people of necessity must become informed of the salient elements of the Gospel. Until they realize that they are shortchanging themselves and are jeopardizing their future, that they have brought the eternal wrath of God upon themselves, there is little likelihood of their becoming convicted and turning to Christ as Saviour. Consequently, there is urgency that every means available should be used to proclaim and to live the Gospel, so as to lay the groundwork for the Holy Spirit to use the truth so disseminated to induce conviction and conversion. Jesus depicted graphically and bluntly the terrible doom that awaits the impenitent: "And they will go away into eternal punishment, but the righteous into eternal life."[10]

Not only do men need to know that their sins will bring the inescapable judgment of God upon themselves, but also that they can never enjoy life in its fullness here and now until they become converted and experience God's marvelous transforming grace. Jesus offered a better existence when he declared, "I came that they may have life and have it abundantly."[11] And he promised: "that my joy may be in you, and that your joy may be full ... and your sorrow will turn into joy ... and no one will take your joy from you."[12] And the Apostle Paul described this experience in these words: "Wherefore if any one is in Christ he is a new creature; the old has passed away, behold it has become new."[13]

The only normal man is the converted man. Only then is he most free from the tensions and frustrations of life. He is most likely to be at peace with both God and men. Then only does he enjoy in its fullness a clear conscience and freedom from guilt and fear. For the first time he is living in harmony with God's will for his life. The realization that God's favor is upon him and that "all things will work together for his good" cheers his spirit and fills his life with joyful expectancy. Like the Psalmist, he visualizes as his possession the "goodness and mercy" of God and expects to "dwell in his house forever."

Erik Routley in *The Gift of Conversion*, in describing the benefits of conversion, has stated: "Personality is not blurred or made negative in conversion. On the contrary, the converted man is more of a person than he was. The tension between what he is and what he would wish to appear to his neighbors is eased, and the result is a simpler, more direct, more clearly drawn personality. Confusion is replaced by in-

[10] Matt. 25:46.   [11] John 10:10.
[12] John 15:11; 16:21, 22.   [13] II Cor. 5:17.

tegration and harmony." In Galatians 5:23, the Apostle Paul has mentioned nine exceedingly precious acquisitions of life and character that become one's immediate or potential possession when he is truly converted: "love, joy, peace, patience, kindness, goodness, faithfulness, gentleness, self-control." How lovely life would be if we and all our associates always manifested such gracious characteristics!

> *Sinners, turn, why will you die?*
> *God, your Saviour, asks you—Why?*
> *He who did your souls retrieve,*
> *Died himself that you might live.*
> *Will you let him die in vain?*
> *Crucify your Lord again?*
> *Why, you ransomed sinners, why*
> *Will you slight his grace and die?*
>
> —John Wesley

BIBLIOGRAPHY

W.D. Chamberlain: *The Meaning of Repentance*
R.O. Ferm: *The Psychology of Christian Conversion*
E. Price: *The Burden Is Light*
E. Routley: *The Gift of Conversion*

30

FAITH

✛

CALVIN D. LINTON

Calvin D. Linton, Dean and Professor of English Literature at Columbian College of Arts and Sciences, George Washington University, Washington, D.C., received his general and theological education at George Washington University (A.B., 1935) and Johns Hopkins University (M.A., 1939; Ph.D., 1940). He is the author of *Keys to Literature, How to Write Reports,* and articles on Elizabethan drama.

In dealing with so vast a subject as faith in so narrow a space, one's first need is to limit the area of discussion without thereby distorting or falsifying the true nature of the subject. Our analytical age is all too prone to divide to conquer, only to find that the sum of the parts divulges no deep truth about the original reality. We must avoid this danger in speaking of faith, for faith is more than the sum of those of its elements which can most readily be detected and analyzed—knowledge, reason, will, love, emotion, and others. "You may think that it is very easy to explain faith," wrote C. H. Spurgeon many years ago, "and so it is; but it is easier still to confound people with your explanation."[1]

[1] C.H. Spurgeon: *What Is Faith?*, p. 13.

DEFINITION

Faith is a channel of living trust and communion between morally conscious free beings. The dimension of moral consciousness must exist if there is to be communion,[2] and freedom must exist if the unity of the society produced by faith (faulty on earth; perfect in heaven) is to be that of dynamic life, not of soulless machines. Because living faith permits each soul to extend its dimensions of existence into the souls of others and into the Infinite Dimension of God, there is irretrievable commitment and consequent hazard in faith. True faith, in the words of T.S. Eliot, costs not less than everything. It also gains everything, if the object of faith is faithful.

The life, the power which flows through the channels of faith is the ultimate energy of the universe: God's love, the love which God *is*. Where love is perfect, faith is perfect, as in the ineffable beatitude of the Trinity.

Every dimension of reality, whether material or spiritual, is compatible with faith, when that dimension is truly understood. That is, faith is harmonious with reason, with knowledge, with "science," with "psychology"—with all truth, ancient or modern—though it is dependent on none of them.

When God's love is permitted, through faith, to permeate existence, life manifests the qualities inherent in divine creation: harmony, beauty, holiness, joy. When man, through a defect of love wilfully wrought, blocks the channel of faith in the Fall, faith ceases in man to reach wholly outward and instead turns in upon itself, where it must sicken and die. The limit of our faith is the limit of our life. It is unimaginable that any man should have faith literally in nothing except himself and continue to "live."

Self-severed from God by disbelief in God's veracity, man is doomed, so far as his own power is concerned, to wander forever in darkness and spiritual death. Any solution must be entirely of God and entirely of grace, without merit on man's part. Even man's assent to the free offer of redemption and salvation from God is a gift of God;[3] the Saviour Who[4] works our redemption is a gift,[5] and man's empowering in the transaction is by the Holy Spirit.[6] It is all of God.

Of the utter centrality of faith in Christian theology there can be no question. So long as man is, by sin, displeasing to God and at en-

[2] Gen. 2:7: ". . . and man became a living soul."
[3] Eph. 6:23; 2:8, 9; Phil. 1:29.   [4] *alone*—John 14:6; Matt. 11:27.
[5] II Cor. 9:15.   [6] II Cor. 4:13; Gal. 5:5.

mity against Him, man is without all hope; and without faith, it is impossible to please God.[7] The rays of divine love come to their sharpest focus in the simple words, "For by grace are ye saved through faith . . ."[8]

FAITH AND KNOWLEDGE

The role of knowledge in faith, and the difference between the two, may perhaps best be discussed by noting the difference of meaning between two terms commonly used to define faith: *belief* and *trust*. In this context, we use *belief* in its narrow, secondary meaning of "intellectual assent, based on a sufficiency of evidence." *Trust* we use in its meaning of reliance upon and commitment to.

Upon sufficient evidence, I am prepared to *believe* that Jesus existed and that during certain years He walked the roads of Palestine. This takes no commitment on my part, involves me in no hazard. My conduct need not be altered by it, nor my boundaries of trust (life) extended, nor my sinful condition modified. This belief is not accounted to me for righteousness, as was Abraham's,[9] for I have not believed God, but evidence. Indeed, no matter how much I believe in this way, I shall always be inferior to the fallen angels and to Satan, for they believe, and tremble.[10]

Knowledge, therefore, may compel the assent of the intellect, but it cannot compel that act of the will which constitutes trust. Our stony natural hearts must be softened by a more powerful solvent than knowledge, "for with the heart"—not the head—"man believeth unto righteousness.[11]

But if knowledge is not of itself sufficient to produce reliant trust, it is, in greater or lesser quantity, an absolutely essential precondition to trust. "How then shall they call on him in whom they have not believed? and how shall they believe in him of whom they have not heard?"[12] The basic imperative in this area is, "Acquaint now thyself with him, and be at peace."[13] Our Lord Himself taught the value of objective evidence in developing reliant trust, when He commanded doubting Thomas to reach forth his hand and feel the evidence of the wounds in Christ's body. Saul of Tarsus, smitten to earth on the Damascus road, asked for one key bit of information: "Who art thou,

7 Heb. 11:6.
8 Eph. 2:8.
9 Gal. 3:6.
10 James 2:19.
11 Rom. 10:10.
12 Rom. 10:14.
13 Job 22:21.

Lord?" The answer, "I am Jesus whom thou persecutest,"[14] gave him the object of his trust.

To scorn knowledge is to make faith a purely subjective experience, which is as fatal as to seek salvation in knowledge alone. Modern Christian existentialism may be useful in reminding us that faith must be an inner reality, and in warning us against faith in human reason; but when it denies the reality of the objective source of knowledge, which God has provided in His Word, and when it suggests that faith is a self-authenticating inner awareness, it cuts us off from the power of God by cutting us off from the historical Christ, Who is the wisdom of God.[15]

The knowledge which leads to belief in scientific laws and principles is available to him who seeks, but the knowledge of the Person of God, which must be the basis of our trust, is given as an act of divine grace. We must learn of God by believing what He says of himself. "God, who at sundry times and in divers manners spake in time past unto the fathers by the prophets, hath in these last days spoken unto us by his Son"[16] and from this source alone does perfect knowledge flow, the knowledge without which, no matter what our intellectual attainments, we walk in darkness.

There is no quantitative relationship between our knowledge and that act of trust through which we are saved. It was not ignorance which caused Adam to fall,[17] but the sin of disbelief committed as an act of will. Thus, man born of Adam is in his fallen condition turned away from God and unable by his own powers to find God, for "he that believeth not God hath made him a liar."[18] When we have received sufficient knowledge to know to whom we speak (as did Saul of Tarsus), we then are no longer in a position to demand more knowledge but simply to confront commands which are in effect gracious invitations: "Trust in the Lord with all thine heart, and lean not unto thine own understanding."[19]

FAITH AND REASON

What stacks of books and what quantities of heat have been produced by the debate over the role (if any) of human reason in Christian faith! Positions have ranged from Tertullian's "*Certum est quia impossibile est*"[20] to the Cambridge Platonists' "nothing truly religious

---

[14] Acts 9:5.
[16] Heb. 1:1, 2.
[18] I John 5:10.
[20] Tertullian: *De Carne Christi*, 5.

[15] I Cor. 1:24.
[17] I Tim. 2:14.
[19] Prov. 3:5.

is irrational and nothing truly rational is irreligious." Each extreme has produced its own sickness: superstition, dependence on ecclesiastical authority, or pure subjectivism, on the one hand; rational skepticism, materialism, or nihilism, on the other.

The contemporary Protestant climate is suspicious of rational (or "natural") theology as a basis for faith. In its place, the tendency today is to stress faith as a product of "direct confrontation" of God subjectively, and to consider the "quality" of that experience as self-authenticating.

First, if it be granted that any degree of knowledge whatever is a precondition to faith, then some role, however small, must be assigned to reason, for only reason knows how to identify and evaluate information.

Second, human reason, created in Adam and Eve as a trustworthy servant of the will, is in fallen man depraved and incapable of finding God.[21]

But though depraved, reason is not destroyed. Paul was not wasting his time when he spent hours and days arguing and debating in the synagogues. The remnant of right reason, though "aimed" away from God, may, like conscience in fallen man, give some light.

FAITH AND LOVE

To quote Spurgeon again: "Although we may not perhaps see it, there lies at the bottom of all love a belief in the object loved, as to its loveliness, its merit or capacity to make us happy. If I do not believe in a person, I cannot love him. If I cannot trust God, I cannot love Him." As a corollary, we are moved to trust those whom we love. Indeed, we may say that faith is embraced in love, and thus the basic exhortation of both Testaments is "Thou shalt love." True, love is not to be commanded, but it may be overwhelmingly attracted. That which attracts it is love, and "herein is love, not that we loved God, but that he loved us, and sent his Son to be the propitiation for our sins. . . . We love him because he first loved us."[22]

HOW FAITH OPERATES

Probably the key word is the preposition "through." "*By* grace are ye saved *through* faith. . . ." On God's side are the unsearchable riches of His grace; on man's side, emptiness, drought, death. If man is to re-

---

[21] Rom. 8:7.　　　　　　　　[22] I John 4:10, 19.

ceive the water of life, there must be a channel, and that channel is faith. That channel need not be large nor perfect, for it is the reviving drop which is pure and efficacious. There is no *merit* in the channel, any more than there is reviving life in the dead pipe through which the water flows.

We must immediately distinguish between *saving* faith ("by grace are ye saved through faith") and *living* faith ("the just shall live by faith").[23]

Saving faith is never spoken of in relative terms, for the consequence of faith is not relative; it is a passing from death unto life. One is either lost or saved, and the scale between the two conditions is not graduated.

Saving faith is not efficacious by reason either of its strength or the degree of its knowledge, but only by reason of its object. The woman who touched Christ's robe did so in almost complete ignorance, but she was healed. And so with Peter, when he began to sink beneath the boisterous waves: "Lord, save me." And *immediately* Jesus stretched forth His hand, and caught him, and said unto him, "O thou of little faith, wherefore didst thou doubt?"[24]

Saving faith, therefore, is nothing more nor less than reliant trust in the Person of the Lord Jesus Christ. "He that believeth in me, though he were dead, yet shall he live."[25] It need be nothing more than this, for "by him, all that believe are justified from all things . . ."[26] "I give them eternal life; and they shall never perish, neither shall any man pluck them out of my hand."[27] It can be nothing less than this, for "this is the stone which was set at nought of you builders, which is become the head of the corner. Neither is there salvation in any other: for there is none other name under heaven given among men, whereby we must be saved."[28] "No man cometh unto the Father but by me."[29] "Through his name whosoever believeth in him shall receive remission of sins."[30]

The difference between saving faith and living faith is the difference between a channel first opened, bringing life; and a channel continuingly and increasingly used, bringing power, victory, and honor. Just as Adam's faith before the Fall manifested itself in deeds of

[23] Heb. 10:38.
[25] John 11:25.
[27] John 10:28.
[29] John 14:6.

[24] Matt. 14:30, 31.
[26] Acts 13:39.
[28] Acts 4:11, 12.
[30] Acts 10:43.

obedience and fulfillment, so the regenerate, now *in* Christ, saved by His perfect obedience and made partakers of the divine nature, *live* in ever-broadening dimensions. The inexhaustible riches of God's power are available through faith,[31] and on the degree of our appropriation of that power, through the channel of faith, depends our earthly blessedness and our heavenly rewards.[32]

All may be summed up in two passages:

Saving faith: "This is the record, that God hath given to us eternal life, and this life is in his Son. He that hath the Son hath life; and he that hath not the Son of God hath not life."[33]

Living faith: "I am crucified with Christ: nevertheless I live; yet not I, but Christ liveth in me: and the life which I now live in the flesh I live by the faith of the Son of God, who loved me, and gave himself for me."[34]

BIBLIOGRAPHY

G.C. Berkouwer: *Faith and Sanctification*
J. Bright: *The Kingdom of God*
E.J. Carnell: *Christian Commitment*
J. Hick: *Faith and Knowledge*
J.G. Machen: *What Is Faith?*
C.B. Martin: *Religious Belief*
A. Richardson: *An Introduction to the Theology of the New Testament*
C.H. Spurgeon, et al.: *What Is Faith?*
S.M. Thompson: *A Modern Philosophy of Religion*
B.B. Warfield: *Biblical and Theological Studies*, S.G. Craig, ed.

[31] Matt. 17:20.   [32] I Cor. 5:10.
[33] I John 5:11, 12.   [34] Gal. 2:20.

31

THE MYSTICAL UNION

✝

WILLIAM A. MUELLER

William A. Mueller, Professor of Church History at New Orleans Baptist Theological Seminary, received his general and theological education at Canisius College, Buffalo, New York (M.A., 1927), Union Theological Seminary, New York (S.T.M., 1944), and New York University (Ph.D., 1933). He is the author of *History of First German Baptist Church of Brooklyn, N.Y.*, *Church and State in America*, *Church and State in Luther and Calvin*, and *A History of Southern Baptist Theological Seminary*.

Whenever the word mystical is mentioned in Christian discourse, some people at once become apprehensive. Have not reputable theologians like B.B. Warfield or Karl Barth seriously warned against using this word in our Christian speech? Yet, men like John Calvin, C.H. Spurgeon, and G.A. Barrois, all of them in the Reformed tradition, have unblushingly spoken of the mystical union of the believer with the risen Lord. Where, keeping all of this in view, shall we take our stand?

Let us from the outset be clear on this: mystical union with Christ does not describe the total absorption of the believer in Christ or Deity. No identity philosophy as expressed in neo-Platonism or classical Hinduism is either possible or permissible in an evangelical Christian experience. Nevertheless, we do affirm the possibility and reality of a highly personal and intimate union of the believer with the crucified, risen, and exalted Lord.

The word mystical in this context is used to suggest the *wonder* of our communion with Jesus Christ. For this union, of a redeemed sinner with a pardoning Saviour, transcends all human apprehension. It is created of God, a gift of His supreme love, not for selfish contemplation, but for the energizing, through the Holy Spirit, of the whole of man for fruitful service to God and man.

THE SCRIPTURAL TEACHING ON THIS UNION

The Bible testifies on every page to God's longing for fellowship with His creatures. God created man for fellowship with Himself and his neighbor. Man's fall shattered His relationship with the Lord, but God unceasingly agonized in order to restore man to blessed fellowship with Himself. Abraham, like Enoch of old, walked and talked with God, as friend with friend. God called Israel out of Egypt's bondage to be His chosen people, a nation of kings and priests, to be the herald of His will. Moses communed with God face to face, and prophets like Isaiah and Hosea, Jeremiah and Ezekiel, knew something of this close and holy fellowship with Jehovah God. And, yet, it is finally in Jesus Christ, the incarnate Word, that God's passionate longing for an enduring fellowship with His lost creatures comes to its highest expression.

THE FOUR GOSPELS AND THIS UNION

The informed reader of the New Testament realizes at once that Jesus, through concrete acts and explicit teachings, aimed at the most intimate union of His followers with Himself and God the Father. It is Jesus Who calls, commissions, and sanctifies His disciples. Under various metaphors and pictures, Christ illustrates the depth and scope of His relationship to His own. In Luke 12 and 14, as in Matthew 10 and numerous other passages, Jesus describe the strong bond between His disciples and Himself in terms of the *cost* of discipleship. For His sake, men are to forsake all—father, mother, brother, sister, house, and home! For His sake, they must be willing to endure the crucifixion of self to the point of martyrdom. And the Apostles and early disciples forsook all and followed the divine Master. In fact, Jesus so completely identified Himself with His disciples that He could say, "Whatsoever ye shall ask in *my name*, that will the Father give unto you." When Christ's followers herald the gospel of grace and judgment, they do so with the assurance that "he that heareth *you* heareth *me*, and he that despiseth *you*, despiseth *me* and *him* that sent me."[1] Whether Jesus speaks of *Nachfolge* or following in His steps, of enduring in affliction, of speaking in His name, of suffering for His sake, of sharing in His glory, or of always abiding in Him, this intimate, personal, indestructible union of the believer with Christ is in evidence. Jesus is the light of the world: His disciples, in turn, are to be the light shining in darkness. Jesus is the vine; and we are the branches. He is the shepherd; we are His sheep. He is the Master; we are His servants. As our elder brother, He is not ashamed to call us His brethren. As Christ *is* in the Father, so *are* we in Him.[2] His glorification, through cross and death, involves our own glorification and ultimate salvation. What could be more holy than Jesus through his bloody passion purchasing our redemption and through His glorious resurrection making us eternally His own? In the explicit teachings of our Lord, there is the joy of salvation, the gift of eternal life, fortitude in trial, and the promise of ultimate, culminating fellowship with God through the grace and power of His Son and our Saviour Jesus Christ.

THE MYSTICAL UNION IN PAUL'S LETTERS

Critical scholarship has established the fact of the priority of the epistolary literature of the New Testament over the four Gospels. Paul's letters are no doubt older than either the Synoptic Gospels or that of John. Yet, there is a remarkable harmony between these two parts of the New Testament. While the imagery differs, the substance is basically the same. It is *one* Gospel that is proclaimed, whether we study the Synoptics or the doctrinal or hortatory letters of the Apostles. With regard to mystical union of the believer with Christ, Paul is explicit.

It was Adolf Deissmann, eminent New Testament scholar, who, in 1892, pointed out the extreme importance of the Pauline formula "in Christ Jesus." By this formula, which occurs 164 times in Paul's writings, Paul sought to express the intimate, mystical union between Christ and himself and every true believer.

[1] Luke 10:1-16.   [2] John 17.

In Christ, thus Paul teaches, we were chosen,[3] called,[4] foreordained,[5] created unto good works,[6] have obtained an inheritance,[7] "being predestinated according to the purpose of him who worketh all things after the counsel of his own will, that we should be to the praise of his glory . . ."[8]

In Christ, each believer is justified,[9] sanctified,[10] but also crucified, as attested through the symbolism of our baptism into Christ's death,[11] and enriched in all utterance and knowledge.[12] We are declared to be one in our relationship with men of all races and tongues.[13] If American Christians, North and South, and Christians everywhere, could realize the impact of this word of the Apostle, racial pride and arrogance, antisemitism, and all non-Christian attitudes toward those of a different color from ours would be radically changed.

The Apostle is deeply convinced that *in Christ* and in Him alone we have redemption,[14] eternal life,[15] righteousness,[16] wisdom for our folly,[17] liberty from the law;[18] and *in Christ*, God, the Father, "has blessed us with all spiritual blessings in heavenly places."[19] Paul is sure that God causes us to triumph *in Christ*, and that always, without failure.[20]

The intimacy of our union with Christ is suggested also in the Pauline writings through various suggestive metaphors. What could be more tender and personal than the relationship between bride and bridegroom, between husband and wife? Paul uses this picture in both Ephesians and II Corinthians. "For I am jealous over you with a godly jealousy: for I espoused you to one husband, that I might present you a pure virgin to Christ."[21] God's family, the church, has its existence *in* Christ; hence, it must live a Christ-like life.

Still another figure in Paul's writings which bears on our subject is that of the body and its members. Both in I Corinthians 11 and 12 and in his Ephesian letter, Paul speaks of Christ as the head of the church and of the believers as members of the body, i.e., the church.

[3] Rom. 16:33. [4] I Cor. 7:22.
[5] Eph. 1:11. [6] Eph. 2:10.
[7] Eph. 1:11. [8] Eph. 1:11, 12.
[9] Gal. 2:17. [10] I Cor. 1:2.
[11] Rom. 6:1–11. [12] I Cor. 1:5.
[13] Gal. 3:28, 29. [14] Rom. 3:24.
[15] Rom. 6:23. [16] I Cor. 1:30.
[17] I Cor. 4:10. [18] Gal. 2:4.
[19] Eph. 1:3. [20] II Cor. 2:14.
[21] II Cor. 11:2.

Theologians have spoken of the body of Christ, the church, as the mystical bride of Christ. And well they might. *Ubi Christus ibi ecclesia!* Where *Christ* is, there is the *church!* Even though, as Luther intimated, only two or three simple folk are gathered *in his Name!* Moreover, believers individually and collectively are called in Paul's letters to the Corinthians "the temple of God." Here again, our high calling and the holiness of Christ's church is set forth.

But the highest expression of the believer's union with Christ is found in Paul's passion mysticism. No one can read those moving verses in Colossians 1:23-28 without realizing how deeply Paul had understood the Master whom he had never known in the flesh. Paul rejoices in his sufferings for the Colossians. Daringly, he speaks of filling "up that which is behind of the afflictions of Christ in my flesh for his body's sake, which is the church."[22] All with this end in view: that "Christ be formed in them," and that his readers might fathom the depth of the mystery hid from past generations but now made manifest to the saints—*Christ in you, the hope of glory.*

Someone else has said that in every age some part of the church of Jesus Christ must endure suffering in fulfillment of God's one increasing purpose. William Carey, pioneer missionary in India, had to sail on a Danish boat because the East India Company denied him passage on its ships. On arrival in Calcutta, he was harassed for years. Later his own brethren in Britain severed their connection with Carey. Robert Morrison's Chinese tutors carried poison on their bodies, fearing torture if they were discovered by the authorities teaching a foreigner the Chinese language. Robert Moffat in Africa, Nommensen in Indonesia, evangelical missionaries in Latin America in most recent times, Russian believers under Stalin, and Christians in Nazi Germany and now in East Germany—these and many others mark "the trail of blood" of the Christian witness through the centuries. The servant is not above his Master. If they have blasphemed Him, so they will His followers. Yet, where in our country is there a serious grappling with this side of the church's mission? There is, instead, far too much status-seeking, compromise with the world's standards and values, and, often, open betrayal of the Lord. Paul, Peter, John, and the early church unite in this testimony: Unless we suffer with *Him,* we may not be glorified together.[23]

Was Paul a mystic? Galatians 2:20 comes to mind, for there the

---

[22] Col. 1:24.   [23] Rom. 8:17b.

Apostle writes: "I am crucified with Christ: nevertheless I live; yet not I, but Christ liveth in me: and the life which I now live in the flesh I live by the faith of the Son of God, who loved me, and gave himself for me." Let us remember that Paul is also the Apostle of faith and of the infinite grace of God in Jesus Christ. His mysticism, to cite Deissmann, is a reacting mysticism. In it, God ever has the initiative. And though Paul experienced such exaltation as being transported into the third heaven, he did not boast of vision or high revelations, but rather of the grace of God, Whose strength is made perfect in weakness.[24] Not in ecstactic elevations is the Christian's glory, but in the cross of Christ and his own self-crucifixion and his anticipation of God's glory amidst the flux of time. Neither is the church now a church of glory, but a church which through many tribulations must enter the Kingdom of heaven.

CONCLUSION

From the foregoing, it becomes clear that the mystical union between Christ and the believer, Christ and the church, is a *unique* relationship, incomparably wonderful, and bound up with the deepest intentions of God's grace and pupose. It is also an *inward*, not merely external, union, which under the influence of God's Spirit and the Christian's self-discipline may organically grow in scope and meaning. It is, moreover, a *spiritual* union, since our being strongly and enduringly wedded and joined to Christ is the work of the Holy Spirit by whom we have been sealed unto the day of our final redemption. It is finally an *indissoluble* union, which the believer sustains to Jesus Christ his head. For we have the promise that we shall never perish, provided we endure to the end. Nothing is ever to separate the believing soul from God's love, which is *in* Christ Jesus.[25]

This doctrine of the mystical union of the believer with Christ ought to be a perennial source of strength in temptation, a clarion call to holy living in season and out, and a summons to realize an ever-closer fellowship with our Lord. This doctrine also ought to make us realize our rich heritage of faith and love, of liturgy and praise, of missions and evangelism, of theology and Christian ethos, that we share with all those who, in churches of Jesus Christ around the world, are united with us in the one body of Christ, the church. Moreover, as A.J. Gordon has well put it, "to be in Christ is not only to be in union with his divine nature,

[24] II Cor. 12:1-10.   [25] Rom. 8:38, 39.

but also because He is the son of man as well as the Son of God, it is to be in truest union with human nature. We never get so near the heart of our sorrowing humanity as when we are in communion with the heart of the man of sorrows." May our awareness of being joined with Jesus the Christ impell us to pray with John Woolman, "Lord, baptize me this day afresh into every condition and circumstance of men!" Let us cast aside all lethargy, put on the whole armor of God, and, as those who have their very existence in Christ, act, pray, live, witness, die and triumph in His name, until faith shall be sight and the kingdoms of this earth shall have become the Kingdom of our Lord. *Sursum corda!* Lift up your hearts! *Regem habemus!* We have a King, even the King of kings and Lord of lords. He will banish all our fears, conquer all sin and evil, for He has conquered it already on Calvary and on Easter morning. His purpose will yet be realized, when a redeemed, united, and glorified humanity shall dwell, by His grace, on a redeemed and new earth.

BIBLIOGRAPHY

J. Calvin: *Institutes*, II, iii, 2
B.B. Warfield: *Biblical and Theological Studies*
A.J. Gordon: *In Christ*
J.S. Stewart: *A Man in Christ*
G.A. Barrois: "Mysticism," *Theology Today*, July, 1947
A. Wickenhauser: *Pauline Mysticism*
K. Barth: *Die kirchliche Dogmatik*, IV, pp. 620 ff.

3 2

JUSTIFICATION BY FAITH

✛

H.D. MCDONALD

H.D. McDonald, Vice-Principal and Professor of Historical
Theology and Philosophy of Religion at London Bible College,
London, England, received his general and theological education
at the University of London (B.A., 1947; B.D., 1953; Ph.D.,
1957). He is the author of *Ideas of Revelation.*

This doctrine with which we are concerned is both the divine heart
of the Gospel and the Gospel for the human heart. To seek an answer
to the question, How can a man be just before God? is to be launched
out into the profundities of our faith and to be occupied with the deep
things of the spirit. Virtually every great truth of the Gospel is
grounded upon and linked up with this. Justification by faith—the answer of God to the needs of man—is the one unchanging message and
method by which God receives sinful men.

But men readily forget, as William Temple has said, that "The only
thing of my very own which I can contribute to my redemption is the
sin from which I need to be redeemed."[1]

Justification is that judicial act of God's free mercy whereby He
pronounces guiltless those sinners condemned under the law, con-

[1] W. Temple: *Nature, Man and God*, p. 401.

stitutes them as actually righteous, once and for all, in the imputed righteousness of Christ—on the grounds of His atoning work, by grace, through faith alone apart from works—and assures them of a full pardon, acceptance in His sight, adoption as sons, and heirs of eternal life, and the present gift of the Holy Spirit; and such as are brought into this new relation and standing are by the power of this same Spirit, enabled to perform good works which God hath before ordained that we should walk therein. Yet, such works performed, as well as the faith out of which they spring, make no contribution to the soul's justification, but they are to be regarded as declarative evidences of a man's acceptance in the sight of God.

A number of very important points present themselves in this comprehensive definition.

THE NATURE OF JUSTIFICATION

The Hebrew term *tsadek,* and its Greek equivalent *dikaioō,* must be understood, in the context of our discussion, in a legal as distinguished from a moral sense. It is true, of course, that in every instance the forensic connotation cannot be insisted upon; there are passages in which it could with as much assurance be read "to make righteous" as "to declare righteous." It is on the strength of this that Roman Catholic and some "Protestant" writers seek to establish their view that man is justified by his own righteousness as infused and inherent, rather than by a divine righteousness vicarious and imputed.

To remain good Protestants and "Paulinists," however, it is not necessary to prove that the term in every instance means "to declare righteous" and nothing else. The fact is that "all parties must be held to admit that, when a sinner is justified, he is, in some sense, both made and accounted righteous; and the real difference between them becomes apparent only when they proceed to explain in what way he is made righteous, and adjudged so to be."[2]

Yet, it is important to observe that in those passages of Scripture which deal specifically with the question of man's acceptance before God the forensic sense of the term is clearly in mind, and for a correct exegesis must be so understood. When, for example, an antithetical expression, such as the word "condemnation," is used, the forensic meaning is certainly present.[3] A forensic idea is essential in those pas-

[2] J. Buchanan: *The Doctrine of Justification,* p. 228.
[3] *See,* e.g. Deut. 25:1; Prov. 17:15; Isa. 5:23; Matt. 12:37; and especially in reference to God, Rom. 5:16; 8:33, 34.

sages where correlative expressions appear.[4] There are also passages in which a synonym for justification is used, which make it evident that the justified man is brought into a changed judicial relation to God and that the word does not relate to a change in his moral and spiritual character.[5]

The doctrine of justification has often been stated in such a way as to leave the impression that it is a "legal fiction." This idea of a *fictio juris* arises when it is taught that God merely declares a man righteous when he is not. The truth is that God sees the believing man as constituted righteous in Christ, and, accepting him "in the Beloved," He pronounces him to be what he is—in Christ. Here is the paradox of the Gospel—a man is a sinner, yet perfect. Yet, it is only a "righteous" man who can be declared righteous. The vital question then is, whose is the righteousness on account of which God gives His verdict, "Not Guilty" and "Acceptable"?

THE GROUNDS OF JUSTIFICATION

Two issues may be distinguished here, referred to as the ultimate and immediate grounds of God's act of justifying the sinner. The ultimate ground lies in the will and the mercy of God.[6] Upon these great facts, our justification is ultimately based. Here might be considered, in the light of the Scriptures, the disclosures of the eternal covenant between the Persons in the triune Godhead by Whom and through Whom the plan and the purpose of salvation for sinful men were forever made sure.[7] In that eternal covenant of grace, salvation was rendered certain.

More particularly, however, it need only be stated here that our justification is based solely and squarely upon the objective mediatorial work of Christ for us. It is with our Lord's deed on the cross that it is connected. This means that our justification is something external to ourselves. It is not something done either *by* us or *in* us. It is what was done—once and for all—*for* us. We are justified, it is declared, "by the blood of Christ,"[8] by His "righteousness,"[9] by His "obedience,"[10] "in the name of the Lord Jesus Christ."[11]

[4] *See*, e.g., Gen. 18:25; Ps. 32:1; 143:2; Rom. 2:2, 15; 8:33; 14:10; Col. 2:14; I John 2:1.
[5] *See*, e.g., Rom. 4:3, 6–8; II Cor. 5:19, 30.
[6] Cf. John 1:13; James 1:18; Titus 3:5–7; Rom. 9, especially v. 16: "So it depends not on human will or exertion, but on the mercy of god" (Goodspeed).
[7] Cf. Eph. 1:3 f.; 3:2; etc.
[8] Rom. 5:9.   [9] Rom. 5:18.
[10] Rom. 5:19.   [11] I Cor. 6:11.

The more immediate grounds, however, of the sinner's justification is the imputed righteousness of Christ. Some have erroneously made the sinner's justification to be a consequence of a grace infused and a righteousness inherent. It is the fundamental error of the Roman church to substitute the inherent righteousness of the regenerate (in baptism, of course) for the imputed righteousness of the Redeemer. The result is that the forensic nature of justification is lost, and it becomes equated with sanctification.

But there are those, not of Rome, who evade the full implications of the doctrine of justification by making room for the righteousness of man.

Against every attempt to give man a part in his justification, the Epistle to the Romans utters an emphatic denial. It is the righteousness of Christ which is imputed to the believer: the whole righteousness of the whole Christ. Christ is not divided nor can His righteousness be finally distributed. Romans 5:17 speaks of the "gift of righteousness"— the righteousness of "the obedience of one."[12] "It is, therefore, the righteousness of Christ, His perfect obedience in doing and suffering the will of God, which is imputed to the believer, and on the ground of which the believer, although in himself ungodly, is pronounced righteous, and therefore free from the curse of the law, and entitled to eternal life."[13]

This doctrine of the imputation of Christ's righteousness cannot be rejected as being either impossible or artificial. With regard to the first, the passage II Corinthians 5:21 is of decisive significance. Most surely, Christ was not made sin in any moral sense. Nor in our justification are we made righteous in a moral sense. He was made sin by bearing our sins; so we are made righteous by bearing His righteousness. Our sins are imputed to Him and thus become the judicial grounds of His humiliation and suffering; and His righteousness is imputed to us and thus becomes the judicial ground of our justification.

On the other hand, the imputation of Christ's righteousness can only give the appearance of artificiality if divorced from the complementary doctrine of union with Christ. "Justification is not an arbitrary transfer to us of legal fictions in the divine government."[14]

---

12 Rom. 5:19.
13 C. Hodge: *Systematic Theology*, III, p. 151.
14 Cf. A.H. Strong: *Systematic Theology*, p. 479.

THE CHANNEL OF JUSTIFICATION

Roman Catholicism virtually makes the Church's sacraments, working *ex opero operato*, produce and maintain the status by which a man is being made acceptable with God. But the Scriptures declare justification to be "by faith."[15] This faith is "fiduciary." It is a living and personal trust in a perfect redemption and a present Redeemer.

"Faith is not a human notion or a dream as some take it to be. Faith is a divine work in us, which changes us and causes us to be born anew from God."[16] James Arminius boldly says that the "author of faith is the Holy Spirit."[17] It is "a gracious and gratuitous gift of God."[18]

In this connection, two facts must be stressed. First, faith is only the channel of our justification. It is, as Arminius says, the "instrumental" and not the "formal" cause. Some have taken the position that our pardon is based sure enough on Christ's atoning work, but justification rests upon faith which God accepts in place of that perfect obedience due from us to the absolute demands of the law.[19] It would be fatal to the full truth of the Gospel thus to turn faith itself into a "work." Abraham's faith was by no means a substitute for obedience.[20] It was, in fact, a faith to (*eis*) righteousness, not instead of (*anti*) righteousness. The position is not made any more acceptable by talking of "evangelical obedience." Faith has no place for any kind of help.

To make faith, then, the only channel of justification means quite literally that all works are excluded.[21] It will stand without emphasizing that the works done by the ungenerate man have no place in his justification. But it should be underlined that if our salvation is to remain a matter of grace alone, by faith alone, this prohibition extends no less to what are called post-regeneration works. The discussion by James about the necessity of works turns not upon their *meritorious* value, but their evidential value. James is condemning a faith merely intellectual, while Paul is rejecting works as having saving merit. James says an inactive faith cannot justify; Paul says meritorious works do not justify. Paul requires a saving faith, therefore a faith apart from works;

---

[15] *See*, e.g., Rom. 3:22, 27; 4:16; 5:1; etc.

[16] John 1:13; M. Luther: *Epistle to the Romans*, Preface.

[17] J. Nichols and W. Bagnall, tr.: *The Works of James Arminius*, Volume II, p. 110.

[18] *Ibid.*, p. 500.   [19] Cf. Rom. 4:3; cf. Gen. 15:6.

[20] Cf. Heb. 11:8.

[21] Cf. Rom. 3:28; Rom. 4; Gal. 2:16; 3; Eph. 2:8; etc.

and James a living faith, therefore a faith which works. And neither contradicts the other.

From the beginning of its rediscovery at the Reformation, the biblical principle of *sola fides* has been compromised. Some have maintained that repentance and love and the new obedience are all to be included in the faith by which a man is justified. Here again, effort is made to share the work between the benefits of Christ and the acts of men, and in this way to give some of the glory to man. Such an idea makes grace no longer grace.

The faith by which a sinner is justified is not, then, itself a work of obedience. "That faith and works concur together in justification, is a thing impossible."[22] But neither is faith an equivalent for obedience; it is rather the germ out of which obedience springs. Faith is the medium or the instrument by which Christ is received and by which we are united to Him. In Scripture, we are never said to be justified *dia pistin*—on account of faith—but only *dia pisteōs*—through faith—or *ek pisteōs*—by faith.

Today, some tend to associate ecumenical love, moral rearmament, and even prayer therapy, with faith as the means of justification. Indeed, in some statements, one or other of these seems to be made a substitute for that faith by which the sinner is justified in the sight of God.

THE RESULTS OF JUSTIFICATION

It certainly includes pardon. Justification relates to the sinner's established and unchanging position *coram Deo;* once established, it remains. But pardon may be renewed. The justified man is certainly accepted "in the Beloved"; not only is he a "child of God" by birth, but he is also a son by adoption. He is *huiothesia*, brought into the enjoyment of all the rights and privileges of the family.[23] "Adoption is a term involving the dignity of the relationship of the believers as 'sons': it is not a putting into the family by spiritual birth, but a putting into the position of sons." Such believers possess eternal life as a present possession.[24] Such, too, have the Holy Spirit, not only as an earnest of our purchased possession,[25] but as the One by whom our sanctification is effected and assured.[26]

[22] J. Nichols and W. Bagnall, *op. cit.,* p. 119.
[23] Cf. Gal. 5:5; Rom. 8.23; Eph. 1:5.
[24] Cf. John 3:15–18; I John 5:10–12; etc.
[25] Eph. 1:14.   [26] I Pet. 1:2; Eph. 3:16.

THE EVIDENCES OF JUSTIFICATION

Good works have a declarative value with regard to a man's justification. Since a man has been taken into union with Christ, righteous though still a sinner, he must work out his own salvation as God works in him.[27] Luther puts the matter in a nutshell: "Oh, it is a living, creative, active, mighty thing, this faith! So it is impossible for it to fail to produce good works steadily. It does not ask whether there is good to do, but before the question is raised, it has already done it, and goes on doing it. Whoever does not do such works is a faithless man."[28]

BIBLIOGRAPHY

J. Arminius: *Works*, Volume II
A.A. Hodge: *Outlines of Theology*
C. Hodge: *Systematic Theology*
J. Buchanan: *The Doctrine of Justification*
A.H. Strong: *Systematic Theology*
L. Berkhof: *Systematic Theology*
J.S. Stewart: *A Man in Christ*

[27] Phil. 2:12, 13.   [28] J. Luther, *op. cit.*

33

ADOPTION

✝

J. THEODORE MUELLER

J. Theodore Mueller, Professor of Systematic Theology at Concordia Theological Seminary, St. Louis, Missouri, received his general and theological education at Concordia College, Ft. Wayne, Indiana, (B.A., 1904), Webster University (Ph.D., 1924), and Xenia Theological Seminary (Th.D., 1927). He is the author of *Christian Dogmatics, Concordia Bible with Notes, Concordia New Testament with Notes, Luther's Commentary on Romans, Commentary on Genesis,* and numerous tracts and articles.

The Christian believer regards it as a most comforting Gospel revelation that in Christ Jesus God from eternity has adopted His chosen saints to be His dear children. It was definitely a manifestation of Christ's sincere love for His disciples when He called them his "friends";[1] but the terms "sons and daughters," which Scripture ascribes to Christian believers, imply far greater privileges than does that of friend. In his well-known monograph, *The Reformed Doctrine of Adoption,* R.A. Webb writes of God's gracious adoption of believers as his dear children: "When we approach Him in the intensity of worship, we gather up all the sweetness involved in Fatherhood and all the

[1] John 15:14.

tenderness wrapped up in sonship; when calamities overcome us and troubles come in like a flood, we lift up our cry and stretch out our arms to God as a compassionate Father; when the angel of death climbs in at the window of our homes and bears away the object of our love, we find our dearest solace in reflecting upon the fatherly heart of God; when we look across the swelling flood, it is our Father's House on the light-covered hills beyond the stars which cheers us amid the crumbling of the earthly tabernacle."[2] It is from the viewpoint of its ineffable solace that the Christian believer gratefully considers the biblical doctrine of adoption.

DEFINITION OF ADOPTION

A.H. Strong briefly defines the doctrine of adoption under the general theme "Restoration to Favor," in connection with justification and reconciliation, as follows: "This restoration to favor, viewed in its aspect as the renewal of a broken friendship, is denominated reconciliation; viewed in its aspect as a renewal of the son's true relation to God as a father, it is denominated adoption."[3] Similar is the definition given in the *Cyclopaedia* of McClintock and Strong: "Adoption in a theological sense is that act of God's free grace by which, upon our being justified by faith in Christ, we are received into the family of God and entitled to the inheritance of heaven."[4] According to these definitions, adoption embraces both the renewal of the soul's true relation to God as a father and the bestowal of the privileges of sonship in this life and that to come. Thus, believers, who by nature were alienated from God and were under His righteous judgment, are received by Him as His dear children and heirs of eternal life.

THE DOCTRINE TAUGHT IN SCRIPTURE

The term *huiothesia*, literally "placing as a son," is used only in the New Testament.[5] It never occurs in the Septuagint, and in the New Testament only in those Epistles which primarily concerned Gentile believers, e.g., Galatians, Romans, Ephesians. Even here, the Apostle's emphasis seems to rest not so much on God's adopting act as on the state of sonship and its prerogatives. Among the Greeks and Romans at

[2] R.A. Webb: *The Reformed Doctrine of Adoption*, p. 19.
[3] A.H. Strong: *Systematic Theology*, Volume III, p. 857.
[4] J. McClintock and J. Strong: *Cyclopaedia of Biblical, Theological, and Ecclesiastical Literature, s.v.*
[5] Cf. J. Orr, ed.: *International Standard Bible Encyclopedia, s.v.*

Paul's time, adoption, that is, "the legal process by which a man might bring into his family and endow with the status and privilege of a son one who was not by nature his son or his kindred,"[6] was so well known that Paul could presuppose that his readers understood what he meant by God's spiritual *huiothesia*. But the question, whether the Apostle was guided in his use of the term by the prevalent custom, is quite another matter. The Old Testament mentions three cases of adoption,[7] though all of them took place outside Palestine. Paul, however, definitely ascribes to chosen Israel the *huiothesia*,[8] just as the Old Testament attributes to believing Israel the prerogative of sonship.[9] In the New Testament the precious Gospel truth, that believers in Christ are God's dear children, is, of course, stressed also in books not written by Paul.[10]

ADOPTION, AN ETERNAL ACT OF DIVINE GRACE

Adoption, according to Scripture, is an eternal act of divine grace, for He "predestinated us unto the adoption of children by Jesus Christ to himself according to the good pleasure of his will."[11] This eternal predestination to adoption, just as God's eternal election to salvation, was, of course, "in him,"[12] that is, in Christ Jesus, and so embraced His incarnation, vicarious atonement, and resurrection—in short, the whole *ordo salutis;* for "when the fullness of the time was come, God sent forth his Son, made of a woman, made under the law, to redeem them that were under the law, that we might receive the adoption of sons."[13] Therefore, the adoption is an act of God's free grace and excludes all human merit; it is absolutely *sola gratia.* As believers have been redeemed purely by grace, so also they have been adopted purely by grace. Thus, God heaps grace upon grace in electing, redeeming, and adopting His elect saints.

While Scripture ascribes to the Father the adoption and to the Son the redemption, it ascribes to the Holy Spirit the sanctifying act by which we become believers in Christ and so God's dear children. The Apostle teaches this truth very clearly when he writes: "For as many as are led by the Spirit of God, they are the sons of God. For ye have not received the spirit of bondage again to fear; but ye have received

6 *Ibid., s.v.*
7 Exod. 2:10; I Kings 11:20; Esther 2:7, 15.
8 Rom. 9:4.   9 Exod. 4:22; Deut. 14:1; 32:5; Jer. 31:9.
10 E.g., Luke 20:26; I John 3:1, 2, 10.   11 Eph. 1:5.
12 Eph. 1:4.   13 Gal. 4:4, 5.

the Spirit of adoption, whereby we cry, Abba, Father. The Spirit itself beareth witness with our spirit that we are the children of God. And if children, then heirs; heirs of God, and joint-heirs with Christ; if so be that we suffer with him, that we may be also glorified together."[14] In this life, of course, the believer's assurance of his adoption is apprehended merely by faith; but on the day of the final resurrection, he will be delivered "into the glorious liberty of the children of God."[15]

THE RELATION OF ADOPTION
TO OTHER BIBLICAL DOCTRINES

The doctrine of adoption stands in close relation to those of justification, reconciliation, regeneration, conversion, and sanctification. The adoption exists objectively *in foro Dei*, because of God's eternal election of grace and Christ's vicarious atonement. But, subjectively, the believer obtains it through faith in Christ or by becoming a believer in Christ, as the Apostle writes: "Ye are all the children of God by faith in Christ Jesus."[16] This means that in the very moment of his conversion to Christ, he is a child of God. But in that very moment, he is also justified or declared righteous before God for Christ's sake, Whose perfect righteousness, procured by His vicarious atonement, he receives by his personal faith in the Redeemer. This comforting Gospel truth the Apostle stresses in Romans 5:1: "Therefore being justified by faith, we have peace with God through our Lord Jesus Christ." But this verse declares also that the believer in the moment of his conversion is in possession of reconciliation with God, for by faith he has "peace with God through our Lord Jesus Christ." According to Scripture, reconciliation is that very act of divine grace through which the believer is granted peace with God by his justification or the forgiveness of his sins.

But by faith in Christ, the believer receives also regeneration or the new birth, as John writes: "Whosoever believeth that Jesus is the Christ is born of God."[17] This, moreover, means that then the believer is converted, since conversion in its proper sense is the "turning from darkness to light" by faith in Christ.[18] The estranged sinner, who was turned away from God, is now turned toward his divine Lord with genuine trust and sincere love. In this sense the Apostle writes: "God

14 Rom. 8:14–17.   15 Rom. 8:21.
16 Gal. 3:26.   17 I John 5:1.
18 Acts 26:18.

... hath shined in our hearts to give the light of the knowledge of the glory of God in the face of Jesus Christ."[19] The regenerated believer is given the firm conviction that Christ is his personal Saviour, who has redeemed him from sin, death, and hell. So, also by faith in Christ, the believer obtains the gift of sanctification or the gradual putting off of the old man, which is corrupt according to its deceitful lusts, and the gradual putting on of the new man, which after God is created in righteousness and true holiness.[20] Thus, the believer's faith in Christ accomplishes his entire renewal: his justification, reconciliation, regeneration, conversion, sanctification, and, last but not least, his adoption to sonship. Paul sums up this whole spiritual process of the believer's turning from unbelief to faith, from sin to holiness, from death to life, when he writes: "For by grace are ye saved through faith; and that not of yourselves; it is the gift of God: not of works, lest any man should boast";[21] or: "Therefore if any man be in Christ, he is a new creature; old things are passed away; behold, all things are become new."[22] As Scripture ascribes the believer's whole salvation to faith in Christ, so also it ascribes to faith in Christ the individual divine acts by which the Holy Spirit works salvation in the believer. It is, therefore, immaterial whether the adoption is linked with regeneration or justification or whether, under a separate head, it is considered as the final goal of man's spiritual reclamation by the Holy Spirit. There is, however, always a note of triumphant rejoicing in the sweet Gospel proclamation that Christian believers are God's dear children.[23] Thus, the adoption may be regarded as the crowning act of God's saving love.

THE BLESSINGS OF THE ADOPTION

Scripture is very explicit in describing the ineffable blessings of the believer's adoption. According to Romans 8:14-17, these are (1) the sanctifying leading by the Holy Spirit; (2) the removal of the servile spirit of fear; (3) the filial trust by which the believer calls God "Abba, Father," the joining of the two words giving emphasis to his endeared relation to God; (4) the witnessing of the Holy Spirit with his spirit that he is a child of God; and (5) the assurance that he is an heir of God and a joint heir with Christ. The blessing of the Spirit's witnessing in the believer's heart is stated with the same emphasis in Galatians

[19] II Cor. 4:6.
[20] Eph. 4:22-24.
[21] Eph. 2:8, 9.
[22] II Cor. 5:17.
[23] Cf. I John 3:2 and similar passages.

4:6; only here the joyous prayer, "Abba, Father," is ascribed directly to the Spirit's witnessing. Accordingly, the believer calls God, "Abba, Father," as the immediate effect of the assuring testimony of the Holy Spirit. The spirit of adoption, therefore, assures the believer of God's fatherly love toward him and of his sure salvation in everlasting glory. In times of trial, the Christian, because of the weakness of his faith, may not always perceive the Spirit's witness, but it is nevertheless there as long as faith in Christ prevails; for in the final analysis, faith itself is nothing else than the Spirit's persuasive witness in the believer's heart.

THE APPLICATION OF THE DOCTRINE

While all Christian theologians glory in the comforting Gospel truth that believers in Christ are God's dear children, they vary greatly in their treatment of the doctrine of adoption. R.A. Webb, in his monograph referred to above, takes note of the fact that Calvin makes no allusion whatever to adoption; while Turretin identifies it as the second element of justification. So also, the thorough dogmatical work of Charles Hodge is silent on the subject, while A.A. Hodge devotes to it a short chapter. None of the ecumenical creeds of Christendom contains a formal confession of adoption, but the *Westminster Confession* and the *Westminster Catechisms* set forth the doctrine as a separate head in theology. The old Dutch theologian Herman Witsius, in his work *The Economy of the Covenants Between God and Man*,[24] gives nineteen pages to the subject of adoption and seventeen to "The Spirit of Adoption."[25]

Luther translated the term *huiothesia* as "filial spirit"[26] or "sonship."[27] According to the classic Lutheran dogmaticians, adoption takes place at the same time as regeneration and justification. The certainty of the believer's adoption, as also the inheritance warranted by it, is counted by them as an attribute to the new birth. Pietism, in its treament of adoption, came somewhat closer to the Reformed presentation. The Reformed theologians, however, do not always consider adoption from the same point of view. While some represent it as the fruit of justification, others regard it as co-ordinate but subject to regeneration. Rationalism wholly discarded the biblical doctrine of

---

24 H. Witsius: *The Economy of the Covenants Between God and Man*, W. Crookshank, tr. and ed., London, 1763.
25 *Ibid.*, volume II, pp. 591 ff.   26 *kindlicher Geist*, Rom. 8:15.
27 *Kindschaft*, Rom. 8:23; 9:4; Gal. 4:5; Eph. 1:5.

adoption. Some of the early church fathers treated adoption as the effect of baptism, since the Apostle in Galatians 3:26, 27 traces the adoption both to faith in Christ and to baptism as the washing of regeneration and renewing of the Holy Ghost.[28] This doctrine was retained by Luther, who regarded baptism as a means of grace that works not *ex opere operato*, or by the mere act, but by the Word of God, which is in and with the water.[29]

The conviction of Christian believers that in Christ Jesus they are God's dear children, is deeply rooted in the hearts of all who "rejoice in hope of the glory of God."[30]

BIBLIOGRAPHY

J. Orr, ed.: *International Standard Bible Encyclopaedia*

J. McClintock and J. Strong: *Cyclopaedia of Biblical, Theological, and Ecclesiastical Literature*

S.M. Jackson, ed.: *The New Schaff-Herzog Encyclopedia of Religious Knowledge*

R.A. Webb: *The Reformed Doctrine of Adoption*

H. Witsius: *The Economy of the Covenants*

W.A. Jarrel: "Adoption Not in the Bible Salvation," *The Review and Expositor*, XV (October, 1918), pp. 459–469

T. Whaling: "Adoption," *The Princeton Theological Review*, XXI (April, 1923), pp. 223–235

[28] Titus 3:5, 6.
[29] Cf. McClintock and Strong, *op. cit., s.v.*
[30] Rom. 5:2.

34

SANCTIFICATION (THE LAW)

✝

JOHN MURRAY

John Murray, Professor of Systematic Theology at Westminster Theological Seminary, received his general and theological education at University of Glasgow (M.A., 1923) and Princeton Theological Seminary (Th.M., 1927). He is the author of *Aspects of Biblical Ethics; Divorce; Principles of Conduct; Redemption, Accomplished and Applied; Commentary on Romans* (two volumes), and numerous articles and tracts.

The battle cry of the Reformation was justification by faith. The issues at stake demanded that this doctrine be made focal. The gospel of grace is polluted at its fountain, when justification of free grace and by faith alone occupies other than a central place. Rome had its doctrine of justification. But it was stated to consist in sanctification and renovation and was construed also as a process outwrought in the works which are the fruit of faith.

It has ever been the objection that justification—complete, perfect, and irrevocable, and by faith alone—is inimical to the interests of holy living. Does not such a doctrine remove the need for and the incentive to good works and the sanctified life evidenced thereby? Paul had to meet this challenge, and the Reformers encountered the same allegation.

In a nutshell, the answer to the charge is the doctrine of sanctification. Justification and sanctification are inseparable, and a faith divorced from good works is not the faith that justifies. Justification is concerned with righteous standing in the sight of God, sanctification with holiness of heart and life. Faith itself is faith in Christ for salvation from sin and acceptance with God. Implicit in the faith by which we are justified is hatred of sin and commitment to God, Whose glory is holiness.

DEFINITIVE SANCTIFICATION

To speak of sanctification as definitive might appear to deny its progressive nature and open the door to the fallacy by which the doctrine has so frequently been distorted. But biblical teaching is not to be suppressed or toned down because of an objection that springs from too restricted an understanding of the biblical witness, nor by fear of the distortions to which the doctrine has been subjected.

When Paul addressed the believers at Corinth as the church of God "sanctified in Christ Jesus, called to be saints"[1] and later reminded them that they were washed, sanctified, and justified,[2] it is obvious that he co-ordinated sanctification with effectual calling, with their identity as saints, with regeneration, and with justification.[3] It would be a deflection from biblical patterns of thought to think of sanctification exclusively in terms of a progressive work. What is this definitive sanctification?

There are various ways in which it can be characterized. The specific and distinguishing action of each person of the Godhead at the inception of the state of salvation contributes to the decisive change which this sanctification denotes, and not only contributes to but insures the decisive nature of the change itself. But perhaps the most significant aspect of New Testament teaching and the aspect requiring particular emphasis is that a believer is one called by the Father into the fellowship of his Son.[4] Union with Christ is the pivot on which the doctrine turns, specifically union with Him in the meaning of His death and the power of His resurrection. When Christ died, He died to sin once for all.[5] And the believer, called into union with Christ, dies with Christ to sin. "We died to sin"[6] is the answer to all licentious abuse of the doctrine of grace. If we died with Christ, we must also live with

[1] I Cor. 1:2.   [2] I Cor. 6:11.
[3] Cf. Acts 20:32; 26:18; II Tim. 2:21; I Thess. 4:7; Heb. 10:10, 29; 13:12.
[4] I Cor. 1:9.   [5] Rom. 6:10.
[6] Rom. 6:2.

him, "that like as Christ was raised from the dead through the glory of the Father, even so should we walk in newness of life."[7] No datum is of more basic importance than the definitive breach with sin and commitment to holiness secured by identification with Christ in His death and resurrection. And this relation of the believer to Christ's death and resurrection is introduced by the Apostle not in reference to justification but to deliverance from the power, defilement, and love of sin. The breach with sin and the newness of life are as definitive as were the death and resurrection of Christ. Christ in His death and resurrection broke the power of sin, triumphed over the prince of darkness, executed judgment upon this world, and by this victory delivered all those who are united to Him. Believers are partakers with Him in these triumphal achievements. The virtue accruing from the death and resurrection of Christ affects no phase of salvation more directly than that of insuring definitive sanctification. If we do not reckon on and with this relationship, we miss one of the most cardinal features of redemptive provision.[8] Believers have the fruit unto holiness.

PROGRESSIVE SANCTIFICATION

It might appear that the emphasis placed upon definitive sanctification leaves no place for what is progressive. Any such inference would contradict an equally important aspect of biblical teaching. No New Testament writers accent the definitive more than Paul and John. Yet, John in the same Epistle in which he says that everyone born of God does not commit sin and cannot sin[9] says also, "If we say that we have no sin, we deceive ourselves, and the truth is not in us,"[10] and he sets before the believer the consolation that "if any one sins, we have an advocate with the Father, Jesus Christ the righteous."[11] For John, there is likewise the self-purifying aspect of the believer's life: "Every one that has this hope in him purifies himself even as he is pure."[12]

When we take account of the sin that resides in the believer and of the fact that he has not yet attained to the goal of conformity to the image of God's Son,[13] his condition in this life can never be conceived of as static. It must be one of progression, a progression both negative and positive, consisting, thus, in both mortification and sanctification.

[7] Rom. 6:4.
[8] Cf. II Cor. 5:14, 15; Eph. 2:1–6; Col. 3:3, 4; I Pet. 4:1, 2; I John 3:6, 9.
[9] I John 3:9; cf. I John 3:6.   [10] I John 1:8.
[11] I John 2:1.   [12] I John 3:3.
[13] Cf. Rom. 8:29.

Paul's references to mortification are striking because of the contexts in which they occur. In the contexts, the once-for-all death to sin and the translation thereby to the realm of new life in Christ are in the forefront. No place might appear to be left for mortification of sin. It is not so. "But if by the Spirit ye put to death the deeds of the body, ye shall live."[14] We are to "cleanse ourselves from all filthiness of flesh and spirit."[15]

Sanctification involves more than cleansing from sin. It is eloquent of something more positive that Paul should have added "perfecting holiness in the fear of God." The most expressive term used in the New Testament to indicate the progression that terminates in conformity to the image of Christ is that of transformation. "Be ye transformed by the renewing of your mind."[16] "But we all with unveiled face beholding as in a glass the glory of the Lord are being transformed into the same image from glory to glory, even as from the Lord, the Spirit."[17] No text defines for us the fact and mode of progressive sanctification more specifically than the latter. Whether the precise thought is that we *reflect* the glory of the Lord Christ or that we *behold* His glory, the outcome is the same. If we behold His glory we also reflect it; and if we reflect it, it is because we first of all behold it.[18] It is a law of our psychology that we become like that in which our interests and ambitions are absorbed. That law is not suspended in this case. But the Apostle reminds us that natural factors are not the secret of this transformation; it is from the Spirit of the Lord that the transformation proceeds.

The progression which must characterize sanctification has respect not only to the individual but also to the church in its unity and fellowship as the body of Christ. Believers may never be regarded as independent units. In the eternal counsel, they were chosen in Christ; in the accomplishment of redemption, they were in Christ; in the application, it is into the fellowship of Christ they are ushered. And sanctification moves to a consummation which will not be realized for the individual in his own particularity until the whole body of Christ is complete and presented in its totality, faultless and without blemish. The practical implications of this corporate relationship for responsibility, privilege, and opportunity become immediately apparent.[19]

---

[14] Rom. 8:13; cf. Col. 3:5.
[16] Rom. 12:2.
[18] Cf. John 1:14.

[15] II Cor. 7:1.
[17] II Cor. 3:18.
[19] Cf. Eph. 4:11-16.

No concept is of more significance, as sanctification is viewed in this perspective, than that of "the fulness of Christ."[20] The stature of Christ's fullness unto which believers are to attain, not as discrete individuals but in the unity and fellowship of the church, is the stature of being filled with the grace and virtue, truth and wisdom, righteousness and holiness, which have their abode in Christ as the firstborn from the dead.

The process which sanctification involves is, therefore, nothing less than conformity to the image of God's Son, a conformity realized not through external initiative assimilation but through an impartation of the fullness that is in Christ,[21] an impartation which flows through a life organism that subsists and operates on an immensely higher plane than any form of organic or animate life with which we are acquainted in our phenomenal earthly experience. Christ and the church are complementary: there is no need of ours, no exigency arising from the high calling of God, no demand flowing from membership in Christ's body, and no office which we are called upon to discharge that is not supplied out of the fullness that resides in Christ as the head of the church.

THE AGENCY IN SANCTIFICATION

In definitive sanctification the pivotal consideration is that believers died with Christ and rose with Him to newness of life. From whatever perspective this relationship is viewed, we are compelled to recognize our passivity. From the perspective of the past and finished historical, it is apparent that our activity was not enlisted in the death and resurrection of Christ. On the other hand, when these events are viewed as taking effect actually and practically in the persons concerned, we are not permitted to think of human agency as enlisted in the decisive breach with sin and commitment to holiness. Even faith may not be construed as the agency in death to sin and in life to righteousness. The language used is clearly to this effect.[22] Furthermore, the bond that makes effective in us the efficacy of Jesus' death and resurrection is union with Him. It is by the call of the Father that this union is established. And this call may never be defined in terms of human agency. Again, the operative principle by which we are freed from the law of

[20] Eph. 4:13; cf. Eph. 1:23.   [21] Cf. John 1:16.
[22] Cf. Rom. 6:3, 4, 6, 17, 18; 7:4; Eph. 2:4, 5.

sin and death is the Holy Spirit.[23] Thus, the agency of all three Persons is brought to bear upon this decisive change.

What is the agency in progressive sanctification? It is to God the Father that Jesus addressed the intercession: "Sanctify them in the truth: thy word is truth."[24] And it is of the Father He speaks when He says: "Every branch that beareth fruit, he purgeth it, that it may bring forth more fruit."[25] Paul points to the same truth—that the Father sanctifies.[26] By way of eminence, however, the Holy Spirit is the agent. The Holy Spirit is brought into relation to the transforming process by which believers come to reflect the glory of the Lord.[27] It is the Holy Spirit Who is the Spirit of wisdom and revelation in the knowledge of Christ.[28] It is by the Spirit we put to death the deeds of the body.[29] The virtues which are both the marks and fruits of sanctification are the fruit of the Spirit.[30] It is by the Holy Spirit that the igniting flame of God's love to us is shed abroad in our hearts.[31] It is the distinctive prerogative of the Holy Spirit to abide in believers, to work effectually in their whole personality to the end that they might be filled unto all the fullness of God and attain to the goal appointed for them. Sanctification progresses not by some law of renewed psychology but by the indwelling and constantly renewing activity of the Holy Spirit.

We are always liable to distort emphases. Out of deference to all the stress that falls upon God's agency in sanctification we must not fall into the error of quietism and fail to take account of the activity of the believer himself. The imperatives directed to the believer imply nothing less.[32] Perhaps the most instructive text is Philippians 2:12, 13, a text frequently misapplied. The salvation spoken of is not initial salvation, but that to be attained at the revelation of Jesus Christ.[33] It is salvation as completed and consummated that we are to work out. And this means that our agency and activity are to be exercised to the fullest extent in the promotion of this salvation. Hence, the implications: our working is not dispensed with or made superfluous because God works; God's working is not suspended because we work. There is the correlation and conjunction of both. The fact that God

23 Rom. 8:2.   24 John 17:17.
25 John 15:2.   26 I Thess. 5:23.
27 II Cor. 3:18.   28 Eph. 1:17.
29 Rom. 8:13.   30 Gal. 5:22.
31 Rom. 5:5.
32 Cf. Rom. 6:13, 19; 8:13; II Cor. 7:1; Gal. 5:16, 25.
33 Cf. Rom. 13:11; I Thess. 5:9; Heb. 1:14; 9:28; I Pet. 1:5; 2:2.

works in us is the encouragement and incentive to our working. Indeed, God's working is the energizing cause of our working both in willing and doing. Our working is the index to God's working; if we do not work, the working of God is absent. Presumptuous self-confidence is excluded; fear and trembling in us are the reflection of our helplessness. Yet, the more assured we are that God works in us, the more diligent and persistent we are in our working. Our whole personality is not only drawn within the scope of but also enlisted in all its functions in that process that moves to the goal of being conformed to the image of God's Son.

BIBLIOGRAPHY

G.C. Berkouwer: *Faith and Sanctification*
J.C. Ryle: *Holiness: Its Nature, Hindrances, Difficulties, and Roots*
A. Köberle: *The Quest for Holiness*
A.W. Pink: *The Doctrine of Sanctification*
W. Marshall: *The Gospel-Mystery of Sanctification*
J. Fraser: *A Treatise on Sanctification*

35

THE PERSEVERANCE OF

THE SAINTS

✚

W. BOYD HUNT

W. Boyd Hunt, Professor of Theology at Southwestern Baptist Theological Seminary, Fort Worth, Texas, received his general and theological education at Wheaton College (B.A., 1939) and Southwestern Baptist Theological Seminary (Th.M., 1942, Th.D., 1944). He is the author of *Sixteen to One*.

Perseverance is a key idea in the Christian revelation. God's unique love is known as a steadfast love. Jesus, having loved His own, loved them to the end. Paul's ultimate word is that the love which the believer learns at the cross "endures all things." Judas betrayed his Lord. Demas forsook Paul. But in Revelation, those who endure to the end are robed in white. Small wonder that Shakespeare calls perseverance a "king-becoming" grace.

In theological discussion, however, perseverance is used not in this ordinary sense but in a technical sense, for the Calvinistic doctrine that God preserves to final salvation each of the elect whom He calls and regenerates. Popularly expressed, this is the doctrine of "once saved—always saved."

PERSEVERANCE AND APOSTASY

In its technical sense, perseverance stands opposed to the idea of apostasy, or the doctrine that it is possible for believers to fall from grace, either temporarily, so as to alternate from a state of grace to a state of lostness and back to a state of grace again, or finally, so as to have been once saved and yet finally be damned. Those who insist on the possibility of apostasy do not entirely eliminate the idea of perseverance. But they use the term in its ordinary sense only, thinking of perseverance as an obligation resting on the believer to persevere in believing. They deny its technical use.

Each of these doctrines claims to be rooted firmly in Scripture. Perseverance points to the passages underscoring the believer's sure persuasion that God takes the initiative in perfecting, as well as originating, man's salvation: He who has begun a good work in the believer performs it to the end;[1] God keeps His own;[2] nothing can separate the believer from the love of God;[3] and the Holy Spirit seals the believer to the day of redemption.[4] From the perspective of the perseverance doctrine, the mere initiation of a process without its consummation[5] should not be called salvation, since there is no salvation apart from endurance.[6] Yet, it is possible for believers to retard God's work[7] and hence, the repeated warnings and exhortations to Christians.[8] Defenders of this view, instead of interpreting such passages as Hebrews 6:4-6 and 10:26, 27 as teaching apostasy, understand these passages as referring either to a hypothetical possibility[9] or to the failure of those who were never genuinely converted. There is no easy interpretation of many of these passages.

In the history of doctrine, the perseverance-apostasy issue is best understood not merely as a difference between Calvinists and Arminians, but more fundamentally as a difference between Protestants and

[1] Phil. 1:6; cf. I John 3:6-9; 4:4.
[2] John 10:28, 29; Col. 2:2 [note the strong expression, "full assurance"; cf. Heb. 6:11; 10:22]; II Tim. 1:12; I Pet. 1:5.
[3] Rom. 8:34; Heb. 7:24; I John 2:1; cf. Luke 22:31, 32; John 17:11-15.
[4] II Cor. 1:22; 5:5; Eph. 1:13, 14; 4:30.
[5] E.g., Mark 4:16, 17; II Pet. 2:20; I John 2:19.
[6] Matt. 10:22; 24:13; Mark 13:13; I Cor. 15:2; Col. 1:23; Heb. 3:6, 14; 10:38; Rev. 2:7, 10, 11, 17, 25, 26; 3:5, 11, 12, 21.
[7] I Cor. 3:1-3; Heb. 5:12 to 6:8.
[8] Matt. 5:13; I Cor. 3:11-15; 9:27; 10:12; Gal. 5:4; Phil. 2:12, 13; Heb. 2:1-3; 3:12-14; 6:4-6, 9-12; 10:26-29; II Pet. 1:8-11.
[9] See W. Manson: The Epistle to the Hebrews, p. 15.

Catholics, whether Roman or Greek, and hence, broadly speaking, as a difference between Augustinians and Pelagians.

PRE-REFORMATION VIEWS

Patristic thought[10] was largely an anticipation of or a practical agreement with Pelagius,[11] the British monk who, in opposition to Augustine,[12] minimized sin and overemphasized man's freedom. By and large, the possibility of apostasy was an assumption common to the earliest writers.

It was left to Augustine to speak a clear word for perseverance in pre-Reformation times. Starting with predestination, he saw that election to eternal life inevitably involves final perseverance. Since salvation is always God's gift, he entitled his work on perseverance *On the Gift of Perseverance*. He denied, however, that the believer can have any assurance of his final salvation.

Medieval Romanism was the heir not of Augustinian predestinarianism but of a semi-Pelagian optimism regarding man's freedom and ability. According to the *Canons and Decrees of the Council of Trent*,[13] man freely co-operates with justifying grace. God does not forsake those who have been once justified by grace "unless he be first forsaken by them." This leads to a doctrine of apostasy, "By every mortal sin grace is lost," and of restoration, ". . . those who, by sin, have fallen from the received grace of Justification, they may be again justified. . . ." Believers "ought to fear for the combat which yet remaineth." On the latter point, J.S. Whale says, "The medieval Church came to trade on this insecurity."[14]

REFORMED VIEWS

Against this semi-Pelagianism of Rome, the Reformers rediscovered the Augustinian and Pauline stress on grace. Luther,[15] carrying out only partially the implications of this rediscovery, failed to develop a doctrine of perseverance.[16] Lutheran symbols are agreed in allowing for the possibility of apostasy.[17] Melanchthon's[18] synergism, or his teaching that

---

[10] Roughly 100–500.   [11] Pelagius, *ca.* 360–420.
[12] Augustine, 354–430.   [13] 1563.
[14] J.S. Whale: *The Protestant Tradition*, p. 67.
[15] Luther, 1483–1546.
[16] *See* M. Luther: "The Greater Catechism," *Luther's Primary Works*, H. Wace and C.A. Buchheim, ed. and tr., pp. 141 f.
H. Wace and C.A. Buchheim, ed. and tr.
[17] *The Augsburg Confession*, 1530, Article XII; *The Formula of Concord*, 1576, Article IV, Negative III; *The Saxon Articles*, 1592, Articles IV, III.
[18] Melanchthon, 1497–1560.

the human will co-operates with the divine will in salvation, reflects a more semi-Pelagian emphasis within Lutheran theology.

Calvin[19] worked out the Reformation stress on grace with greater logical consistency. He may be said to be the first to develop a full doctrine of perseverance. Subscribing to "the inflexible constancy of election," he affirms the believer's sure persuasion of present and future salvation.[20] Strict Calvinistic orthodoxy received its classical definition at the Synod of Dort.[21] In answer to the moderate Calvinism of the Arminian *Remonstrance*,[22] Dort formulated its position in five canons: unconditional election, limited atonement, total depravity, irresistible grace, and the final perseverance of the saints. Under the last or fifth head of doctrine, which follows logically from the first, Dort summarized in fifteen articles the definitive statement of perseverance. Strict Calvinism tended to dwell on the mystery and the theological, as over against the inner or psychological, certainty of the divine preservation. According to the *Wesminster Confession*,[23] "This perseverance of the saints depends, not upon their own free-will, but upon the immutability of the decree of election, etc."[24]

The most signficant development of an Arminian or moderate type of Calvinism was the original Wesleyanism. Repelled by the antinomian extremes of some hyper-Calvinists, John Wesley[25] stressed the necessity of human perseverance and allowed for the possibility of apostasy. Yet, he more than any other recaptured the New Testament emphasis on the believer's joyous inner or psychological certainty of salvation. Wesley even allows that a full conviction of future perseverance is possessed by some.[26] Later, Methodism tended toward semi-Pelagianism, as indicated in its neglect of grace and preoccupation with freedom.[27] By an irony of history, Arminianism came to stand for this later semi-Pelagianism rather than for a moderate type of Calvinism.

MODERN DEVELOPMENTS

Until about the third decade of the twentieth century, the Calvinistic-Arminian controversy dominated the theological scene within

[19] Calvin, 1509–1564.
[20] J. Calvin: *Institutes*, III, xxiv, 10; III, ii, 16, 40 (Beveridge, tr.).
[21] Synod of Dort, Netherlands, 1618–1619.
[22] 1610.   [23] 1647.
[24] Chapters XVII, II.   [25] Wesley, 1703–1791.
[26] *See* J. Telford, ed.: *The Letters of the Rev. John Wesley*, 1931, Volume III, pp. 305 f.
[27] *See* R.E. Chiles: "Methodist Apostasy: From Free Grace to Free Will," *Religion in Life*, XXVII (Summer, 1958), pp. 438–449.

Protestantism, particularly in America. On the Calvinistic side ranged the Reformed, Presbyterian, Free, Puritan, Congregational, and most of the later Baptist groups. On the Arminian side, in the limited sense of defending the possibility of apostasy, stood the Lutheran, Anabaptist (Mennonite), General and Free Will Baptist, Methodist, Holiness, and Disciple groups. The position of the Anglican communions remained ambiguous.

Today, many of the older issues are being superseded. As P.T. Forsyth foresaw, "The centre of majesty has passed, since Calvin, from the decrees of God to his Act of redemption in Christ."[28]

THE NEED FOR RESTATEMENT

Some suggestions pointing toward a contemporary restatement of the doctrine should include the following: (1) The urgency of reconsidering the problem can hardly be overemphasized. Seen in its biblical perspective, the perseverance issue strikes at the heart of one of the most dire problems of Christendom, the tragedy of uncommited church members. When perseverance is conceived in its ordinary sense as heroic, self-sacrificing constancy in the face of bitter opposition and despairing discouragements, how can we speak of the perseverance of today's saints?

This is obviously no light matter. Nor is there significant evidence that nominal Christianity is any less an inadequacy of either the Calvinists or the Arminians. Presbyterians are hardly more or less courageous than Methodists. Baptists are hardly more or less inwardly confident of God's certain victory over all his enemies than Lutherans. Puritan hyper-Calvinists agonized over assurance of personal salvation, while it was Luther, with his belief in the possibility of apostasy, who wrote "A Mighty Fortress Is Our God."

As evangelicals, we glory in our freedom in Christ. But is it really the liberty we have in Christ, Forsyth asks, "when we feel more free than obedient, and more released than ruled?"[29]

(2) Christian experience involves both the divine initiative in grace and man's free response, and in this order. Because of the former, Christian theology affirms that though hypothetically man can fall from grace, since he remains free as a Christian, experientially the grace of God prevents it. A biblically grounded faith is confident that God's

---

[28] P.T. Forsyth: *Faith, Freedom, and the Future*, p. 277.
[29] *Ibid.*, p. 291.

faithfulness prevails over our faithlessness. We have assurance, J.S. Whale says, because "God is trustworthy and unchanging.... The grace of God is not capricious, and therefore intermittent and precarious; it abides, even though we still fail and fall."[30]

Yet, because Christian experience is also man's free response, this security is always the security of the believer. God secures through man's faith, not without it.

(3) Since there is no state of final perfection in this life, it follows that neither is there any final inner security. The believer can never simply sit back, as though the full experience of his faith were already realized. He has Christ, yet he needs Christ. He has salvation, yet he needs salvation. On the one hand, his confidence in Christ is intimately real. Martyrs have sung triumphantly as they faced torture and death. On the other hand, his confidence needs repeatedly to be rewon. Man is never freed from the causes of anxiety and the threats to his security, a fact contemporary existentialists have helped us to see more clearly. But as a believer, man no longer faces these threats alone. Now there is Another who stands with him.

(4) Two other aspects of the doctrine of perseverance can be only mentioned. First, God honors the believer's perseverance with an increased spiritual capacity for receiving the divine blessings. This is Jesus' principle, that to him who has is given. Second, perseverance as preservation has its corporate aspect. As God preserves the individual, so he preserves the church as the fellowship of believers in the Holy Spirit. Again and again, God resurrects the church to a new life of victory over its would-be destroyers. (According to Roman theology, the church cannot apostatize, but believers can. According to Calvinistic theology, the institutional church can apostatize, but individual believers cannot.)

In conclusion, perseverance is no easy doctrine. God preserves; the believer perseveres. God preserves through the believer's perseverance. The believer's perseverance is God's gift.

It is not an easy doctrine, nor is it a soothing doctrine. It probes the soul that is at ease in Zion with a holy disquiet, asking whether a believer has been to the cross, whether he knows the quality of love that is there laid bare, whether he has learned the basic fidelity that in the

---

30 J.S. Whale, op. cit., p. 83. Whale calls the assurance that our salvation is untouchable by human weakness the glory of Protestantism and describes it as "fatal to all papal, hierarchical and sacerdotal pretensions" [p. 144].

end includes all other marks of Christian character, until he has persevered.

Speaking of the quality of the dedication of the men and women who lived from Peter to Polycarp,[31] Guy Schofield declares that no triumph has been like their triumph, and then he explains: "They were clothed in flesh no less sensitive than is our own to heat and frost and blade and whip. But they endured all things and never quit the field."[32]

BIBLIOGRAPHY

G.C. Berkouwer: *Faith and Perseverance*, R.D. Knudsen, tr.
J.F. Green, Jr.: *Faith to Grow On*
G.S. Hendry: *The Westminster Confession for Today*
R. Shank: *Life in the Son*
J.S. Whale: *The Protestant Tradition*
A.S. Yates: *The Doctrine of Assurance*

[31] *Ca.* 69–155.
[32] G. Schofield: *It Began on the Cross*, p. 244.

36

THE NATURE OF

THE CHURCH

✚

JAMES I. PACKER

James I. Packer, Lecturer at Latimer House, Oxford, England, received his general and theological education at Corpus Christi College, Oxford (B.A., 1950; M.A., 1952; D.Phil., 1954). He is the author of *Fundamentalism and the Word of God* and the translator (with O.R. Johnston) of Luther's *Bondage of the Will*.

The Church of God, "that wonderful and sacred mystery,"[1] is a subject that stands at the very heart of the Bible. For the church is the object of the redemption which the Bible proclaims. It was to save the church that the Son of God became man, and died;[2] God purchased His church at the cost of Christ's blood.[3] It is through the church that God makes known his redeeming wisdom to the hosts of heaven.[4] It is within the church that the individual Christian finds the ministries of grace, the means of growth, and his primary sphere for service.[5] We cannot properly understand the purpose of God, nor the method of grace, nor the kingdom of Christ, nor the work of the Holy Spirit,

[1] Aquinas.   [2] Eph. 5:25.
[3] Acts 20:28.   [4] Eph. 3:10.
[5] Eph. 4:11–16.

nor the meaning of world history without studying the doctrine of the church.

But what is the church? The fact that we all first meet the church as an organized society must not mislead us into thinking that it is essentially, or even primarily, that. There is a sense in which the outward form of the church disguises its true nature rather than reveals it. Essentially, the church is not a human organization as such, but a divinely created fellowship of sinners who trust a common Saviour, and are one with each other because they are all one with Him in a union realized by the Holy Spirit. Thus the church's real life, like that of its individual members, is for the present "hid in Christ with God,"[6] and will not be manifested to the world until He appears. Meanwhile, what we need, if we are to understand the church's nature, is insight into the person and work of Christ and of the Spirit and into the meaning of the life of faith.

THE COVENANT PEOPLE OF GOD

The church is not simply a New Testament phenomenon. An ecclesiology which started with the New Testament would be out of the way at the first step. The New Testament church is the historical continuation of Old Testament Israel. The New Testament word for "church," *ekklesia* (in secular Greek, a public gathering) is regularly used in the Greek Old Testament for the "congregation" of Israel. Paul pictured the church in history, from its beginning to his own day, as a single olive tree, from which some natural (Israelite) branches had been broken off through unbelief, to be replaced by some wild (Gentile) branches.[7] Elsewhere, he tells Gentile believers that in Christ they have become "Abraham's seed," "the Israel of God."[8]

The basis of the church's life in both Testaments is the covenant which God made with Abraham. The fundamental idea of biblical ecclesiology is of the church as the covenant people of God.

What is a covenant? It is a defined relationship of promise and commitment which binds the parties concerned to perform whatever duties toward each other their relationship may involve. The two main biblical analogies for God's covenant with sinners are the royal covenant between overlord and vassal and the marriage covenant between husband and wife, the former speaking of God's sovereignty and lordship,

[6] Col. 3:4.   [7] Rom. 11:16–24.
[8] Gal. 3:29; cf. Rom. 4:11–18; Gal. 6:16.

the latter of His love and saviourhood. By His covenant, God demands acceptance of His rule and promises enjoyment of His blessing. Both thoughts are contained in the covenant "slogan," "I will be your God, and ye shall be my people";[9] both are implied whenever a believer says "my [our] God."

God expounded his covenant to Abraham in Genesis 17, a chapter of crucial importance for the doctrine of the church. Four points should be noticed here. First, the covenant relationship was announced as a *corporate* one, extending to Abraham's seed "throughout their generations."[10] Thus, the covenant created a permanent community. Second, the relationship was one of *pledged beneficence* on God's part: He undertook to give Abraham's seed the land of Canaan.[11] This, as He had already told Abraham, would involve redeeming them from captivity in Egypt.[12] Third, the end of the relationship was *fellowship* between God and His people: that they should "walk before" Him, knowing Him as they were known by Him.[13] Fourth, the covenant was confirmed by the institution of a "token,"[14] the *initiatory rite* of circumcision.

Later, through Moses, God gave His people a *law* for their lives and authorized forms of *worship* (feasts, exhibiting His fellowship with them, and sacrifices, pointing to the bloodshedding for sin which alone could provide a basis for this fellowship). Also, He spoke to them repeatedly, through His prophets, of their glorious *hope* which was to be realized when the Messiah came.

Thus, emerged the basic biblical notion of the church as the covenant people of God, the redeemed family, marked out as His by the covenant sign which they had received, worshiping and serving Him according to His revealed will, living in fellowship with Him and with each other, walking by faith in His promises, and looking for the coming glory of the Messianic kingdom.

NEW TESTAMENT FULFILLMENT

When Christ came, this Old Testament conception was not destroyed, but fulfilled. Christ, the Mediator of the covenant, was Him-

[9] Cf. Exod. 29:45; Lev. 26:12; Jer. 31:33; II Cor. 6:16; Rev. 21:3; etc.
[10] Gen. 17:7.
[11] Gen. 17:8, a type of heaven; cf. Heb. 11:8–16.
[12] Gen. 15:13–21; cf. Exod. 2:24.   [13] Gen. 17:1.
[14] Gen. 17:11.

self the link between the Mosaic and Christian dispensations of it.[15] The New Testament depicts Him as the true Israel, the servant of God in Whom the nation's God-guided history is recapitulated and brought to completion,[16] and also as the seed of Abraham in Whom all nations of the earth find blessing.[17] Through His atoning death, which did away with the typical sacrificial services forever, believing Jews and Gentiles become in Him the people of God on earth. Baptism, the New Testament initiatory sign corresponding to circumcision, represents primarily union with Christ in His death and resurrection, which is the sole way of entry into the church.[18]

Thus, the New Testament church has Abraham as its father,[19] Jerusalem as its mother[20] and place of worship,[21] and the Old Testament as its Bible.[22] Echoing Exodus 19:5f. and Hosea 2:23, Peter describes the Christian church in thorough-going Old Testament fashion as "a chosen generation, a royal priesthood, an holy nation, a peculiar people; . . . Which in time past were not a people, but are now the people of God."[23]

A NEW CREATION IN CHRIST

The New Testament idea of the church is reached by superimposing upon the notion of the covenant people of God the further thought that the church is the company of those who share in the redemptive renewal of a sin-spoiled creation, which began when Christ rose from the dead.[24] As the individual believer is a new creation in Christ,[25] raised with Him out of death into life,[26] possessed of and led by the life-giving Holy Spirit,[27] so also is the church as a whole. Its life springs from its union with Christ, crucified and risen. Paul, in Ephesians, pictures the church successively as Christ's *building*, now growing unto "an holy temple in the Lord";[28] His *body*, now growing toward a state of full edification;[29] and His *bride*, now being sanctified and cleansed in readiness for "the marriage supper of the Lamb."[30]

---

[15] I.e., the "old" and the "new" covenants of Heb. 8–10, chapters which build upon Jer. 31:31 ff.

[16] Cf. Matt. 2:15; etc.　　　　　　　　[17] Gal. 3:8 f., 14–29.

[18] Rom. 6:3 ff.; Gal. 3:27 ff.; Col. 2:11 ff.

[19] Rom. 4:11, 16.　　　　　　　　　　[20] Gal. 4:26.

[21] Heb. 12:22.　　　　　　　　　　　[22] Rom. 15:4.

[23] I Pet. 2:9 f.　　　　　　　　　　　[24] Cf. I Cor. 15:20; Col. 1:18.

[25] II Cor. 5:17.　　　　　　　　　　　[26] Eph. 2:1 ff.

[27] Rom. 8:9–14.　　　　　　　　　　[28] Eph. 2:21.

[29] Eph. 5:25 ff. cf. Rev. 19:7 ff.

[30] Found, as well as in Ephesians, in Rom. 12, I Cor. 12, and Col.

Some modern writers in the "catholic" tradition treat Paul's body metaphor[31] as having a special "ontological" significance, and indicating that the church is "really" (in a sense in which it is not "really" anything else) an extension of the manhood and incarnate life of Christ. But, according to Paul, the church's union with Christ is symbolically exhibited in baptism; and what baptism symbolizes is not incorporation into Christ's manhood simply, but sharing with Him in His death to sin, with all its saving fruits, and in the power and life of His resurrection. When Paul says that the Spirit *baptizes* men into one body, he means that the Spirit makes us members of the body by bringing us into that union with Christ which baptism signifies.[32] Scripture would lead us to call the church an extension of the resurrection rather than of the incarnation! In any case, Paul uses the body metaphor only to illustrate the authority of the Head, and His ministry to His members, and the various ministries that they must fulfill to each other; and we have no warrant for extrapolating it in other theological directions.

MINISTRY IN THE CHURCH

The New Testament conceives of all ministry in the church as Christ's ministry to and through the church. As the church is a priestly people, all its members having direct access to God through Christ's mediation, so it is a ministering people, all its members holding in trust from Christ gifts of ministry (i.e., service) for the edifying of the one body.[33] Within the context of this universal ministry, Christ calls some specifically to minister the Gospel,[34] giving them strength and skill for their task[35] and blessing their labors.[36] As spokesmen and representatives of Christ, teaching and applying His Word, church officers exercise His authority; yet they need to remember that, as individuals, they belong to the church as its servants, not the church to them as their empire. The church is Christ's kingdom, not theirs.[37] This is a basic point which Luther accused the Papacy of forgetting.

UNIVERSAL AND LOCAL

Paul speaks not merely of the whole body but also of local groups in an area, and even of a Christian household, as "*the* church." No local group is ever called "*a* church." For Paul does not regard the church

[31] I Cor. 12:13.
[32] I Cor. 12:4–28; Rom. 12:6–8; cf. I Cor. 16:15; II Cor. 9:1.
[33] Eph. 4:11; cf. Rom. 1:1, 5, 9; 15:16.
[34] I Cor. 3:10; 15:10.   [35] I Cor. 3:6 f.
[36] Cf. II Cor. 4:5.   [37] Matt. 18:20.

universal as an aggregate of local churches (let alone denominations!);
his thought is rather that whenever a group of believers, even Christ's
statutory two or three,[38] meet in His name, they *are* the church in
the place where they meet. Each particular gathering, however small,
is the local manifestation of the church universal, embodying and dis-
playing the spiritual realities of the church's supernatural life. So Paul
can apply the body metaphor, with only slight alteration, both to the
local church (one body in Christ)[39] and to the universal church (one
body *under* Christ).[40]

VISIBLE AND INVISIBLE

The Reformers drew a necessary distinction between the church
visible and invisible; that is, between the one Church of Christ on earth
as God sees it and as man sees it; in other words, as it is and as it seems
to be. Man sees the church as an organized society, with a fixed structure and roll of members. But (the Reformers argued) this society can
never be simply identified with the one holy catholic Church of which
the Bible speaks. The identity between the two is at best partial, indirect, and constantly varying in degree. The point is important. The
church as God sees it, the company of believers in communion with
Christ and in Him with each other, is necessarily invisible to men, since
Christ and the Holy Spirit and faith, the realities which make the
church, are themselves invisible. The church becomes visible as its
members meet together in Christ's name to worship and hear God's
Word. But the church visible is a mixed body. Some who belong,
though orthodox, are not true believers—not, that is, true members of
the church as God knows it—and need to be converted.[41] The Reformers' distinction thus safeguards the vital truth that visible church
membership saves no man apart from faith in Christ.

Another matter on which this distinction throws light is the question of church unity. If a visible organization, as such, were or could
be the one church of God, then any organizational separation would
be a breach of unity, and the only way to reunite a divided Christendom would be to work for a single international super-church. Also,
on this hypothesis, it would be open to argue that some institutional
feature is of the essence of the church and is therefore a *sine qua non*

[38] Rom. 12; I Cor. 12.   [39] Eph. 4.
[40] Cf. Matt. 13:24 ff., 47 ff.; II Cor. 13:5; I Cor. 15:34.
[41] Cf. Eph. 4:3.

of reunion. (Rome, for instance, actually defines the church as the society of the faithful *under the Pope's headship;* some Anglicans make episcopacy in the apostolic succession similarly essential.) But, in fact, the church invisible, the true church, is one already. Its unity is given to it in Christ.[41] The proper ecumenical task is not to create church unity by denominational coalescence, but to recognize the unity that already exists and to give it worthy expression on the local level.

In the purposes of God, the church, we have seen, is glorious; yet on earth it remains a little flock in a largely hostile environment. Often, its state and prospects seem to us precarious. But we need not fear. Christ Himself, the King who reigns on Zion's hill, is its Saviour, its Head, its Builder, its Keeper. He has given his promise: "the gates of hell shall not prevail against it."[42] And He is not accustomed to break His word.

BIBLIOGRAPHY

J. Bannerman: *The Church of Christ*
C. Hodge: *The Church and Its Polity*
A.M. Stibbs: *God's Church*
R.B. Kuiper: *The Glorious Body of Christ*
E. Best: *One Body in Christ*

[42] Matt. 16:18.

37

THE GOVERNMENT OF

THE CHURCH

✝

EDWARD JOHN CARNELL

Edward John Carnell, Professor of Ethics and Philosophy of Religion at Fuller Theological Seminary, Pasadena, California, received his general and theological education at Wheaton College (A.B., 1941), Westminster Theological Seminary (Th.B., Th.M., 1944), Harvard University (S.T.M., 1945; Th.D., 1948), and Boston University (Ph.D., 1949). He is the author of *Television: Servant or Master?*, *The Theology of Reinhold Niebuhr*, *A Philosophy of the Christian Religion*, *The Case for Orthodox Theology*, and *The Kingdom of Love and the Pride of Life*, among other works.

As in other matters pertaining to faith and practice, the evangelical looks to Scripture when he defines the boundaries of acceptable church government. At first glance, however, Scripture seems disturbingly indecisive, for no *specific* government is legislated for the church. The general principles of polity are clear, but not the details. This is one reason why questions of government have caused such deep and lasting divisions in the church.

It seems that the Spirit of God has been pleased to allow a certain flexibility in matters of form and order. In any case, we have no right to boast, for no branch of Christendom has precisely the same kind of government as that which existed in the early church.

THE NECESSITY OF GOVERNMENT

According to the Apostles' Creed, the church is a communion of the saints. This view comports with Scripture. True believers are a fellowship in Christ. This fellowship is not an external society whose rights dissolve when the corporation dissolves; it can exist without any organization at all.

But if this be true, why should the church be yoked with ecclesiastical rule? Why not let the fellowship carry itself? The answer is that government keeps the affairs of the church decent and orderly, in order that the ministry of the Word might not be hindered.

Although the church is not an external society, it is a vital society with a normative ground of existence. Christ is the head of the church, and Christ is confronted in and through Scripture. This is why the ministry of the Word is so essential to the fellowship. Unless Scripture is studied and preached with diligence, Christians will not know what God requires of them.

But if the ministry of the Word is to prosper, it must be delivered from the distractions of secondary duties. Hence, the Lord has been pleased to ordain auxiliary ministries in the church—those of serving, teaching, and rule. These ministries, taken together, form the substance of church government. They give stability to the fellowship.

THE MINISTRY OF SERVING

Scripture tells us that the ministry of serving was created to resolve a conflict of interests in the church.[1] The Hellenists murmured against the Hebrews, because their widows were neglected in the daily distribution. Charges of injustice threatened the fellowship. The Apostles knew that something had to be done about the matter and done at once. But they also knew that it would be wrong for them to leave the ministry of the Word to serve tables. Therefore, deacons were appointed to oversee the practical affairs of the church. *Nothing* must come between a pastor and his task of preaching the Gospel.

There is no limit to the ways in which the ministry of serving can

[1] Acts 6:1–6.

lift burdens from the ministry of the Word. When a pastor is cumbered by much serving, he neglects his duties as a shepherd of the flock. Rather than giving himself to prayer and meditation, he types stencils for the bulletin, does janitorial work, or coaches a basketball team. Or his strength may be depleted by larger distractions such as fund-raising, building church properties, or managing a complex educational system. A pastor must follow the example of the Apostles: he must practice the art of delegation. Christian education directors and psychiatrists may be as necessary to the ministry of serving in the modern church as deacons were in the early church.

THE MINISTRY OF TEACHING AND RULE

Although the Apostles entrusted the ministry of teaching and rule to elders, the appointment of elders—unlike that of deacons—did not arise out of a specific incident in the life of the fellowship. We are not told *when* the first elders were set apart or *why*. We are simply told that when relief was sent to the distressed brethren in Judea, the money was delivered to the elders by the hands of Barnabas and Saul.[2] It appears that the office of elder belonged to the government of the church from the earliest times.

When Christ founded the church, He drew on a fellowship which was already in existence. This fellowship was formed of Israelites who were accustomed to the mode of government that prevailed in the synagogue. Therefore, it was only natural that this mode would be carried into the new communion. The office of elder "continued, in substance, what it had been hitherto under the Jewish synagogue system in its best days, with suitable modifications and developments in accordance with the free spirit of the Gospel and the Providential circumstances in which the Christian congregations found themselves placed. This presumption is confirmed by all the evidence, direct and indirect, bearing upon the point in the New Testament documents which belong to this period of the history."[3]

Although the Apostles outranked the elders in authority, the elders were destined to become the highest permanent officers in the church. There is no record that the office of Apostle continued after the death of John; Scripture neither commands such a continuance nor does it specify the qualifications of those who should seek the office.

[2] Acts 11:29, 30.
[3] D.D. Bannerman: *The Scripture Doctrine of the Church*, p. 416.

But the qualifications of those who seek the office of elder (or bishop) are specifically set down in Scripture.[4] The question was not left to chance. The Apostle Paul appointed elders in the places where he had preached, and at great personal risk. We could ask for no more forceful proof that the Gentile churches were to be governed by the same polity that prevailed in the Jewish churches.

THE PURPOSE OF ELDERS

The elders were entrusted with the tasks of teaching and rule. "This double function appears in Paul's expression 'pastors and teachers,' where, as the form of the original seems to show, the two words describe the same office under different aspects. Though *government* was probably the first conception of the office, yet the work of *teaching* must have fallen to the presbyters from the very first and have assumed greater prominence as time went on."[5] The ministry of teaching and rule had exactly the same goal as the ministry of serving: to keep the affairs of the church decent and orderly, that the ministry of the Word might not be hindered.

After the elders were appointed by the Apostles, they served as a self-acting body. They could take the needed steps, with the concurrence of the congregation, to add to their number or to create any subordinate offices that might be needed for the more perfect life of the church.

It should be observed, however, that though the elders were to teach and rule, Scripture does not spell out their specific duties. Scripture assumes, as it does in the case of the deacons, that as long as the elders are full of the Spirit and wisdom, they will not only see what is required of them but they will discharge their duties with cheerfulness and dispatch.

THE FUNCTIONAL ELEMENT IN CHURCH GOVERNMENT

The church is presently divided on whether the ministry of rule requires a separate officer, such as bishop or superintendent, or whether this ministry belongs to pastors or elders who enjoy parity of rank. Two points should be noted in this connection.

First, the New Testament equates the offices of "elder" and

[4] I Tim. 3:1-7.
[5] J.B. Lightfoot: *Saint Paul's Epistle to the Philippians,* "The Christian Ministry" p. 194.

"bishop." Therefore, any distinction between these officers is based on expedience, not principle. "There was in apostolic times no distinction between elders [presbyters] and bishops such as we find from the second century onwards: the leaders of the Ephesian church are indiscriminately described as elders, bishops [i.e., superintendents] and shepherds [or pastors]"[6] The validity of this exegesis is generally acknowledged.

Second, and more important, the ministry of rule, like other auxiliary ministries in the church, is free to develop its office according to the needs of the times. In the actual life of the fellowship, therefore, divergent modes of government may emerge. These modes may be the result of rich cultural and social influences. Or they may simply grow out of the dictates of expediency.

There may be times when a fellowship is so small that all the prescribed ministries in the church—that of the Word, serving, teaching, and rule—may devolve on the pastor himself. As he succeeds in training others, he can delegate the auxiliary ministries. But he must proceed slowly, for it is not wise to lay on hands hastily.[7]

When a fellowship reaches vast proportions, however, expedience may dictate that a separate office of rule be created. And it makes precious little difference what name is given to the officer in charge— whether bishop, archbishop, superintendent, or state secretary.

In some cases it may be more expedient to vest the office of rule in a group of men—a council of pastors or elders, a pastor and his deacons, etc. Neither the number of men nor their title is important. The important thing is that the office of rule is founded on biblical principles.

CHURCH DISCIPLINE

When church members are guilty of gross immorality, they must be excluded from the fellowship until they give signs of evangelical repentance. The New Testament is clear on this point.[8] Gross immorality cannot be ignored, and neither can it be tried by just anybody. If the fellowship is to be kept decent and orderly, specific persons must be vested with authority to administer discipline. Spheres of lawful jurisdiction *must* be defined.

When church members follow false teaching, however, the New Testament is not so clear. On the one hand, Christians are commanded

[6] F.F. Bruce: *Commentary on the Book of Acts*, p. 415.
[7] I Tim. 5:22.   [8] *See,* for example, I Cor. 5.

to continue in the teaching of Christ and the Apostles. But on the other hand, they are not told precisely what doctrines are essential to fellowship, nor are they told precisely what to do with errorists. For example, certain Judaizers went about teaching the necessity of circumcision.[9] The Apostles denounced the error, but they did not excommunicate the Judaizers. Again, there were some in Corinth who denied the resurrection.[10] The Apostle Paul was shocked by such a denial, but he did not command the Corinthians to undertake heresy proceedings. And so it goes.[11]

Since the data in the New Testament are not decisive, it is only natural that the church will be divided on how far to go when confronting errorists with the evil of their ways. Some denominations will create elaborate judicial machinery, while others will try to exclude errorists by the use of moral pressures alone. The mechanics of discipline are not important. The important thing is that the church is sincerely trying to continue in the teaching of Christ and the Apostles. Complacency and indifference are the attitudes most to be feared.

CONCLUSION

Since church government is a servant of the fellowship, it is a means and not an end. This is an important point. We must not separate from one another because we do not agree in details of government. If we do, we forget that *love*, not skill in ecclesiastical rule, is the sign of a true disciple. Worldwide Christian fellowship is the ideal for the church. Whatever hinders this ideal should be brought under the scrutiny of Scriptures.

Instead of boasting about superior polity, we ought to occupy ourselves with the weightier matters of the law: justice and mercy and faith. "Happier are they whom the Lord when he cometh, shall find doing in these things, than disputing about 'doctors, elders, and deacons.' "[12]

Devising new offices is not the whole answer to problems arising out of the complexity of the modern church. The offices in the New Testament are simple and effective. The sheer multiplying of offices may be a sign that the church is substituting human wisdom for a life of faith and grace.

[9] Acts 15:1–5.　　　　　　[10] I Cor. 15:12.
[11] *See*, e.g., Rom. 16:17; II Thess. 3:14, 15; I Tim. 6:3–5; II Tim. 2:14–19; Tit. 3:9–11; and II John 9–11.
[12] R. Hooker: *Of the Laws of Ecclesiastical Polity*, Preface VI, p. 5.

We do not need additional officers as such. What we need is prophets of God who can call existing officers back to biblical standards. As long as rulers are filled with the Spirit and wisdom, *any* form of government will do. And if rulers lack these virtues, even the most cleverly devised polity will be found wanting.

Too much government leads to tyranny, whereas too little government leads to anarchy. Either extreme disrupts the fellowship. Good rulers will not only steer the course between these extremes, but they will cheerfully acknowledge that their own authority is derivative and subordinate. Ecclesiastical rule has no independent rights. It exists as a handmaid to the ministry of the Word.

BIBLIOGRAPHY

G.W. Bromiley: *Christian Ministry*

S.M. Jackson: *The New Schaff-Herzog Encyclopedia of Religious Knowledge*, Volume VIII, article "Organization of the Early Church" by A. Harnack

C. Hodge: *Discussions in Church Polity*

T.W. Manson: *The Church's Ministry*

———: *The Chicago Lutheran Theological Seminary Record*, article "The Ministry in the New Testament" Volume LVII, Number 3, July, 1952 [a study prepared for the Commission on the Doctrine of the Ministry of the United Lutheran Church in America]

———: *The Expository Times*, article "The Church and the Ministry" by V. Taylor, Volume LXII, Number 9, pp. 269–274

38

BAPTISM AND

THE LORD'S SUPPER

✚

MERRILL C. TENNEY

Merrill C. Tenney, Dean of the Graduate School at Wheaton College, received his general and theological education at Gordon College (Th.B., 1927), Boston University (M.A., 1930), and Harvard University (Ph.D., 1944). He is the author of *Resurrection Realities, Galatians: The Charter of Christian Liberty, Interpreting Revelation,* and *The Word for this Century,* among other works.

Two ritual observances, baptism and the Lord's Supper, are maintained by members of the church of Christ irrespective of their denomination or of their personal spiritual maturity. Whether these observances are regarded as possessing only symbolic value or whether they are sacraments which confer spiritual grace directly, they are central to the worship of all groups. In them, the heart of Christian doctrine is enacted in visible form.

BAPTISM

This is the rite by which a professed believer was inducted into the fellowship of the New Testament church. By submitting to immersion in water, pouring, or sprinkling, he confessed publicly his need of cleansing from sin and his faith in Christ. Peter instructed his audience on the day of Pentecost to "Repent, and be baptized ... in the name of Jesus Christ for the remission of sins,"[1] and each subsequent stage of the church's growth was marked by baptism of the believers.[2]

The concept of baptism is rooted in the Old Testament law, which prescribed certain washings for the cleansing of diseased persons.[3] Proselytes entering Judaism were expected to strip themselves of their former clothing, submit to circumcision, and bathe themselves completely, after which they were reckoned members of the Jewish community. The rite was acknowledgment of defilement and of the acceptance of the law as a purifying agent. The baptism of John must have been founded upon current usage, for his hearers were not surprised when he proclaimed it, and the Scriptures take the significance for granted.[4] John the Baptist, however, realized that his ministry of baptism was only preparatory, for he expected the advent of another who would baptize "in the Holy Spirit."[5]

Jesus' personal acceptance of John's baptism was a public avowal of His consecration to God and of His mission to men. By taking His stand with sinners, although He was sinless, He provided a link between the symbol repentance and the fuller significance implied in the final commission to His followers. He enjoined them to "make disciples of all the nations, baptizing them into the name of the Father and of the Son and of the Holy Spirit."[6] By this command, He related baptism to the total work of the Trinity in salvation, and prescribed it as the universal practice of the church.

The key passage on baptism is connected with Paul's argument for holiness in Romans 6:4-6:[7] "We were buried therefore with him through baptism into death: that like as Christ was raised from the dead through the glory of the Father, so we also might walk in newness of life."

Assuming that the Roman Christians were familiar with the ceremony, he explained it in terms of death and resurrection. Since the claims of retributive justice cannot be executed upon a dead person, the union of the Christian with Christ in His death frees him from con-

---

[1] Acts 2:38.
[2] Acts 8:12, 38; 9:10; 10:47, 48; 16:33; 18:8.
[3] Lev. 14:8.   [4] Mark 1:4, 5.
[5] Mark 1:8.   [6] Matt. 28:19.
[7] ARV.

demnation, and through the resurrection he shares in a new life. By the rite of baptism, he enacts this experience symbolically and accepts its reality by faith, though his full realization of the truth may develop gradually.

Parallel with the baptism by water is the baptism of the Holy Spirit, which insures this progressive experience of union and which constitutes the Christian an active member of the body of Christ.[8] The same term, "baptism," is used of both the external rite and the internal reality, as if to indicate that they are interdependent and equally necessary. The internal experience necessitates outward confession; the external confession must be supported by inward reality.

The efficacy of baptism lies in the relation of the individual to God, rather than in any property of the water. The only passage in the New Testament that connects salvation directly with baptism is I Peter 3:20, 21:[9] "wherein few, that is, eight souls, were saved through water: which also after a true likeness doth now save you, even baptism, not the putting away of the filth of the flesh, but the interrogation of a good conscience toward God. . . ." Although the translation seemingly conveys the idea that baptism saves men, a careful study of the context reveals that "saved through" does not mean "saved by" but "preserved through." The baptismal water does not provide the means of our salvation, but is rather representative of the peril through which we are brought into a new life, as Noah passed through the waters of the flood to safety. Obviously, water cannot save any man; salvation is by the grace of God.

The long dispute over the proper mode of baptism will probably never be settled satisfactorily to all concerned. The Greek verb *baptizo*, which has been transliterated rather than translated, means fundamentally to *dip, plunge, immerse*. After making allowance for certain occasional exceptions, such as passages where washing is implied, the etymological meaning indicates that baptism was originally by immersion. Historically, this mode has been perpetuated by the Eastern Church, and it prevailed in the West until the Middle Ages. Pouring, or affusion, according to the *Teaching of the Twelve Apostles*, a second-century document, was permissible if water were scarce, and sprinkling was a later substitution developed in the Middle Ages.

Of greater importance than the mode of baptism is the question of the proper candidates. Where the New Testament speaks clearly, it

[8] I Cor. 12:13.   [9] ARV.

emphasizes the personal belief of those concerned. Faith must precede commitment; the external act of water baptism will not transform an unbeliever into a Christian. Can infants, incapable of an individual act of faith, rightfully receive baptism? On this question the Scriptures make no direct pronouncement. The mention of the Philippian jailor's household[10] does not necessarily imply that infants were included, nor is there any other passage that affords an obvious answer. The varying views on baptism are the logical consequences of attempts to interpret the implications of the Scriptures.

At the moment of baptism, the Christian makes an irrevocable commitment to Christ, whose death is the means of his redemption and whose life will be the continuing dynamic of his career. He takes a step in spiritual experience which he cannot retrace, and need not, if he is sincere. He enters a new relationship with God and with other members of the redeemed community who constitute the church.

Having accepted baptism and having agreed to all that it means, the Christian is, henceforth, destined for a life of progress in holiness. He cannot logically revert to the old sins which he has abandoned, but he must rather devote himself to holiness and to conscious spiritual growth. The teaching of Paul in Colossians 2:12, 13, 20–3:2 indicates that the baptized believer is obligated to put away his former loose thinking and conduct and to adopt the standards of the new fellowship of the regenerate into which he has been inducted. Such a life is not negative asceticism, but is rather the spontaneous response of a renewed conscience to the ethical revelation of God. Baptism, according to the New Testament, is not merely a religious ceremony, but it is also a moral and spiritual pledge of devotion to holiness.

THE LORD'S SUPPER

The second ordinance is the memorial feast instituted by Jesus on the eve of His death. As He celebrated the passover with His disciples, He gave them bread and wine, saying, "This is my body," and "This is my blood of the new covenant which is shed for many."[11] The Pauline record[12] shows that the Lord's Supper had become the focal point of worship in the early church[13] and that it was observed regularly. Justin Martyr states in his *First Apology* that Christians met on

[10] Acts 16:33, 34.
[12] I Cor. 11:23–26.
[11] Mark 14:22, 24.
[13] Ca. 50 A.D.

the first day of the week to worship and to break bread. With few exceptions, the sacred meal has been perpetuated in all denominations to the present day.

The primary significance of the Lord's Supper is its representation of Christ's death as the seal of the new covenant between God and man. The breaking of Christ's body and the shedding of His blood made the sacrifice by which atonement for sin was accomplished, thereby reconciling man to God. As the bread and wine are assimilated into the physical body to contribute to its well-being, so the person of Christ enters spiritually into the life of the communicant. By this impartation, the saving power of Christ is constantly appropriated and His strength becomes the source of the believer's life.

Although the Lord's Supper is not a sacrifice offered by a priest, since the death of Christ occurred once for all, its origin implies that it is more than a social meal. The bread and wine were part of the passover feast, which was itself symbolic of Israel's deliverance from Egypt and of the beginning of new life as a redeemed nation. By analogy, "Our passover hath been sacrificed, even Christ,"[14] so that the elements of which we partake imply union in a body of individually redeemed men who are bound together into the church of God.

The bread and wine cannot be fragments of the literal body and blood of Christ, for when He said, "This is my body" and "This my blood," He was reclining at the table with His disciples. They would have understood that the bread and wine were only representative of His physical being, as a picture represents the person whose likeness it reproduces. This figure of speech was discussed by Jesus in His discourse on the bread of life: "Except ye eat the flesh of the Son of man and drink his blood, ye have not life in yourselves."[15] His language created consternation among His hearers, who took it with absolute literality. Jesus provided the initial clue to its meaning by adding: "As the living Father sent me, and I live because of the Father; so he that eateth me, he also shall live because of me."[16] The relation between the Father and Himself was so close that the same relationship, expressed by the figure of "eating," should obtain between Him and His disciples. When they grumbled at the obscure expression, He replied, "It is the spirit that giveth life; the flesh profiteth nothing."[17] The eating of the

[14] I Cor. 5:7.
[15] John 6:53.
[16] John 6:57.
[17] John 6:63.

material emblems is both a reminder and a pattern of this appropriation of the spiritual essence of Christ.

Jesus also intended by the observance to keep alive His memory and the obligation of His disciples to serve Him until He should return. "Ye do show forth the Lord's death until he come" was His final word. Although He did not reveal the details of His purpose at that time, Jesus contemplated a program extending beyond His death and resurrection to the establishment of His kingdom. Knowing that His departure would remove Him from visible companionship with His disciples, He gave them this stimulus to hope that they might not become discouraged nor forget the true objective of their calling.

The table of the Lord establishes also a new basis of fellowship. Those who partake of it cannot consistently maintain evil associations; complete severance from all defilement is required. Paul, in reproving the Corinthians for idolatry, says, "Ye cannot partake of the table of the Lord, and of the table of demons."[18] Furthermore, it creates a bond of union between believers, for hatreds, jealousies, and divisions are incompatible with the principle of love which was the very motive for Christ's sacrifice. Negatively and positively, Christians are bound into one fellowship around the center of His living person.

Participation in the Lord's Supper was therefore limited to believers who receive the elements in a spirit of thankfulness and honesty. Absolute sinlessness was not a prerequisite, else there would be none to partake; but careless indifference or willful impenitence unfits the spirit for joining others who assemble in humility and sincerity to celebrate the feast. Flagrant sin was adequate cause for exclusion from the Lord's table, the last and most drastic step in the discipline of the church.

By these means of grace the life of the believer was initiated and sustained. His public declaration of faith in deliverance from sin and possession of a new life is manifested in baptism; his public avowal of dependence upon Christ and association with others of like faith is maintained in communion.

Dr. G.W. Bromiley, in his work on *Sacramental Teaching and Practice in the Reformation Churches,* has well summarized the value of these rites:

"To know their meaning and purpose is to be helped to their true enjoyment... But properly to use them... is to do so with a readiness to see Christ Himself and His saving work, and therefore with prayer

[18] I Cor. 10:21.

to the Holy Spirit that He may dispose of the means which He Himself
has chosen and of which He Himself is the Lord."[19]

BIBLIOGRAPHY

J.H. Blunt, ed.: *Dictionary of Doctrinal and Historical Theology*, article
"Baptism"

K. Barth: *The Teaching of the Church Regarding Baptism*

A. Carson: *Baptism in Its Modes and Subjects*

O. Cullmann: *Baptism in the New Testament*, J.K.S. Reid, tr.

W. Flemington: *The New Testament Doctrine of Baptism*

G.H.W. Lampe: *The Seal of the Spirit*

J.G. Lawson: *Did Jesus Command Immersion?* [revised edition]

J. Warns: *Baptism*, G.H. Lang, tr.

A.J.B. Higgins: *The Lord's Supper in the New Testament*

J. Jeremias: *The Eucharistic Words of Jesus*

C.L. Wallis: *The Table of the Lord*

[19] G.W. Bromiley: *Sacramental Teaching and Practice in the Reformation
Churches*, p. 106.

39

OTHER MEANS OF GRACE

✛

FRANK E. GAEBELEIN

Frank E. Gaebelein, Headmaster at the Stony Brook School, Stony Brook, Long Island, New York, received his general and theological education at New York University, College of Arts and Pure Science (B.A., 1920), Harvard University (M.A., 1921), Wheaton College (Litt.D., 1931), Reformed Episcopal Theological Seminary (D.D. [honorary], 1951), and Houghton College, New York, (LL.D. [honorary], 1960). He is the author of *Down Through the Ages, Exploring the Bible, Christian Education in a Democracy,* and *Philemon, The Gospel of Emancipation,* among other works.

Baptism and the Lord's Supper are, by Christ's own appointment, means whereby His grace is imparted to the members of His body—the one relating to entrance through union with Christ in His death and resurrection into newness of life and the fellowship of the church, the other relating to the nourishment of that life through believing participation in the elements of bread and wine as showing forth the Lord's death till He come. But there are, apart from the two sacraments, other means whereby God's grace is imparted to men. As Charles Hodge says, "A work of grace is the work of the Holy Spirit; the means of grace are the means by which, or in connection with which, the influence of the Spirit is conveyed or exercised."[1] Thus, the sacraments or ordinances, although unique in their institution, are not the only agencies through which divine grace is received. For both Scripture and life bear witness to the fact that the Holy Spirit influences men in many different ways.

So manifold are these other means of grace that to discuss them within the compass of a brief essay imposes a problem of selection. But the problem may be solved, in part at least, by considering first those means which, although different from the sacraments, or ordinances, are in particular relation to them, namely, the Word of God, prayer, and fellowship (communion of the saints); and then by considering some of the many means that come through common grace.

Baptism and the Lord's Supper do not stand in isolation. They are intimately related within the church to the Word of God. Thus Calvin declared, "Wherever we see the Word of God purely preached and heard, and the sacraments administered according to Christ's institution, there, it is not to be doubted, a church of God exists."[2] And, as R.S. Wallace shows,[3] much of the great reformer's thought rests upon this indissoluble relationship of Scripture and sacrament.

THE WORD OF GOD

Foremost, then, among the other means of grace is the Word of God, not only in its true preaching and faithful hearing but also in its daily use by the individual believer. Church history from apostolic times[4] down through the ages testifies to the preached Word as a means of grace unto the salvation and nourishment of souls. If the first-century church "continued stedfastly ... in breaking of bread,"[5] the same text tells us that it did so in conjunction with "the apostles' doctrine and fellowship" and "in prayers." Indeed, the book of Acts is in large part a record of the apostolic preaching of the Word.[6] Following the pattern established in Acts, God has made faithful preaching and obedient hearing of the Word a blessing to His people. Therefore, the integrity of Scripture is crucial for the life of the church, and to impugn the authority of the Word is to call in question one of God's chief means of grace.

[1] C. Hodge: *Systematic Theology*, II, p. 654.
[2] J. Calvin: *Institutes*, Volume II, p. 1023, J.T. McNeill, ed.
[3] R.S. Wallace: *Calvin's Doctrine of the Word and Sacrament*.
[4] I Cor. 1:17, 21, 23, 24.   [5] Acts 2:42.
[6] Acts 2:14–35; 3:12–26; 4:31; 7:2–53; 8:4, 35; 10:34–43; 13:16–41; etc.

But it is not just in its public preaching and hearing that Scripture is a means of grace; in its private use, the Bible is no less an instrument of the Spirit. Recall the relation of the Word of God to some of the *loci classici* of Christian experience: Augustine in the garden at Rome hearing the childish voice repeating, *"tolle, lege,"* and going into the house to find deliverance through reading Romans 13:13, 14; Luther in the Black Monastery at Wittenberg converted through meditation on Romans 1:16, 17; Bunyan finding spiritual peace through I Corinthians 1:30. What happened to these men has been paralleled countless times by the experience of Christians in all ages and among all peoples. Moreover, along with this function in God's gracious work of regeneration,[7] Scripture is also daily food whereby the believer is nourished. The exhortation, "Grow in grace and in the knowledge of our Lord and Saviour Jesus Christ,"[8] goes hand in hand with the injunction, "As newborn babes, desire the sincere milk of the word, that ye may grow thereby: if so be that ye have tasted that the Lord is gracious."[9] Daily reading of the Word is beyond question a continuing means of grace for untold multitudes of God's people.

FELLOWSHIP, PRAYER, WORSHIP

Turning again to the record in Acts, we observe that fellowship and prayer accompanied teaching and the sacrament: "And they continued stedfastly in the apostles' doctrine and fellowship, and in breaking of bread and prayer."[10] Surely the most inclusive of the other means of grace is that of fellowship (*koinonia*). Samuel Rutherford quaintly said, "Many coals make a good fire and this is part of the communion of saints."[11] The worshiping, serving fellowship of the church is surely among the other means of grace. It is significant that in the new translation of Calvin's *Institutes*[12] the original title of Book IV, which deals with the church, is for the page headings shortened from "The External Means or Aids by Which God Invites Us Into the Society of Christ and Holds Us Therein" to "Means of Grace: the Holy Catholic Church." In the comprehensive sense, the church is indeed a chief means for the Spirit's influence upon men. Proper recognition of this fact is a corrective to the extremes of individualism into which certain forms of evangelicalism may possibly lapse.

[7] Jas. 1:18; I Pet. 1:23.   [8] II Pet. 3:18.
[9] I Pet. 2:2, 3.   [10] Acts 2:42.
[11] A. Bonar, ed.: *Letters* [of S. Rutherford], #286.
[12] J. Calvin: *Institutes*, J.T. McNeill. ed.

Again, prayer, public as well as private, is a means of grace. For while prayer offered, as our Lord instructed, behind the shut door is the most intensely personal of spiritual exercises, no believer anywhere prays only as an individual but always as a member of the body of Christ. Nor does he pray apart from the Word of God. The promises of Scripture constitute the warp and woof of prayer. Feeding the soul on the Bible leads to prayer, and prayer leads to the Bible. From the perfect prayer life of our Lord on through the intercessions of the great saints of Scripture—among them Abraham, Moses, David and the other psalmists, Elijah, Isaiah, Jeremiah, Daniel, Jonah, Ezra, Peter, Paul—Scripture is the book of prayer. Nor is it answered prayer alone that is a means of grace, but rather the act of praying in the sense of adoration of God, praise to God, communion with God, which also brings blessing to the soul.

At this point, special mention should be made of corporate worship, including as it does the preaching and hearing of the Word of God, and public prayer. For this, too, is a means of grace, and a great one. In the words of Calvin, "Believers have no greater help than public worship, for by it God raises his own folk upward step by step."[13]

However, to subject these other means of grace to strict analysis is difficult, if not impossible. Just as in man the physical, mental, and spiritual components are united, so these agencies of the Spirit's working are interrelated and interdependent. The Word of God is spiritual seed and spiritual food; prayer is made according to its promises and teaching; the sacraments are administered as it directs; and all this is under Him who is at the center of the Word and who is the great Head of the church in which believers find gracious fellowship.

ADDITIONAL MEANS IN RELATION TO COMMON GRACE

God also confers His benefits to men through common grace, by which is meant the "general influences of the Holy Spirit which to a greater or lesser degree are shared by all men."[14] Included in these influences of the Spirit are not only the blessings of the natural order, epitomized in our Lord's words in the Sermon on the Mount, "He

[13] J. Calvin: *Institutes*, Volume II, p. 1019.
[14] L. Boettner: *The Reformed Doctrine of Predestination*, p. 179; cf. also C. Hodge: *Systematic Theology*, Volume II, pp. 654–675; M.E. Osterhaven: "Common Grace," *supra*, pp. 171 f.

maketh his sun to rise on the evil and on the good, and sendeth rain on the just and on the unjust,"[15] but also the talents God bestows upon men, whether artistic, as typified by Bezaleel,[16] or administrative, as in the case of Moses and Joshua and David, or in the many other kinds of human ability. Thus considered, all human progress intellectually and culturally, science not excepted, stems from common grace. In this fact lies the answer to the parochialism of judging a work of litera-ture or art by the life of its human creator or of relegating scientific advances wholly to the secular realm. For if God gives ability, then the products of that ability, provided that it is used in the integrity of the truth, are to be accepted as gifts of God's grace. As Justin Martyr put it, "All that has been well said belongs to us Christians."[17] Therefore, music, not simply in conjunction with sacred words but in its own right, may be, under common grace, an uplifting and ennobling influence. Likewise, with the other arts. For the title of C.G. Osgood's little book, *Poetry As a Means of Grace*, is more than figurative, and points to the spiritual use of culture as a whole.

NATURE

But while the arts and sciences are necessarily subject to limitations of opportunity and ability, there are even more spacious areas of common grace that are open to all, regardless of education and culture. In the forefront of these are the works of God in nature. To go down to the sea in ships and to behold the wonders of the deep;[18] to lift up one's eyes unto the hills;[19] to consider the heavens, the moon, and the stars which God has ordained[20]—these and experiences like them are also, in their wordless but eloquent communication of the greatness of the living God, means of grace.

WORK AND SERVICE

Of great importance among the agencies of common grace is work. Faithful doing of the daily task brings satisfaction gained in no other way, while even the humblest work done for the glory of God may become a pathway to lofty Christian experience, as with Brother Lawrence.[21] But, especially, work in the form of selfless service for

[15] Matt. 5:45b.
[16] Exod. 31:2-4.
[17] J. Martyr: *Second Apology*, p. 13.
[18] Ps. 107:23, 24.
[19] Ps. 121:1, 2; Ps. 36:6.
[20] Ps. 8:3.
[21] Cf. Brother Lawrence: *The Practice of the Presence of God.*

others, done out of love and compassion, is a means of blessing both to doer and recipient. If some forms of present-day evangelicalism lack social concern, the remedy lies in renewed sensitivity to human need. Said our Lord to those who gave food and drink to the hungry and thirsty, sheltered the stranger, clothed the destitute, and visited the sick and imprisoned, "Inasmuch as ye have done it unto one of the least of these my brethren, ye have done it unto me."[22] And James, the brother of the Lord, wrote, "Pure religion and undefiled before God and the Father is this, To visit the fatherless and widows in their affliction and to keep himself unspotted from the world."[23] After describing how a group of British officers who, having suffered unspeakable degradation in the notorious Japanese prison camp at Chungkai, shared food and water with destitute Japanese casualties and bound up the wounds of these their enemies, Ernest Gordon declares, "We had experienced a moment of grace.... God had broken through the barriers of our prejudice and had given us the will to obey His command, 'Thou shalt love.' "[24]

SPECIAL HUMAN RELATIONSHIPS

Other means of grace include the wide range of human relationships. The sacred union of husband and wife, bearing the precious analogy of the union of Christ with His church,[25] surely conveys a special measure of grace to those who live within it in the fear of the Lord. And additional relationships, such as that of parent and child, friend and friend, employer and employee, doctor and patient, teacher and pupil, citizen and civil authority—all of these may be used by the Spirit to bring blessing to men.

The fact is that the breadth of divine grace is immeasurable. In His sovereignty, God is able to make any circumstance a vehicle of good for His children.[26] Even the bitter experiences of life—disappointment and misunderstanding, sorrow and tragedy—may become means of grace through him who is able to sanctify to us our deepest distress. There is no limit to the wideness of God's mercy. His grace has infinite horizons, and the agencies through which it is conveyed are as varied and multiform as life itself.

[22] Matt. 25:40.   [23] Jas. 1:27.
[24] E. Gordon: *Through the Valley of the Kwai*, p. 222.
[25] Eph. 5:22-33.   [26] Rom. 8:28.

USE OF THE OTHER MEANS OF GRACE

A final comment is in order regarding use of the other means of grace. Here the reference, although including the special nonsacramental means, such as the Word of God and prayer, which are no more to be neglected than the sacrament, cannot be restricted to these special means. Clearly, there is for Christians the continuing obligation to use talents, to do work, to serve others, to enjoy the beauty and fruits of creation, to live with others, and to experience every contingency of life as unto the Lord. Only by the unremitting practice of Paul's advice, "Whatsoever ye do in word or deed, do all in the name of the Lord Jesus, giving thanks to God and the Father by him,"[27] can believers use, as they should, the other means of grace.

BIBLIOGRAPHY

L. Boettner: *The Reformed Doctrine of Predestination*
J. Calvin: *Institutes*
C. Hodge: *Systematic Theology*, II
Brother Lawrence: *The Practice of the Presence of God*
R.S. Wallace: *Calvin's Doctrine of the Word and Sacrament*

[27] Col. 3:17.

40

DEATH AND THE STATE OF THE SOUL AFTER DEATH

✝

J.G.S.S. THOMSON

J.G.S.S. Thomson, Minister of St. David's Church, Glasgow, Scotland, received his general and theological education at the University of Edinburgh (M.A., B.D., and Ph.D.) and Oxford University (B.A.). He is the author of *The Praying Christ, The Old Testament View of Revelation, The Word of the Lord in Jeremiah,* and *A Devotional Commentary on St. Matthew's Gospel.*

Death is a universal experience, yet men will not think about it until compelled to. They plead that death is incomprehensible, that there is no evidence of survival after death. They are offended by the thought of hell and embarrassed by the thought of heaven. The triumphs of modern science and the secular and atheistic philosophies of life and of the state have produced this reaction. The weakening of man's personal dignity, wholesale extermination by means of the atomb bomb, slave-labor camps, the secularization of human life, have blurred the concept of eternal life. Many, including religious people, are not interested in, attracted by, or concerned about a future life. Belief in immortality may not have been extinguished, but it has been eclipsed.

Meantime, death remains an ineffaceably solemn fact. Why? Because of the relation between death and sin. Men die because of sin. Man's creation in the *imago Dei* probably implies a relation between God and man in which death had no part. Man was not originally immortal; death is not now inescapable, but it was probably inoperative in man's original perfection. But with sin came death. Death is inevitable not because man is a creature of nature but because he is a sinner. Sin makes death a "bondage of corruption" and gives it its painful power and penal character. Death, being separation from God,[1] is both a physical and a spiritual event. Christ triumphed over sin by triumphing over death. Sin's curse "compelled" Christ to die a death that destroyed death and him who had power over death. Death's solemnity stems from its connection with sin.

The solemnity arises from man's ineradicable conviction that he survives death. In spite of death's inevitability and seeming finality, man knows he is deathless. In their best moments even agnostics and rationalists find their certainty of extinction after death fading. Belief in survival after death is not only universal but very ancient. The Egyptians held it; in Greece it was adopted by the Orphics, from whom Plato received it; the Hebrews accepted it; Jews in Christ's day held it; Christianity has always believed it; and for primitive man, too, immortality was a certainty, not a conjecture. Survival after death was how man interpreted the ineradicable intuition rooted in the imperishable core of his being.

Yet there is no scientific "proof" or material knowledge of immortality. The belief cannot be based upon scientific discovery or philosophical conclusions. Life after death belongs to a realm of experience of which science knows nothing. Even the psychical researches of the spiritists have produced little of real value. Their claim to have proved the soul's survival after death is not made out. Certainty of identification of any disembodied spirit is rarely claimed.

Is there, then, no certainty of hope of immortality? There are three considerations: (1) *Man's personality*. Doubt that there exists as the core of the personality a persistent entity called the soul or the self is a rejection which goes back to David Hume. For Bertrand Russell, "the most essential thing in the continuity of a person is memory." If, then, memory does not survive death, the hope of immortality is groundless.

[1] Ps. 88:3–5; Isa. 38:9–20.

Personal identity and continuity in life after death imply memory since, if a person's memories of life on earth are eliminated at death, he would not be the person identical with the earthly counterpart. But since memory is closely connected with the brain, memory should disappear when the brain disintegrates; hence belief in immortality has no scientific basis. But this ancient objection assumes that the brain is *causally* related to the mind; in fact, science does not know how they are related. At best, scientific evidence against immortality is negative, in that the evidence against it is not forthcoming.

(2) *Man's rationality*. Mind and body are interdependent, but does a physiological change in the brain produce thought? If so, how do physical changes produce psychical phenomena? Materialists answer that man's mental life springs from entirely physical changes, but that this causality does not work in reverse. Some psychologists reply that mental and physical events are not interdependent; at best, there is a correspondence between them. Others suppose an interaction between the physical and psychical. That is, the first view denies life after death; the other two, especially the third, support such a hope by implying that mind is a higher mode of existence than body and is not necessarily dependent on the physical organism for existence.

(3) *Man's morality*. Since the source and satisfaction of moral principles transcend this time-space world, they commit men to living as if they were immortal. Morality means that if man is not immortal, then he ought to be. Morality is a guarantee that life is worth living. But this also means that religious faith is an indispensable factor in the hope of immortality. Faith in God commits one to the belief that the universe is rational and moral; that it is on the side of justice and truth; and that in a life beyond death, evil and good shall receive their just reward. Faith finds, in the revelation of God to the Hebrews and through Christ, God's pledge and promise that life survives death. Several things call for attention here.

SCRIPTURE

(1) As for immortality in the Old Testament, there, death as well as life involves men in relations with God. At death, the body remained on earth; the *nephesh* passed into Sheol;[2] but the breath, spirit, or *ruach*, returned to God,[3] not Sheol. But in Sheol, a place of darkness, silence, and forgetfulness, life was foreboding and shadowy. In spite of con-

[2] Isa. 38:17; Pss. 16:10; 86:13.   [3] Eccl. 12:7.

sciousness, activity, and memory, the "dead" subsisted rather than existed.[4] Death was a passing beyond Jehovah's hand[5] forever,[6] hence, the despair in Psalm 88:10-12 and the not very bright hope in Job 7:9. Sheol had little religious significance. The prophets are all but silent on the subject, although when the hope of individual immortality clarified, the prophetic insistence on the value of the individual contributed to the hope. But through the dark despair attaching to life in Sheol gleams of hope appear.[7] God's presence, providence, and guidance throughout life guarantees that death is not extinction. "Afterward thou wilt receive me into glory." Belief in immortality springs from faith in God, from the nature and fidelity of the God with whom one fellowships daily.

(2) In the apocryphal[8] and apocalyptic literature the hope of immortality is clarified still further. When the resurrection was more clearly formulated, the question of the dead sharing Messiah's Kingdom was raised. Would the body be raised along with the soul and spirit, and would it be identical with the earthly? The answer was that the resurrected would have angelic bodies.[9] Here, also, the fusing of Jewish national and individual hopes of immortality was effected.

(3) Jesus' argument against the Sadduces.[10] It is really based on Psalm 73:23 f. The Sadducees rejected belief in immortality on the assumption that life after death would be merely continuous with the life in this world. In reply, Christ says two significant things: (a) Life after death is different from life in this world. After death, men will be "as the angels"; therefore marriage, for example, in the hereafter becomes unthinkable. To reject belief in this new mode of existence is "not to know the power of God." (b) The Sadducean rejection also revealed ignorance of "the Scriptures." The presuppositions from which belief in immortality springs have been present from the patriarchal period. The God of Abraham, Isaac, and Jacob is the God of the living, which includes the "dead" patriarchs. God called them into fellowship with Himself; therefore, they were dear to him, and He could not possibly leave them in the dust. That is, Christ based belief in immortality upon God's faithfulness, the only finally valid argu-

---

[4] Job 10:21 f.; Pss. 39:12 f.; 115:17 f., Isa. 14:9–12.
[5] Isa. 38:10 f., 18.   [6] Job 7:9.
[7] Pss. 16:8–11; 73:23 f.   [8] Cf. II Esdras 7:43; Wisdom 9:17.
[9] Enoch 51:4; 62:15 f.   [10] Mark 12:18–27.

ment for life after death. The only alternative is to deny its premises.

(4) The church argued from the same ground. Why was Christ's resurrection the ground of the Christian's resurrection?[11] Because God loosed the bonds of death from Jesus, since "it was not possible that he should be holden of it."[12] Otherwise, God's own nature, His sure mercies toward His own, the meaningfulness of the incarnation would have been denied. So Christ's resurrection guarantees the Christian's immortality, since Christ pledged him a share in His risen life[13] and joined him to Himself by unbreakable bonds.[14] That is, the Christian's belief in immortality, Christ's resurrection, and the Old Testament patriarchs' hope all stand on the same foundation.

(5) Natural immortality and eternal life are not synonymous. The first makes it possible to receive the latter, which is God's gift. Eternal life is both infinity and a quality of life. It is life lived now, but in a new dimension.[15] It consists in a knowledge of God,[16] which, though imperfect, is true. It is heart knowledge, not head knowledge. In this world it issues in morality, in that it issues in love;[17] in the hereafter, it will find an environment consistent with itself and will issue in absolute perfection.

(6) Judaism teaches that the dead are in Sheol awaiting resurrection, or are in an intermediate state of imperfect bliss, or are already in the Kingdom, though not till the Last Day do they attain to perfect bliss. Here again, Judaism insists upon the immortality of the community and the individual; without the former, the latter is imperfect. In orthodox Christianity, the dead, redeemed, and unredeemed are in their final abode, and are disincarnate until the general resurrection, when their mortal shall put on immortality. Both Jesus and the New Testament church treated the present condition of the dead with marked reserve. Although in heaven or hell,[18] their fate is declared only at the judgment.[19] The Christian at death confidently resigns his spirit to the Father,[20] and enters the blessedness of fellowship with Him.[21] Neither the Roman doctrine of purgatory nor intercession for the dead has any biblical foundation.

[11] I Cor. 15:20–22; 6:14; II Cor. 4:14; Rom. 8:11.
[12] Acts 2:24.   [13] John 14:1–3.
[14] John 6:39, 40, 44, 54.   [15] Rom. 14:17; Col. 1:13; 2:12 f.; 3:1 f.
[16] John 17:3; 5:24.   [17] I John 3:14.
[18] Luke 16:19 ff.   [19] Matt. 25:31 ff.
[20] Luke 23:46.   [21] Luke 23:42 f.; Phil. 1:23.

RESURRECTION

The resurrection impinges upon the subject of immortality. In the future state, existence will not be patterned upon the Hebraic hope nor upon the Hellenic divorce between the spiritual and the physical. Continuity and identity, some form of physical likeness, an assurance of mutual recognition are implied in the phrase "a spiritual body." The continuity and identity may be in moral personality rather than in material particles, but a "bodily" form "as the angels,"[22] infinity with loss of finitude is assured. Scientific study and philosophical thought to-day support the credibility of this hope. No longer is personality divorced from the physical organism. Matter is energy, organizing itself in particular patterns. The body is not identical with a particular collection of molecules. Through a seven years' mutational period, the body remains identically itself, not because material particles are immutable but because they are organized after the principle of the body's self-identity. The body is essential to the self. Consciousness involves body as well as mind. The physical body's identity and continuity with the spiritual body, and the transmutation that will be involved is "a mystery," but a relation between the self here and the self there is certain. "The law of the spirit of life" is now operative in the body. "This mortal" is significant for the future "immortality." It secures not only survival of the soul, but the future life of the whole man, the restoration and recognizability of the total personality clothed in "a spiritual body."

DESTINY

If, then, our continuity and identity between this life and the here-after is primarily moral, this world must be moral and this life must be a period of probation. Moral choices between right and wrong determine character and eternal destiny. After death, we shall be seen for what we are, and judged for what we have become as moral personalities. Christ taught the possibility of the loss of the soul in hell. All will not end well, irrespective of choice and conduct. Hell is the sinful self existing in separation from God, since man, being moral and spiritual, can find no satisfaction except in God. To reject the gift God desires to give—Himself—is the fire that dieth not. But this is self-inflicted alienation. Darkness is given to those who prefer it. By contrast, heaven is the beatific vision, ever deeper communion with God, the perfection

[22] Mark 12:25.

of God's image, the fulfillment of spiritual nature, the maturing of higher capacities, the perfection in holiness, "serving God day and night." Death, then, is the most solemn crisis of the soul, the entrance to judgment, the step into eternity. If, in this life only, we have hope, death is terrible tragedy, unrelieved pessimism, the dark night of the soul. If Christ is our hope, death has already lost its dominion;[23] it is the threshold of life; death is "present with the Lord" and reunion with the blessed dead, in communion with whom the beatific vision will be shared.

BIBLIOGRAPHY

C.R. Smith: *The Bible Doctrine of the Hereafter*
J. Baillie: *And the Life Everlasting*
W.A. Brown: *The Christian Hope*
C. Allington: *The Life Everlasting*
W.R. Matthews: *The Hope of Immortality*
W. Milligan: *The Resurrection of Our Lord*
M. Ramsey: *The Resurrection of Christ*
J. Denney: *Studies in Theology*
H.V. Hodson, ed.: *The Great Mystery of the Hereafter*

[23] Rom. 8:2.

41

THE SECOND COMING:

MILLENNIAL VIEWS

✦

WILLIAM M. ARNETT

William M. Arnett, Professor of Christian Doctrine at Asbury Theological Seminary, Wilmore, Kentucky, received his general and theological education at Asbury College (B.A., 1940), Asbury Theological Seminary (B.D., 1943), Princeton Theological Seminary (Th.M., 1944), and Drew Theological Seminary (Ph.D., 1954).

The explicit teaching of Holy Scripture is that Jesus Christ will come a second time from heaven to earth—personally, bodily, and visibly. This marvellous and climactic event is called "the blessed hope" of the Christian church by the Apostle Paul.[1] Christ appeared once on earth in *grace;*[2] He will appear a second time in *glory.*[3] Both of His appearings, one of which is past, the other which is a future cosmic event, are prophetically foretold in Scripture. A summary of the two Advents of Jesus Christ is made in Hebrews 9:28: "Christ was once [i.e., "once for all"] offered to bear the sins of many, and unto them that look for

[1] Titus 2:13. [2] John 1:14, 17; Titus 2:11.
[3] Matt. 16:27; 24:30; 25:31; Luke 21:27.

him shall he appear the second time without [i.e., "apart from"] sin unto salvation." In view of the many scriptural references to the Second Advent of our Lord, particularly in the New Testament, Dr. James Denney has declared with scholarly earnestness that we cannot "call in question what stands so plainly in the pages of the New Testament—what filled so exclusively the minds of the first Christians—the idea of a Personal Return of Christ at the end of the world. . . . If we are to retain any relation to the New Testament at all, we must assert the personal return of Christ as Judge of all."[4]

THE MEANING OF CHRIST'S SECOND COMING

As already indicated, the Second Coming means that Jesus Christ will come again to this world in His personal and bodily form, glorified and deathless. The word *parousia* is used frequently in the New Testament as a technical term to denote the return of Christ at the end of the age.[5] His second appearing will be personal,[6] unexpected,[7] sudden,[8] visible,[9] and glorious.[10]

This great truth has been subject to misunderstanding and abuse. Christ's Second Coming is not identical with the coming of the Holy Spirit at Pentecost, nor is it the same as the conversion of the individual. Neither is it to be equated with some calamity, such as the destruction of Jerusalem. It is not to be identified with the death of a believer or with the spread of the Gospel throughout the world. "Realized" eschatology—a present-day emphasis which denies future apocalyptic events—likewise evaporates the truth of the Second Coming. The keystone of this doctrine is the fact of the personal nature of Christ's return at the end of the age, as described in the words "this same Jesus . . . shall so come in like manner as ye have seen him go into heaven."[11]

THE IMPORTANCE OF CHRIST'S SECOND COMING

The prominent place this subject occupies in the Scripture gives some indication of its importance. All but four of the New Testament books refer to it, with a total of 318 verses in which it is set forth within the 216 chapters of the New Testament. A broad approxima-

---

[4] J. Denney: *Studies in Theology*, p. 239.
[5] E.g., Matt. 24:3, 27, 37, 39; II Pet. 3:4, 12; I John 2:28.
[6] Acts 1:11; John 14:3; 21:20-23. [7] Matt. 24:32-51; 25:1-13.
[8] Matt. 24:27; Luke 17:24. [9] Matt. 24:30; Rev. 1:7.
[10] Mark 8:38; Luke 9:26. [11] Acts 1:11.

tion is that one-fifth of the Bible is prophecy, that one-third of prophecy relates to Christ's return, and that one-twentieth of the New Testament deals with the subject. Another approximation is that it is mentioned twice as much as the atonement, and eight times as much as Christ's first coming.

Its importance is also observed in the fact that it is bound up with the great doctrines of the Christian faith, such as the Deity of Christ,[12] the atonement,[13] Sonship with God,[14] sanctification,[15] the resurrection,[16] final judgment,[17] and the promise of rewards.[18] Above all, its importance is seen in the fact that Christ declared it.[19]

The great ecumenical creeds of the Christian church have briefly but clearly included the expectation of Christ's return. The Apostles' Creed declares that Christ "ascended into heaven; and sitteth at the right hand of God the Father Almighty; from thence He shall come to judge the quick and the dead." The Nicene Creed states that "he shall come again with glory to judge both the quick and the dead." Again, the Athanasian Creed says, "at whose coming all men shall rise again with their bodies, and shall give account for their own works."

Official declarations of various groups in Christendom have presented this doctrine, such as the *Augsburg Confession*,[20] the *Thirty-Nine Articles of the Church of England*,[21] the *Westminster Confession*,[22] and the *Articles of Religion* of the Methodist Church.[23] To this, there could be added the vast volume of testimony from the theologians and hymn writers of the universal Church of Christ. The lines of Charles Wesley's great hymn reflects the glowing essence of that testimony:

Lo, He comes with clouds descending,
Once for favored sinners slain;
Thousand, thousand saints attending,
Swell the triumph of His train;
Hallelujah!
Jesus comes, and comes to reign.

[12] Matt. 26:63, 64.
[13] Heb. 9:13-28.
[14] I John 3:1, 2.
[15] I Thess. 3:12, 13; 5:23.
[16] I Cor. 15:23.
[17] II Tim. 4:1.
[18] II Tim. 4:7, 8; Rev. 22:12; I Pet. 5:4.
[19] E.g., Matt. 24, 25; Luke 21; Mark 13; John 14.
[20] *Augsburg Confession*, Part I, Article XVII.
[21] *Thirty-Nine Articles of the Church of England*, Article IV.
[22] *Westminster Confession*, Chapters 32, 33.
[23] *Articles of Religion*. Article III.

THE PURPOSE OF CHRIST'S SECOND COMING

There is a divergence of interpretation regarding the details of the Second Coming. However perplexing the fitting together of various details may be, it is clear that Christ will come for His own.[24] It is also obvious that the judging and rewarding of men are related to Christ's return.[25] Divine redemption is unfinished until the last enemy is beneath the Redeemer's feet and God is all in all.[26]

Although there is agreement in the belief among evangelicals that Christ will return to judge the world, there is a difference of opinion regarding the events before and in connection with His Second Coming. These differences are largely due to various interpretations of an interlude of a thousand years, spoken of in Revelation 20, which has been called "the Millennium."[27] There are three generally accepted views concerning this passage:[28] postmillennialism, amillennialism, and premillennialism.

(1) *Postmillennialism.* The term covers "that view of last things which holds that the kingdom of God is now being extended in the world through the preaching of the Gospel and the saving work of the Holy Spirit, that the world eventually is to be Christianized, and that the return of Christ will occur at the close of a long period of righteousness and peace, commonly called the millennium."[29] Evangelicals who embrace this interpretation are quick to point out the difference between this view and that of liberals who emphasize human progress and social betterment, by virtue of which the Kingdom of God on earth will be achieved through a natural, rather than a supernatural, process.

The postmillennialists insist that Revelation 20 should be understood figuratively, that the words "a thousand years," which occur six times in the first seven verses, mean an indefinitely long period of time, and embody, among other things a spiritual kingdom in the hearts of men. It will be a golden age of spiritual prosperity, which culminates with the Second Coming of Christ, the general resurrection, and last judgment. Both the Old and New Testaments give evidence of a future golden age. Isaiah 11:9 anticipates the day when "the earth shall be full of the knowledge of Jehovah, as the waters cover the

[24] I Thess. 4:16, 17; John 14:3; Matt. 25:6; Luke 19:15.
[25] Matt. 25:31–46; II Tim. 4:1; Rev. 22:12.
[26] I Cor. 15:25–28.   [27] From Latin *mille*, a thousand.
[28] Rev. 20:1–7.   [29] L. Boettner: *The Millennium*, p. 4.

sea." In Psalm 22:27, we are informed that a day will come when "all the ends of the world shall remember and turn unto the Lord: and all the kindreds of the nations shall worship before thee." For the postmillennialist, the parable of leaven in the New Testament teaches the universal extension and triumph of the Gospel, as society is transformed by the Kingdom's power and influence.[30] Admittedly, this involves a long and tedious process through the centuries, but the ultimate goal is certain and the outcome is assured.

(2) *Amillennialism.* Sometimes called the nonmillennarian view, this interprets the disputed passage in Revelation 20 symbolically and spiritually, and omits an earthly millennium. Amillennialists reject the notion of a "golden age" which represents the hope of a converted world. Rather, they believe that the Scripture teaches that good and evil will continue side by side, but eventually there will be a sudden personal eruption of Christ into the midst of the world's scene of conflict, with a swift sifting and separation of souls at the final judgment. Hence, the millennial reign of Christ in Revelation 20 is given a spiritual interpretation. Following a view which originated with Augustine, it may refer to the present reign of Christ in the world through the church and in the lives of Christians, or it may refer to the souls of Christians who have been martyred as they now reign with Christ in heaven in the intermediate state. Those who follow this particular teaching insist that a literal and temporal interpretation of the millennium is erroneous.

(3) *Premillennialism.* This is a view of last things which insists that the millennial passage in Revelation 20 must be interpreted literally and that the Second Coming of Christ will inaugurate His reign as King in person on the earth. There are two phases involved in His Coming: the first is called the "rapture," when Christ comes *for* His bride, the church, and the second is called the "revelation," at which time Christ returns *with* His bride to the earth. At that glorious appearing, He subdues the antichrist and establishes His reign over the earth during the millennium. At the close of the millennium, there will be a brief but fierce rebellion led by Satan, which is quickly quelled, and which is followed by the bodily resurrection of the wicked and the final White Throne Judgment.

The premillennial view also involves a very definite teaching concerning the tribulation period which precedes the millennial reign of

[30] Cf. Matt. 13:33; Luke 13:20, 21.

Christ. There is disagreement among premillennialists, however, regarding the "rapture," in relation to the period of tribulation which is predicted in the Scripture.[31] One group believes that the "rapture" will take place before the tribulation period, and this view is known as a pretribulation rapture. Others insist that the "rapture" takes place after the tribulation period, and is, therefore, a posttribulation rapture. Still others believe that the "rapture" will take place during the tribulation period, and their view is a midtribulation theory.

It should also be noted that among premillennialists there are those who regard Revelation 20 from a dispensational point of view, with the millennial Kingdom being the last of seven dispensations which they believe are revealed in Scripture.

THE TIME OF CHRIST'S SECOND COMING

Although our Lord's return occupies a prominent place in Scripture, the time of His return is not specified.[32] Hence, the necessity of preparedness.[33] From the standpoint of God's evaluation of what we call time, Christ's return has been "imminent," or near, ever since He went away. Although the time of the Second Coming is unknown, various "signs" of its approaching hour are indicated in Scripture. Among these "signs" are the recurrence of war and commotion,[34] the growing apostasy in the church,[35] the foregathering of God's covenant people to the promised land of their fathers,[36] and the spread of the Gospel.[37]

THE GOAL OF HISTORY

In conclusion, it is well to note that the subject of the Second Coming involves the meaning and goal of history. Scripture indicates that history is built along redemptive lines, and that, in moving to its final goal, it is a conflict of opposing forces heading toward a crisis. To the end of time, a mixed condition will prevail: wheat and tares,[38] love and hate, peace and war, faith and apostasy, righteousness and iniquity.[39] In the end, however, God will prevail, for the final word in the conflict rests with Him—a word that will be spoken in judgment

[31] Matt. 24:21; Dan. 12:1.

[32] Mark 13:32; I Thess. 5:1, 2.

[33] Matt. 24:44.

[34] Luke 21:9.

[35] Luke 18:8; I Tim. 4:1.

[36] Matt. 24:32, 33; Luke 21:29–31.

[37] Matt. 24:14; cf. *also* Mark 13; I Tim. 4:1–3; II Tim. 3:1–7; II Pet. 3.

[38] Matt. 13:24–30.

[39] E.g., the Book of Revelation.

through His Son.[40] The immense drama of human history, with its perennial conflict between good and evil, will not go on forever. In the end, God and righteousness will triumph.[41]

The truth of Christ's Second Coming is a glorious and comforting revelation to all believers, as well as a stimulus and encouragement to Christian service and holy living.[42] For unbelievers and Christ-rejecters, it is a solemn warning.[43] But to the child of God, who trusts utterly and completely His Son and His atoning death for salvation, it is the "blessed hope." It is a thrilling prospect! "Even so, come, Lord Jesus."[44]

BIBLIOGRAPHY

J.H. Snowden: *The Coming of the Lord: Will It Be Premillennial?*
L. Boettner: *The Millennium*
G.E. Ladd: *The Blessed Hope*
J.F. Walvoord: *The Return of the Lord*
G. Vos: *The Teaching of Jesus Concerning the Kingdom of God and the Church*
O.T. Allis: *Prophecy and the Church*

[40] Acts 17:31; Rom. 2:16.
[41] I Cor. 15:24–28; Acts 15:14–18; II Tim. 2:19; Rev. 11:15.
[42] Luke 21.28; I Cor. 1:7; Phil. 3:20; Col. 3:4, 5; I Thess. 1.10; 4:18; Heb. 9:28; Jas. 5:7; II Pet. 3:12; I John 3:2, 3.
[43] Mark 13:35, 37; John 3:18; II Thess. 1:7, 8; II Pet. 3:3, 4, 9, 10; Jude 14, 15; Rev. 6:12–17.
[44] Rev. 22:20.

42

THE RESURRECTION OF THE
DEAD AND FINAL JUDGMENT

✛

WALTER W. WESSEL

Walter W. Wessel, Associate Professor of Biblical Literature at Bethel College and Seminary, St. Paul, Minnesota, received his general and theological education at the University of California, Los Angeles (B.A., 1946; M.A., 1950) and the University of Edinburgh, Scotland (Ph.D., 1953). He has contributed articles to *The Biblical Expositor, The Wycliffe Bible Commentary,* and *Baker's Dictionary of Theology.*

We are not far removed from the time when in theological circles eschatological themes were considered unimportant and irrelevant. An apocalyptic world and a new emphasis on biblical theology have combined to change this situation radically. Theologians have again been brought to consider soberly the great eschatological themes of the New Testament, and to ponder carefully their meaning and significance for our age. Two of the most important of these eschatological themes are the resurrection of the dead and the final judgment.

THE RESURRECTION OF THE DEAD

Although belief in the resurrection of the dead has been generally unacceptable to both ancient and modern man, A.M. Ramsey is right when he says that for Christianity to have succumbed to the opponents of this truth would have been disastrous for the church. "It would have blunted the cutting edge of the Gospel and removed a doctrine which sums up the genius of Christianity in its belief about man and the world."[1] Indeed, Reinhold Niebuhr states that "there is no part of the Apostolic Creed which . . . expresses the whole genius of the Christian faith more neatly than . . . 'I believe in the resurrection of the body.' "[2]

The Old Testament is strangely silent about the future life. It has been suggested that this silence may have been a reaction against the Canaanite cults of the dead. Whatever the reason, the Old Testament usually describes the afterlife in terms of a shadowy existence in Sheol, the abode of the dead. When it does speak of resurrection, most often it is the resurrection of the nation, as distinguished from the individual, which is in mind. The well-known "valley of dry bones" passage in Ezekiel 37, and probably the resurrection passage in the Isaiah apocalypse,[3] fit into this category. The only clear statement of a resurrection for individuals is Daniel 12:2: "And many of those who sleep in the dust of the earth shall awake, some to everlasting life, and some to shame and everlasting contempt."

Significant developments in the doctrine of the resurrection of the body took place during the intertestament period, particularly during the time of the Maccabees. The intense suffering and persecution under Antiochus Epiphanes provided a stimulus for the further refinement of this doctrine. This is most evident in such apocryphal books as the Wisdom of Solomon and II Maccabees and the pseudepigraphical Psalms of Solomon and I Enoch.

It is not until we reach the New Testament that the full flower of belief in the resurrection of the dead appears. References to it appear in every stratum of the New Testament, from the words of Jesus, as found in the Synoptics, to the visions of the seer in the Apocalypse.

The basis of all New Testament belief in the resurrection of the dead is the fact of Christ's resurrection. I Corinthians 15 is the classic passage. Paul's answer to those who denied a future resurrection was Christ's resurrection. "Now if Christ is preached as raised from the dead, how can some say that there is no resurrection of the dead? But if there is no resurrection of the dead, then Christ has not been

[1] A.M. Ramsey: The Resurrection of Christ, p. 100.
[2] R. Niebuhr: Beyond Tragedy, p. 290.   [3] Isa. 26:19.

raised."[4] But Christ has been raised and has become "the first fruits of those who have fallen asleep."[5]

Dr. Cullmann has underscored the difference between the Greek idea of the immortality of the soul and the biblical concept of the resurrection of the dead.[6] The Bible does not embrace the Greek dualism of body and soul. The human body, in biblical thought, resulted from the creative activity of God, and as such is good. Thus, man is not conceived of as a soul housed in an evil body, from which he constantly seeks release. He is a body-soul, and the redemptive process includes his material as well as his immaterial self, a process climaxed by the resurrection of the body.

Very little is said by Jesus about the nature of the resurrection body. His most significant statement arises in answer to the question of the Sadducees as to whose wife the woman would be in the resurrection who had married seven brothers in succession. Jesus replied that because of an inadequate knowledge of the Scriptures and the power of God, they were wrongly limiting the conditions of the future life to those of the present. "In the resurrection they neither marry nor are given in marriage, but are like the angels in heaven."[7] Resurrection life is of a new and different order of existence.

The Apostle Paul says essentially the same thing in I Corinthians 15:35-50 in answer to the questions: "How are the dead raised? With what kind of body do they come?" These were pertinent questions at Corinth, since the Greeks denied the resurrection of the body on the ground that corruptibility and bodily existence could not be disassociated. How could the future life have anything to do with a corruptible body? Paul concedes that the earthly body of man is corruptible.[8]

But there is more than one kind of body. Although the resurrection body has a certain continuity with the earthly body—Paul likens this continuity to that between the seed which is planted and the ear of grain which springs from it—yet there is a vast difference between the present body and the resurrection body. This difference is emphasized in a series of contrasts in verses 42-45. "What is sown [our earthly bodies] is perishable, what is raised is imperishable. It is sown

---

[4] I Cor. 15:12, 13.   [5] I Cor. 15:20.
[6] O. Cullmann: *Immortality of the Soul or Resurrection of the Dead?*
[7] Matt. 22:30.
[8] I Cor. 15:50: "Flesh and blood cannot inherit the kingdom of God."

in dishonor, it is raised in glory. It is sown in weakness, it is raised in power. It is sown a physical body, it is raised a spiritual body." Corruptibility, dishonor, weakness and a psychical (AV "natural") nature are all ascribed to our earthly body. In contrast, incorruptibility, glory, power, and spirituality (*pneumatikos*) are ascribed to the resurrection body.

This last mentioned characteristic has led to much misunderstanding. How can a body be "spiritual"? G.E. Ladd's answer is to the point: "The 'spiritual body' of I Corinthians 15:44 is not a body made of spirit, anymore than the 'natural' [literally, *psychical*] body is a body made of psyche.... However, it is a *literal, real body*, even though it is adapted to the new order of existence which shall be inaugurated at the resurrection for those who experience it."[9] "Spiritual" in this context is probably best taken to mean "dominated by the Holy Spirit," or perhaps as Leon Morris suggests, "adapted to the needs of the spirit" [i. e., the human spirit]. "The spiritual body ... is the organ which is intimately related to the spirit of man, just as his present body is intimately related to his earthly life."[10] Whatever "spiritual" means here, Paul is convinced that the future life will be so glorious that our present earthly bodies will have to be radically changed in order for us fully to enjoy what God has prepared for us.[11]

Although all evangelicals believe that the resurrection of the dead will be closely associated with the return of Christ,[12] there are numerous differences in details. Some hold to one general resurrection of all men at Christ's return. Others, on the basis of Revelation 20 in particular,[13] see two resurrections, one (of just men) at Christ's return, but before the millennium, the other (of the unjust) at the end of that period. Dispensationalists split the first resurrection into two phases consistent with their theory of a pretribulation "rapture" and a posttribulation "revelation." Differences in details there are, but these do not prevent evangelicals from unitedly affirming, "We believe in the resurrection of the body."

THE FINAL JUDGMENT

Closely associated with the resurrection of the dead is the final judgment. Our Lord declared: "The hour is coming when all who are

[9] G.E. Ladd: *Crucial Questions Concerning the Kingdom of God*, p. 139.
[10] L. Morris: *The First Epistle of Paul to the Corinthians*, p. 228.
[11] Cf. Phil. 3:20, 21.   [12] Cf. Phil. 3:20, 21.
[13] Cf. also John 5:29; Phil. 3:11; I Cor. 15:23.

in the tombs will hear his voice and come forth, those who have done good, to the resurrection of life, and those who have done evil, to the resurrection of judgment."[14]

The New Testament idea of the final judgment arises out of the Old Testament concept of the Day of the Lord. That Day is the final crisis (the English word "crisis" is simply the transliterated Greek word for judgment) of history, when God will judge all men, with blessing for the faithful and destruction for the wicked.

Judgment is an essential part of biblical religion. In both the Old and New Testaments it inevitably arises out of the nature of God as righteous. A righteous God must judge sin and reward obedience.

The judge is none other than God Himself, and His agent in judgment is Jesus Christ, the Son. Thus God "has appointed a day in which he will judge the world in righteousness by that man whom he has ordained,"[15] and the Father has given to the Son "authority to execute judgment also, because he is the Son of man."[16]

The judgment effected by God through Christ is universal. All men must stand before God's judgment bar.[17] This includes Christians,[18] as well as non-Christians.[19] Whereas it is true that he who believes in Jesus will not experience condemnation,[20] for "there is no condemnation to those that are in Christ Jesus,"[21] these statements are not to be taken to mean that for the Christian there is no future judgment at all. Paul specifically states that "we shall all stand before the judgment seat of Christ,"[22] and "all" in this context means "all Christians." The Christian, however, can face the judgment with confidence.[23] Christ's redemptive work has already acquitted him. It was Thomas à Kempis who said: "The sign of the cross shall be in heaven when the Lord cometh to judgment."

Judgment of Christians will be based on works.[24] The work of some Christians will prove to be superficial ("wood, hay, stubble"). "The Day will disclose it," and it will be destroyed, but the believer himself will be saved, but "only as through fire."[25] Alan Richardson is right when he says that this "works judgment" for Christians "is no mere relic of Paul's Pharisaic ideology; it is no unconscious clinging to a doc-

[14] John 5:28, 29.
[15] Acts 17:31.
[16] John 5:27.
[17] Rom. 2:6-10.
[18] II Cor. 5:10; Rom. 14:10.
[19] Rev. 20:15.
[20] John 5:24.
[21] Rom. 8:1.
[22] Rom. 14:10.
[23] I John 4:17.
[24] II Cor. 5:10.
[25] I Cor. 3:12-15.

trine of works. It is an assertion of the seriousness of the moral struggle of the Christian life . . ."[26] In this judgment, Christ's verdict of blame or praise is itself the punishment or reward.[27]

The final judgment is the climax to a process of judgment which was actually inaugurated by the entrance of Jesus Christ into human history. "For judgment," said Jesus, "I am come into the world."[28] This present aspect of the final judgment is particularly stressed in John's Gospel. He that does not believe in the Son "is condemned already because he has not believed on the name of the Son of God."[29] The final judgment has already begun, and its basis is belief in Jesus. The same teaching is found in the Synoptics: "For whoever is ashamed of me and of my words in this adulterous and sinful generation, of him will the Son of man also be ashamed, when he comes in the glory of his Father with the holy angels."[30]

There are some passages[31] that emphasize works as the basis for the judgment of the unbeliever (as well as the believer). Stauffer understands these passages to refer to those who "have rejected the work of Christ and relied upon their own achievements, and on their achievements they will be judged. . . . But such a judgment will lead inevitably to condemnation, for even the noblest deeds and characteristics are tainted with the poison of self-sufficiency . . ."[32]

No uncertainty exists about the outcome of the final judgment. Both in the teachings of Jesus and in the writings of the Apostles, the ultimate fate of those who persist in their rebellion against God is eternal condemnation.[33]

Differences, similar to those that exist concerning the resurrection of the dead, are found among evangelicals relative to the precise time and number of judgments. But unanimity exists on the great fact of the final judgment, a judgment that involves the end of history and the ultimate separation of souls.

The biblical doctrines of the resurrection of the dead and the final judgment have powerful practical implications for the Christian. Although he anticipates with joy the consummation of his redemption at

[26] A. Richardson: *An Introduction to the Theology of the New Testament*, p. 342.
[27] Matt. 25:21, 23; Luke 19:17.
[28] John 9:39.   [29] John 3:18.
[30] Mark 8:38; cf. Matt. 10:32, 33; Luke 12:8, 9.
[31] Cf. the "Great Assize" passage of Matt. 25:31–46; Rom. 2:6–10.
[32] E. Stauffer: *New Testament Theology*, pp. 221, 222.
[33] Matt. 25:31, 46; II Thess. 1:7–10; Rev. 20:14, 15.

the resurrection and the revelation of the lordship of Christ at the final judgment, aspects of the latter have sobering elements. *He* must stand before Christ to be judged on the quality of his Christian life—a potent incentive for holy living! All men must face the same Lord to be judged on the basis of the gospel of Gods' grace—an urgent plea for an increased effort in the proclamation of the truth concerning Jesus Christ, in Whom there is no condemnation. How true it is that eschatology and ethics can never be disassociated; but neither can eschatology and evangelistic *concern!*

BIBLIOGRAPHY

P. Althaus: *Die letzten Dinge*
O. Cullmann: *Immortality of the Soul or Resurrection of the Dead?*
T.A. Kantonen: *The Christian Hope*
H.A.A. Kennedy: *St. Paul's Conception of the Last Things*
W. Milligan: *The Resurrection of the Dead*
S.D.F. Salmond: *The Christian Doctrine of Immortality*
R. Summers: *The Life Beyond*
G. Vos: *The Pauline Eschatology*
G. Kittel: *Theologisches Wörterbuch zum Neuen Testament* [relevant articles]

43

THE FINAL STATE:

HEAVEN AND HELL

✚

J.A. MOTYER

J.A. Motyer, Vice-Principal of Clifton Theological College, Bristol, England, received his general and theological education at Trinity College, Dublin (B.A., 1947; M.A., B.D., 1951). He is the author of *Introducing the Old Testament* (1961).

Every sensitive person, facing the question of human destiny, must surely long to be a universalist. No one could desire to see another person brought to the end of all existence, whether at death, as conditional immortality teaches, or by the judgment of God after death, as annihilationism teaches; no one could wish to think of the bitter pains of eternal death, consciously and eternally endured by sinners, as traditional orthodoxy insists. Hence, the tremendous human attractiveness of a belief which assures eternal life and bliss to every soul of man!

However, sentiment cannot be exalted into a theological norm, and when one sees the extent to which universalist writings lean upon analogies of human love, one realizes that there is at least a danger of the wish being father to the thought. For the truth is that man, as such, possesses no yardstick whereby to measure eternal issues. We do not know by instinct what the love of God is like, and therefore we need to beware of the human analogy; we certainly do not know for ourselves what the holiness of God is like, and therefore we must beware of giving much weight to what sinners think of the seriousness of sin. Only God can say what precisely are the facts, and what are their implications. We must rigidly adhere to the principle: "To the law and to the testimony!" What has the God of truth written for our learning?

OLD TESTAMENT

The Old Testament insists on the fact of human survival of death. This is asserted as true of godly and ungodly alike. The life in Sheol, the place of the departed, is the expectation of the patriarch Jacob[1] and of King David;[2] equally it is the lot of the heathen king of Babylon[3] and of "the multitude of Egypt."[4] All alike die, and all alike take up their abode in Sheol.

A most important observation follows. It is widely urged by advocates of conditional immortality and of annihilation that death may be defined as "the loss of life or existence."[5] Man is not possessed of an immortal soul; this is only the possession of some, on condition of faith in Christ; for the rest, death is the end. The slight modification of this statement made by adherents of annihilationism—that the soul survives bodily death until it is extinguished by act of God in judgment—is unimportant at the moment. The question is: May we define death as "loss of life"? Clearly not! The Old Testament shows us that death is rather to be seen as an alteration of place, from earth to Sheol; and of state, from the body-soul unity of life on earth to the separate life of the soul in Sheol. Death is defined by God himself as "Dust thou art, and unto dust shalt thou return,"[6] but by virtue of creation man is more than dust.[7] Consequently, the correct balance is set forth in Ecclesiastes:[8] "Then shall the dust return to the earth . . . and the spirit . . . to God. . . ." This meaning of death seems to stand firm throughout the Bible.

The life of the soul in Sheol is revealed as continuous with the present life in terms of character and personality. David expects to meet his lost child and to know him;[9] Samuel, recalled from the grave, is recognizably the Samuel who was known on earth;[10] and Job[11] and the Psalmist[12] expected *personal* survival of death.

---

[1] Gen. 42:38.
[2] II Sam. 12:23.
[3] Isa. 14:9.
[4] Ezek. 32:18 ff.
[5] H. Constable: *The Duration and Nature of Future Punishment*, p. 16.
[6] Gen. 3:19.
[7] Gen. 2:7.
[8] Eccles. 12:7.
[9] II Sam. 12:23.
[10] I Sam. 28:11 ff.
[11] Job 19:25–27.
[12] Ps. 49:15.

This at once leads us to ask if the Old Testament recognizes and provides for distinctions of moral character in the world to come. Only the beginnings of such teaching are to be found. Certainly, in the case of the wicked, there is only the hint of adverse lot after death. There are, for example, certain passages which associate Sheol rather specifically with notable wickedness of life.[13] In the same way, whereas the threat to the wicked,[14] that he shall die in his iniquity, may only mean that his inequity will speedily terminate his life on earth, the general tone of the context rather suggests that there is a special doom awaiting a man who dies unrepentant. Daniel 12:2 is explicit.

The teaching on the reward of the righteous is rather more prominently stated. Of the passages which relate to this point,[15] Psalm 73: 23, 24 is undoubtedly pre-eminent. The problem of this Psalm is the familiar one of the prosperity of the godless and the suffering of the godly. The Psalmist's solution is this: that at every point of life and in all circumstances, the man who has God is richer than the man without God. In the verses mentioned, the godly man counts his wealth: for the present, he has the assurance that God is with him and will not let him go;[16] and as he looks ahead, he sees a life ordered by divine providence,[17] and "afterward" entrance upon "glory." The verb "receive" is also found in Psalm 49:15 and in Genesis 5:24; it is virtually a technical term for the divine act of glorification of the saints.

NEW TESTAMENT

As soon as we set foot in the New Testament we find a plain declaration of the bliss of the people of God and the condemnation of the unsaved. Without prejudice to the task of exegesis, surely the Lord Jesus illuminated immortality when He said, "These shall go away into eternal punishment: but the righteous into eternal life."[18] Along with the clear assertion of opposite eternal destinies, the New Testament is adamant that death, the termination of life on earth, is the end of man's probationary period. As a man dies, so his eternal destiny is decided. The Lord Jesus Christ is once more our teacher in this matter, for in His story of the rich man and Lazarus, He laid particular stress

---

13 Ps. 9:7; Prov. 5:5; Ps. 88:7–12; Job 31:12.
14 Ezek. 3:18.
15 E.g., Isa. 25:8; 26:19; Prov. 14:32; Dan. 12:2; Ps. 16:8 ff.; 17:14 f.; 49:14, 15.
16 Ps. 73:23.   17 Ps. 73:24a.
18 Matt. 25:46.

on the fixity of the great gulf and the impossibility of reversing that situation which death initiated.[19]

What, then, does the New Testament teach about those who die without Christ? It is useful to notice first the emphasis placed on the absolute justice of the judgment which God will pass on such. Revelation 20:12 ff. tells us that it is a judgment based on exact evidence. There is not only the "book of life"; there is also the book of human works. Often the judgment throne of God is wrongly construed at this point. It is fancied that before God's throne those who formerly rejected God, actively or passively, will meantime have undergone a change of mind, will see the error of their ways, and desire to repent and be saved, yet be cut off from all hope. A picture containing all the poignancy of helpless anguish is thus conjured up. But Scripture, in fact, insists on a very different picture: that of the dead appearing before God in exactly the character of God-denying, Christ-rejecting sin which they evidenced on earth. The rich man in the Lord's story bore in hell the same personal marks as he did in life: desire for sensual gratification, subjection of the welfare of others to his personal whim, absence of any regard for the law of God.

The judgment which God passes is in its quality "eternal";[20] and in its form "fire,"[21] "punishment,"[22] "destruction,"[23] and "the second death."[24] It would seem unavoidable that the word "eternal" rules out universalism. It answers to the "great gulf *fixed*" in the story. While every sympathy flows like a tide toward the goal the universalist is trying to reach, he is none the less impotent against the stark assertion that the judgment passed by God initiates an eternal state of affairs. Neither of the two positions adopted by universalists effects anything at this point. They may oppose Scripture to Scripture, urging that, in I Corinthians 15:28, the hope is held out that "God may be all in all" and that this cannot be so if some of God's creatures are eternally alienated from Him. Or, additionally, they may urge that if any are eternally lost, the divine love is deprived of its object and is not almighty. But this is all unbiblical thinking. In the first place, in the Corinthians passage, the "all" who die "in Adam" and the "all" who are made alive "in Christ" are not identical; and, therefore, the inter-

---

[19] Luke 16:26; cf. Heb. 9:27; Rev. 20:12.
[20] Matt. 25:46; II Thess. 1:9; Rev. 20:10.
[21] Matt. 25:41; Rev. 20:14, 15.   [22] Matt. 25:46.
[23] II Thess. 1:9.   [24] Rev. 20:14.

pretation of the total exaltation of God is wrongly made out. Secondly, the Bible teaches holiness as the essential characteristic of God, and displays the truth which, possessing only a sinner's defective notion of holiness, we find unpalatable: that God is *glorified* in judgment.[25] Thirdly, as against the assertion that omnipotent love guarantees the salvation of every sinner, and will after death produce such evidence of love as will win the free response of every heart, Scripture asserts that this evidence has already been given and nothing more can be expected,[26] and that His love is specifically that which prompted God to save a people He freely and mercifully chose for Himself.[27]

However, accepting that an eternal issue is settled, what is the subsequent state of those condemned? Following the word "eternal," annihilationists urge the words "death" and "destruction"; the eternal state of the unsaved is to be totally and eternally extinguished or disintegrated so as to cease to be. But firstly, it does not concur with the meaning of "death" already indicated: not annihilation, but alteration. On this meaning, just as death terminated this life but ushered in the life of the separation of body and soul, so "the second death" will terminate that existence and usher in the "lake of fire." Secondly, it does not concur with the meaning of "destruction" in two of the other three places where the New Testament uses it,[28] where it certainly does not mean a final and complete end of conscious existence. Thirdly, such annihilation is not the lot of the devil, who in the lake of fire is "tormented day and night for ever,"[29] and with whom, in the same fire, according to the Lord Jesus, the wicked have their portion.[30] Fourthly, annihilation is not necessarily—perhaps not at all—"punishment." Conceivably, the thought would bring nothing but relief to some! And, finally, annihilation is not consistent with the principles enunciated by our Lord Himself in the case history of the rich man. It was his lot to know his lost eternity and to experience the pangs of it.

These things are no joy to write, and nothing but a burden to contemplate. Let them urge us on in the task of proclaiming the saving Word, and all the more when we appreciate afresh the glories which God has reserved for those who love Him.[31] "The souls of believers are at their death made perfect in holiness, and do im-

[25] E.g., Ezek. 10:4; Isa. 2:10; etc.
[27] I John 4:9–14.
[29] Rev. 20:10.
[31] I Cor. 2:9.

[26] Rom. 5:8; cf. Mark 12:6.
[28] I Cor. 5:5; I Thess. 5:3.
[30] Matt. 25:41.

mediately pass into glory; and their bodies, being still united to Christ, do rest in their graves till the resurrection,"[32] wherein "the dead in Christ shall rise first: then we that are alive, that are left, shall together with them be caught up in the clouds, to meet the Lord in the air; and so shall we ever be with the Lord."[33] Thus, there is the immediate prospect of the believer at death, and the ultimate prospect at the final resurrection. We are taught by the New Testament that death is followed at once by conscious enjoyment of the presence of the Lord. This was the expectation of Paul, to whom to depart and be with Christ was "better by far,"[34] for he would be "at home with the Lord."[35] It seems innate in these sayings of the Apostle that he did not expect any "sleep of the soul" after death. Such was clearly not the experience of Lazarus.[36]

But even this blissful enjoyment of the Lord does not exhaust God's purposed blessing of His people. The redemption accomplished by the Lord Jesus was total in its efficacy, the redemption of the whole man. Therefore, the New Testament holds before us the prospect of "the redemption of the body,"[37] the consummation of glorification, when we shall see Him and be like Him.[38]

GLORY OF THE LAMB

As regards the personal element of this life, the life beyond will be marked by continuity and transformation,[39] so that just as Moses and Elijah were recognized on the Mount of Transfiguration,[40] in the same way we shall see and know our loved ones. As regards the toils of this life, there is the promise of blessed rest;[41] as regards its deficiencies, clothing;[42] as regards its trials and uncertainties, provision and security; and for its sorrows, comfort and joy.[43] In exchange for the imperfectly realized fellowship of God's people now, there will be "the church of the firstborn,"[44] with their common testimony to the blood of the Lamb;[45] and, more than all else, there will be no longer the intermittent fellowship of the Lord, blighted by sin and defeat, but, there, the Lamb will be all the glory—sin and Satan, death, sorrow, defeat, and

[32] *Westminster Shorter Catechism.*
[33] I Thess. 4:16 f.
[34] Phil. 1:23.
[35] II Cor. 5:6 ff.
[36] Luke 16:23 ff.; cf. Rev. 6:9 f.
[37] Rom. 8:23; Eph. 1:14.
[38] I John 3:2.
[39] I Cor. 15:35 ff.
[40] Luke 9:30.
[41] Rev. 14:13.
[42] II Cor. 5:1, 2.
[43] Rev. 7:14-17.
[44] Heb. 12:23.
[45] Rev. 7:9.

even temptation will be banished—the song of the redeemed will proceed not from faith but from sight, and the brightest jewel will be the word fulfilled, which says: "Forever with the Lord."

BIBLIOGRAPHY

H. Constable: *The Duration and Nature of Future Punishment* [annihilationism]

J.A.T. Robinson: *In the End, God* [universalism]

L. Boettner: *Immortality*

H. Buis: *The Doctrine of Eternal Punishment*

L. Morris: *The Wages of Sin*

———: *The Biblical Doctrine of Judgment*

C. Hodge: *Systematic Theology*

L. Berkhof: *Systematic Theology*

A POSTSCRIPT ON
THEOLOGY

✚

ROGER NICOLE

Roger Nicole, Professor of Theology at Gordon Divinity School, Beverly Farms, Massachusetts, received his general education at the Gymnase Classique, Lausanne, Switzerland (B.A., 1935), the Sorbonne, Paris (M.A., 1937), and the Gordon Divinity School (B.D., 1939; S.T.M., 1940; and Th.D., 1943). He is the author of chapters in *Contemporary Evangelical Thought,* and *Revelation and the Bible.*

DEFINITIONS

Theology is that area of knowledge which is concerned with God, His purpose and relation to the world. This does not deny that in other areas of knowledge one may and should adopt an orientation toward God, but the distinctive of theology is its subject matter.

Systematic theology, in the broader sense, is that branch of theological learning which correlates the data of biblical revelation in order to exhibit the structure of Christianity, viewed as a system of doctrine and morals, and to vindicate this system against any competing view. The word "systematic" does not imply that this branch of theology alone is orderly in its approach; rather, it is meant merely to emphasize that the organic structural character of Christianity is prominently featured here.

Systematic theology, in the narrower sense, or dogmatics, is that department of the previous branch which deals with the exhibition, in a positive way, of the organism of the Christian truth. In the pursuance of this task, it aims to present the truth in its completeness, rather than in fragmentary fashion; in its correlation and proper balance with other truths of the faith, rather than in a disjointed or ill-proportioned way; in its eternal validity, rather than merely in certain historical contexts; on the basis of proper grounds which are normative for the Christian, rather than by appeal to spurious authorities. It is especially in their understanding of this last requisite that evangelicals differ from competing viewpoints.

ENCYCLOPEDIC PLACE

The place of systematic theology and of dogmatics in the structure of theological studies may be portrayed in the following diagram:

	Exegetical	culminates in		Biblical Theology
	Historical	culminates in		History of Doctrine
Theology	Systematic (broader sense)	{ thetic { antithetic		{ Dogmatics { Ethics
	Practical			Apologetics

From this diagram, certain relationships may be discerned at once, but clarification and amplification are desirable here at four points:

(1) *Biblical Theology and Dogmatics.* The adjective "biblical" should not be construed to suggest that other branches of theology are not grounded in Scripture, or even less biblical than this branch. A contrast, commonly made on this score, between biblical theology and systematic theology is very misleading. Biblical theology, as the culminating discipline of exegetical studies, gathers together the scattered results of exegesis, in order to exhibit in articulated form the historical unfolding of special revelation. It is often concerned with the peculiar emphases and insights of individual writers or particular periods.

Systematic theology receives its primary materials from biblical theology and incorporates them into the total perspective of revealed truth. As Warfield so well put it,[1] "We do not make our theology,

---

[1] B.B. Warfield: *Studies in Theology,* "The Idea of Systematic Theology," p. 67.

according to our own pattern, as a mosaic, out of the fragments of the Biblical teaching; but rather look out from ourselves upon it as a great prospect, framed out of the mountains and plains of the theologies of the Scriptures, and strive to attain a point of view from which we can bring the whole landscape into our field of sight."

(2) *History of Doctrine and Dogmatics.* A similar remark may be made here. History of doctrine, as the culminating branch of historical theology, has for its purpose to expound, in its historical unfolding, the impact of the truth of revelation upon God's people. It challenges to many fruitful avenues of thought and manifests many of the dead ends previously explored by the church. Systematic theology draws amply from these insights and derives indispensable instruction from the victories and the failures of the past.

Symbolics, in particular, dealing with the official formulation of the faith given by various branches of the church, is of paramount importance both for the precise expression of certain truths and for an assessment of trends.

(3) *Ethics and Dogmatics.* These two fields are in close relation to each other and have often been treated together in the past. Together, they constitute the positive presentation of the Christian view as a system of faith and life. Dogmatics describes what God does for man, to man, and in man; while ethics describes what man should do in his service of gratitude to God.[2]

(4) *Apologetics and Dogmatics.* There is a considerable difference of opinion as to the nature and function of apologetics, and consequently as to its place in theological science. This is not the place to discuss this topic, but we may point out here that one fundamental feature of apologetics is that it seeks to vindicate what is considered true over against competing viewpoints. These may be false religions or non-Christian philosophies or aberrant positions within Christendom. The approach is thus fundamentally antithetical, while that of dogmatics is basically thetic and positive.

FOUNDATIONAL PRINCIPLE OF DOGMATICS

Presumably, all those who would claim to be theologians would agree in recognizing the authority of God as the supreme norm of truth. There are, however, very considerable differences of conception as to how and where this authority is expressed.

[2] Cf. H. Bavinck: *Gereformeerde Dogmatiek*, 2nd edition, Volume I, p. 41.

(1) The Roman Catholic Church insists that authoritative revelation is embodied in Scripture and tradition as co-ordinate supernatural sources of truth. Both of these are accessible to the individual through the teaching ministry of the church, which determines what is to be received and how it must be interpreted. Ecumenical councils and the Popes, in the discharge of their functions as supreme teachers of the church, have from time to time issued infallible pronouncements, which have made explicit certain aspects of the faith held more or less indistinct until then, but becoming then and there binding upon all faithful at the peril of damnation. This, in the judgment of the Evangelical Protestant, has heavily burdened the Roman Catholic faith with extra-scriptural and even anti-scriptural materials. The Bible has often receded to the background, and the serious charge of our Lord against the scribes and Pharisees appears applicable, that they made void the word of God by their tradition.[3]

The Eastern Church presents an approach which is analogous in many respects, although it acknowledges only seven ecumenical councils (instead of twenty), and rejects the infallibility of the Pope. Nevertheless, here also, tradition and church authority are among the most important factors in dogmatics.

(2) A second basic approach is that of subjectivism, which is the hallmark of theological liberalism. Here, the presupposition is that God's authority is expressed directly in the subject and channeled through one or the other of the key faculties of the human soul: reason, feelings, or conscience.

(a) It has always been particularly tempting to ascribe to reason a place of dominance in the attainment of religious truth. Indeed, it is in the sphere of reason that concepts are formed and that communication, especially verbal communication, from one thinking subject to another is possible. Rationalism, however, goes beyond recognizing reason as an indispensable channel for the reception of truth; it elevates reason into being the supreme and autonomous judge of truth and sometimes even the source of truth. In the final analysis, it makes little difference whether one follows the barren deistic form of approach known as *Rationalismus Vulgaris*, whose chill winds blew over almost all of Christendom in the eighteenth century, or whether one follows Hegel in his venturesome attempts to soar on the wings of "thesis, antithesis, and synthesis," in order to achieve a grasp of the whole of

[3] Mark 7:13.

reality. In either case, reason is the mistress instead of a servant; it insists on speaking when it should listen; and it condemns man to be bound by the narrow limits of his own horizon.

(b) In good part, as a reaction against rationalism, Schleiermacher developed his theology of feeling. In this, he was in tune with the romantic mood of the beginning of the nineteenth century, and he aimed to validate anew the place of emotions in the religious life. Inasmuch as communication is difficult on this level, a major emphasis was placed upon individual experience, as contrasted with any objective norm either of belief or of conduct. A drastically new approach of faith developed, in which the believing subject rather than the truth itself was seen as the proper object of investigation. Religion was lowered to being a branch of anthropology and psychology, perhaps even abnormal psychology!

(c) The third option appears in moralism, in which the importance of conscience and of the norms of ethics is emphasized. Here, one of the great modern leaders was Kant, whose influence was very manifest upon the Ritschlian movement. In this approach, the reliability of our knowledge is heavily discounted, but great confidence is placed in the basic moral instincts of the human soul. Judgments of value, rather than metaphysical judgments, reach the core of faith.

Wide differences separate the various views embraced in this brief survey, but one common feature of all of them is the fact that they all view some aspect of human nature as the source of religious truth. It is this aspect which then becomes determinative, rather than any objective presentation of truth made outside of the individual. The Hebrew-Christian tradition, on the other hand, while recognizing the value of inner voices of the soul, has always made an objective revelation of God in words and in Christ the key and the norm of the true religious approach.

(3) Neo-orthodoxy is classified sometimes with liberalism and sometimes with conservative theology. We need not go on record here with a judgment on this score. Moreover, we should not forget that under this name are commonly grouped thinkers representing a wide range of individual positions. Generally speaking, neo-orthodoxy professes to make a radical break with the various forms of liberalism by denying flatly the adequacy of any approach upward from man to God, and insisting that the approach of true religion is always downward from God to man, at His sovereign good pleasure. In consistency

with this insight, the neo-orthodox are commonly loath to ascribe an absolute character to anything which is accessible to man, be it an historical figure or a book. God communicates Himself, they say, at the point of "crisis," that is, in a personal encounter of a transcendental nature. Without our going further in the analysis of this position, it is clear that it avows a high regard for the divine initiative in revelation, but that, since it provides no external norm by which alleged crisis experiences are to be judged, and since even these experiences do not constitute a permanent deposit of reliable knowledge, the dangers of subjectivism are by no means avoided.

Over against these competing viewpoints, the evangelical is intent upon giving obedient recognition to the authority of the Scripture as the infallible rule of faith. There, he finds the objective revelation of God centering in the redeeming work of Jesus Christ. His primary task is to listen to the voice of God, Who has spoken, then to employ all the resources of a regenerate personality, an enlightened mind, re-oriented emotions, and a conscience cleansed from dead works, in order to set forth this divinely authenticated truth in orderly and correlated fashion. In the pursuance of this task, he will not be unmindful of the valuable lessons of history, nor discard lightly the accumulative weight of insight into the meaning of Scripture gathered over generations of saints, scholars, and martyrs. Furthermore, he does not speak and write merely as an isolated believer, but in the midst of a confessing community and in the strength of the fellowship of the church. Nevertheless, with all due weight being given to the above considerations, it remains that it is the Scripture, and that alone, which is normative. Theology is basically and ultimately always biblical, and the evangelical is confident that in this affirmation he is in line with the great Reformation doctrine of *Sola Scriptura*, yea, with the attitude of the Apostles and of our Lord Himself, when they triumphantly rested their case on the note, "It is written."

BIBLIOGRAPHY

L. Berkhof: *Introductory Volume* (to *Systematic Theology*)

K.E. Kirk, ed.: *The Study of Theology*

A. Kuyper: *Principles of Sacred Theology*

B.B. Warfield: *Studies in Theology*, "The Idea of Systematic Theology" and "The Task and Method of Systematic Theology"

———: *The Right of Systematic Theology*